FRIED & JUSTIFIED

Mick Houghton began his career writing about music before starting out in PR at WEA in 1978. Two years later he set up the independent PR agency Brassneck Publicity. He began writing again in 2001 for *Mojo* and later *Uncut*, and has since published two books, *I've Always Kept A Unicorn: The Biography of Sandy Denny* and *Becoming Elektra: The True Story of Jac Holzman's Visionary Record Label*, as well as being one of the Grammy-nominated compilers of *Forever Changing: The Golden Age of Elektra Records, 1963–1973*.

Mick Houghton

FRIED & JUSTIFIED

HITS, MYTHS, BREAK-UPS AND BREAKDOWNS IN THE RECORD BUSINESS 1978-98

FABER & FABER

First published in the UK in 2019
by Faber & Faber Limited
Bloomsbury House
74–77 Great Russell Street, London WC1B 3DA

First published in the USA in 2019

Typeset by Ian Bahrami
Printed in England by CPI Group (UK) Ltd, Croydon CR0 4YY

All images courtesy of Getty and the author

A CIP record for this book
is available from the British Library

ISBN 978-0-571-33682-1

FSC
www.fsc.org
MIX
Paper from
responsible sources
FSC® C020471

2 4 6 8 10 9 7 5 3 1

To old friends

CONTENTS

ACKNOWLEDGEMENTS

Although I chose not to interview any artists expressly for *Fried &
Justified*, I did draw from interviews, email exchanges and conversations
down the years with Mickey Bradley, Damian O'Neill, John O'Neill, Ian
McCulloch, Will Sergeant, Les Pattinson, Julian Cope, David Balfe, Bill
Drummond, Jimmy Cauty, Lawrence, David Gedge, Bobby Gillespie,
Lee Ranaldo, Euros Childs, Andrew Oldham and Dee Dee Ramone.

Except where sources are credited in the text, all other quotes are
taken from my own interviews and encounters.

Thanks to Max Bell, Jane Burridge, Keith Cameron, Andy Ferguson,
David Gedge, Ian Harrison, Paul McNally, Louise Nevill, Andrew
Oldham, James Oldham, John Reed, Slim Smith, Terry Staunton and, last
but not least, Stuart Batsford for his unfailing help and encouragement.

At Faber & Faber I'd like to thank Dan Papps, Paul Baillie-Lane, Ian
Bahrami and especially Lee Brackstone for his support and reassurance
and for helping to clear a path through the trees. I'm indebted to Dave
Watkins for guiding me through the commissioning stages and making
this book happen.

Special thanks to Bill Drummond and Jimmy Cauty.

During the years *Fried & Justified* covers I worked with five assistants. They don't feature anywhere near enough in this narrative, but we
shared a lot of experiences that I'd like to think were mostly enjoyable;
they also got my back on plenty of occasions. So in chronological order
and without whom . . . I'd like to thank Geraldine Oakley, who brought
order to the chaos of setting up Brassneck Publicity in 1980; Mel Bell,
who took over for much of the rest of the 1980s; Pam Young, who came
on board for eighteen months in 1990, and Louise Nevill, who followed
her. Sara Lawrence joined me in 1995. She stuck around for a good ten

years before she left, but then we got married instead. So there are some happy endings. I'd never have finished this book without her love and understanding.

And, belatedly, I'm grateful to my family. During my mum and dad's lifetime they never understood what I did for a living, yet they were responsible for igniting my passion for pop music in the first place because we had a pile of old 78s at home that were my favourite toys. I'd sprawl on the floor of the living room in front of our hefty gramophone and pretend to be a disc jockey. It was a terrible collection of schmaltzy ballads and novelty hits by the likes of David Whitfield, Mantovani, Dickie Valentine, Ruby Murray, Russ Conway and Winifred Atwell, but sometime in 1956 my dad came home with Bill Haley and the Comets' *Rock Around the Clock* LP. I was six years old, but after hearing its rim-shot percussion, driving slap-bass and frantic guitar solos and puzzling over the language of mysteriously titled songs such as 'Razzle-Dazzle', 'Rock-a-Beatin' Boogie' and 'Shake, Rattle and Roll' nothing was the same again. Then, over the next couple of years, my elder sisters Beryl and Sheila began buying singles. Showing remarkably good taste for an eight-year-old, it was the new 45s by Elvis Presley, the Everly Brothers and Buddy Holly I'd play the most. I was gone . . . real gone, and I was never coming back.

Mick Houghton
November 2018

FOREWORD:
BILLY FURY VERSUS THE WORLD

There are secret histories in pop music.

There is one particular secret history that holds that pop music in Liverpool went straight from Billy Fury singing 'Halfway to Paradise' in 1961 to the release on Zoo Records of 'Sleeping Gas' by the Teardrop Explodes in February 1979, with nothing happening in the intervening eighteen years.

This secret history of pop music can only be glanced at from time to time, and then only by those with gifted vision.

There are those who say, 'What about Rory Storm and the Hurricanes, or the Real Thing, or even Deaf School?' It is best not to listen to those people – their vision is not to be trusted.

I am pleased to note here that Zoo Records was ours.

The founder of Sire Records was Seymour Stein. He was from New York, and thus had never heard of Billy Fury. But I suspected he shared a parallel secret history of pop music, one in which nothing had happened in American rock between Del Shannon's 'Runaway' dropping out of the *Billboard* Hot 100 in 1961 and the release on Sire Records of 'Blitzkrieg Bop' by the Ramones in February 1976.

Come the summer of '79, Seymour Stein was interested in signing one of our other Zoo Records bands – Echo & the Bunnymen – to his Sire Records. We sensed Sire Records might be a good place for Echo & the Bunnymen to explore the possibility of developing other channels in future secret histories of pop music.

Stein was over from New York. We headed down from Liverpool to the Sire Records London office. This was round the back of the then derelict Covent Garden market.

One of the people who Stein introduced us to was a man in his late twenties. As in a couple of years older than me. This man so mumbled his name, I wasn't too sure what it was. I was told he was a press officer and we might be working with him. I assumed a press officer would be the person in the record company who oversaw the pressing of the records. As far as I knew, the main job of a record company was to press records. Bands wrote, played and recorded the songs, record companies pressed those recordings into records, record shops sold the records to people who wanted to play the records at home.

But I was wrong on numerous fronts: mainly about how the record industry worked, but more precisely about what a press officer did. It seemed this man's job had nothing to do with the pressing of records. His job was to put one of each of the newly pressed and soon-to-be-released records into an envelope, seal the envelope, write the address of a music paper on the front of the envelope, stick a stamp on the envelope and finally drop the envelope into a pillar box. At the time there were four music papers in the UK: the *Melody Maker*, *New Musical Express*, *Sounds* and *Record Mirror*. At most, this job would take thirty minutes per newly released record. I did not see how this could amount to a proper full-time job. With the records we had been releasing on Zoo, that is exactly what we did. And a week or so later the record in question would be reviewed as Single of the Week in at least three of those four music papers.

But this man I was introduced to in the Sire office seemed affable enough, and we were soon discussing the merits of the Flying Burrito Brothers' version of 'The Dark End of the Street', compared to the original by James Carr. He then asked me if I had recently listened to *The Sound of Fury* by Billy Fury. This was code. It was then I knew I was talking with a man who had a gifted vision regarding the secret history of pop music.

This man began to turn up at Echo & the Bunnymen and Teardrop Explodes gigs, always unannounced and usually with some music journalist in tow.

And as I became more aware of what his job was, or what it was supposed to be, I began to question his methods. If he was supposed to be convincing the journalist in tow how great the Teardrop Explodes were, why was he talking to the journalist only about the merits of Gram Parsons's second album?

And when Echo & the Bunnymen released their second album, why would I overhear him telling the journalist in tow that this second album was not as good as their first album?

But then a couple of weeks later there would be a five-star rave review of Echo & the Bunnymen's second album by the said journalist in tow.

And so it went on.

But this man's attitude towards his job of putting records into envelopes and posting them to music papers got more extreme.

In the late 1980s I was part of a group myself. Our new album was called *Chill Out*. When this man heard the album called *Chill Out*, he told us, in no uncertain terms, that he was not going to sully his reputation with music journalists by putting this record into envelopes and posting it to them. He suggested we find someone else to do the stamp-licking for us. He recommended someone called Jeff Barrett. Jeff Barrett didn't think *Chill Out* was rubbish and was willing to drop the envelopes into postboxes on our behalf.

Within weeks *Chill Out* was considered seminal by the said music journalists.

Although I had now learnt something of the dark arts, this man's knowledge was at a completely different level to mine.

There was an occasion when this man, no longer in his late twenties, told me he did not suffer fools gladly. I was very aware it was me that was the fool in question. But that was by the by, and somehow we carried on with what was more than a working relationship for what will have been more than forty years by the time you read this.

He has a speciality, and that is troubled singers. He understands them, and they seem to understand him – as, I am sure, Ian McCulloch and Julian Cope will testify.

As yet, I have not read this book by this man, who is no longer in his late twenties but is still only a couple of years older than me. Late last night I was invited to write a thousand words as a possible Foreword to the book. I thought it better if I did not read the book first. I will read it when it comes out. I hope you do as well. But not before you listen to *Billy Fury Versus the World*.

Bill Drummond
October 2018

INTRODUCTION

Spiritualized, the World Trade Center, 16 April 1998

A year after the release of *Ladies and Gentlemen We Are Floating in Space*, Spiritualized's World Trade Center show marked the beginning of the end of one of the most successful and satisfying jobs I'd done in twenty years as a publicist. Just as Johnny Ramone always described Ramones shows as jobs, I always thought of what I did as a job, and one that was best kept simple. I never thought in terms of elaborate press campaigns. Everything about *Ladies and Gentlemen* was near perfect, from its conception to its completion and the reverberations it had over the years to come. The album itself was special, and the record company let it happen without interference. We had fantastic photos taken in a disused hospital pharmacy and magnificent packaging. The CD came in a pill-style tray manufactured under strict pharmaceutical conditions, complete with an information sheet containing dosage instructions and warnings about the possible side effects of listening to the group. The concept played on the notion that Spiritualized, and singer and songwriter Jason Pierce's previous group, Spacemen 3, had a reputation for being drug fiends. Not for nothing did Spacemen 3 release an album called *Taking Drugs to Make Music to Take Drugs to*, and chemical dependency was one of two themes underpinning *Ladies and Gentlemen*. The other was an indie soap-opera back story that jolted Jason out of his usual interview comfort zone. He couldn't just talk about the music, about the buzz of working with New Orleans and Memphis greats Dr John and Jim Dickinson, and he wasn't just being asked about the Cramps, the Gun Club or the 13th Floor Elevators; he had to deal with persistent prying by music journalists about whether this most heart-rending of albums was about

1

the break-up two years earlier of his relationship with Spiritualized's keyboard player Kate Radley, now married to Richard Ashcroft of the Verve.

The album took its title from a chapter in Jostein Gaarder's philosophical fantasy novel *Sophie's World*, which had been given to Jason by Kate's stepfather. Although rarely asked about the book, Jason once explained: 'It's all about looking at the bigger picture rather than the everyday mundane. It didn't mean, as everybody thought, that we were "out there".' Of course, it meant both, but Jason always liked to deflect journalists from the obvious. From the very first interviews, journalists set out their agenda, which was to get Jason to admit that his break-up with Kate inspired songs like 'Broken Heart', in which he sings about being wasted all the time and driven to drink to erase the memory of lost love. The second interview we did was with James Oldham for the *NME*. It took place in small hotel in Chippenham. After a convivial evening of fine dining and good wine, both of which Jason always appreciated, we adjourned to James's room at around midnight. I left them to it as James launched straight into the 'Kate' question, and went to my room next door. Three hours later I could still hear them talking. Maybe it was time to call a halt. The floor of James's room was littered with discarded wine bottles, and he was still trying to wheedle an answer out of Jason to the same question. It was a battle of wills which Jason won every time with a skill and determination that would shame a politician. A year on, he was still being badgered about it and still giving nothing away.

I wasn't a great businessman. I never tried to build up a roster or wanted to run a PR company where I was delegating to others. So I never took risks; I just stumbled along. I could always get by. It was a struggle at times in the early days, but I always believed something would turn up, even though I never made any effort to find it. Usually something special came my way. That certainly happened with Spiritualized. I hadn't wanted to work with the group at first. I'd been warned that Jason was a nightmare to handle. I'd been told by a number of journalists that he was unreliable and inarticulate, and famously once nodded off during an interview with his face in a bowl of soup. Spiritualized's two earlier studio albums hadn't really moved me – although I later saw the error of my ways – but I was working with Sara Lawrence, who was not only my assistant but had become my girlfriend, and she'd have walked out on me if we'd not taken them on. I had to pass an audition and was vetted by Kate, who came up to the warehouse space in Old Street where I lived and worked. There was no inquisition. We sat around drinking tea. I think the three cats I shared the office with won her round as much as anything persuasive I had to say.

So I travelled down to Chippenham, where Jason was living in an idyllic, spacious house with Kate's mother and stepfather. I thought I must have been meeting a different person to the one I'd been told about. He and I just clicked. He was friendly and welcoming, but it probably all came down to the music. It always comes down to the music. I think we bonded initially over Elvis and his 1971 album *Elvis Country (I'm 10,000 Years Old)*. *Ladies and Gentlemen* had originally sampled a line from 'Can't Help Falling in Love', but the Presley estate wouldn't grant permission to use it. Jason even played me some of the demos for his new album. When I told the people at the group's label, Dedicated, about these, they were astonished; they'd heard nothing. You can teach certain aspects of PR, but it's totally about connecting with people – the artist, journalists, even the record label. I've been known to struggle with the latter. PR is about common sense above all else, and a little intuition helps.

So I got the job, and over the next couple of months Jason would invite me along to the studio. I tended not to go there even when asked, because I knew my job didn't start until the album was finished and, frankly, hanging out during recording was usually boring and, more often, fraught. Spiritualized were different. I had a feeling I was going to witness something extraordinary and felt privileged to be there when Jason was recording the string parts with the Balanescu Quartet at Olympic Studios in London, and when he was recording with the London Community Gospel Choir. The session with the choir had him beaming, and with good reason. The singers raised the roof, singing lines that were anything but sacrosanct. Musically, the finished record was astounding. Everything the previous ones had hinted at was magnified, and somehow Jason had managed to retain a minimalist feel but with a huge sound when called for, and all within a context of fifty years of rock 'n' roll history.

I have a thing about defining moments, which often become a millstone rather than a milestone. The Jesus and Mary Chain could never quite get past *Psychocandy*; the Undertones were stultified once 'Teenage Kicks' was immortalised, long after the original group had split up; and Julian Cope created a monster with *Fried* – not the record but its front-cover artwork. For others it was burning a million pounds. Jason might not agree, but *Ladies and Gentlemen* was Spiritualized's defining moment: it presented something that was daringly different in scale and ambition, and which was often genuinely testing for its audience, but conveyed it in a way that made it palatable, to the point where it became a huge success. It topped many end-of-year polls, when it was up against Radiohead's *OK Computer* and the Verve's *Urban Hymns*. By comparison with those albums, it spawned only minor hit singles, but Spiritualized's stirring, challenging live shows provided the momentum. Their Royal Albert Hall show on 10 October 1997 was as moving and momentous as any I'd ever attended, and in November they played the 'Highest Show on Earth', 144 floors up the CN Tower in Toronto. I made sure I had a reason to be there.

The World Trade Center performance was the sequel to the *Guinness Book of World Records*-cited CN Tower gig. It was only the highest gig in New York. They played in the Windows on the World restaurant, where in the afternoon there was a clear view of the Statue of Liberty on the south side and Manhattan on the east. By nightfall it was dark and cloudy. All we could see were lights in the distance, but the thick blanket of cloud magically gave the effect that we were floating in space. Spiritualized were set up in one corner of the room on the 107th floor. Despite a capacity of only around three hundred and fifty people, they still lit up the bar with a blinding light show and an array of colours that bled out of the windows in full view of the outside world.

I was in New York with Neil McCormick from the *Daily Telegraph*. In his piece Neil wrote that he'd been trying to arrange an interview with

4

the elusive Jason Pierce for over a year. It was a touch of journalistic conceit, and I laughed when I read it. A year earlier the *Telegraph* wouldn't have considered running a Spiritualized feature, but the fact that Neil was witnessing the highest gig in New York was the hook that changed their mind. In the year leading up to it Jason had given interviews to just about every other broadsheet and the music press. When I'd started out as a PR twenty years earlier there had been almost no broadsheet coverage of pop music at all. There were no significant monthly music titles either. From being dominated by four weekly music papers – *NME*, *Melody Maker*, *Sounds* and *Record Mirror* – pop music was now absolutely everywhere and in almost every publication on the newsstands. It was one of the major changes that occurred between 1978 and 1998.

This book is my take on twenty years working as a publicist in the music business, and I've been dutifully reliving it for the last couple of years, even dreaming about it. I very rarely remember my dreams, but a few months ago, around my birthday, I woke with a very clear memory of being in Pete de Freitas's hotel room. Hotel rooms are much the same the world over, so it could have been anywhere. I'd find any excuse to join Echo & the Bunnymen on tour, but I like to think this encounter took place sometime in the years between 1981 and 1984, when the Bunnymen could do little wrong and touring with them was such a joy. I'd wandered into Pete's room and was sat in a chair by his bed, where he was sitting up, half asleep and slightly dishevelled, cradling a mug of tea. Typically, Pete's room was a complete mess, his clothes and the rest of his stuff strewn all over the floor. He grinned the boyishly handsome grin that charmed every girl he ever met and asked me, 'Why are you still doing this?' I didn't have an answer, at least not an easy one, beyond a rather clichéd 'It beats working for a living.' It's what Robert Mitchum always said about acting. 'Yeah,' said Pete, 'but this isn't the real world, is it?' I knew exactly what he meant.

I'd like to think my encounter with Pete was mid-morning, after an Echo & the Bunnymen gig, when we were both feeling a little the worse for wear following a night of innocent reverie, ciggies, booze and pot.

Hanging out with the Bunnymen was a unique experience, but as somebody who worked almost exclusively with groups, believe me, every one of them was unique. The delicate balance of personalities is always precarious; the different levels of creative input, the endless touring and travelling, tedious soundchecks, months on end in the studio, who wrote what and who played that – all these come into play. Age, class, educational background, sex, drugs, booze, dietary preferences and foibles in general: any one of these and more can upset that balance. Throw success into the mix – or a lack of it, or a reversal of fortunes – and before long everybody is at each other's throats.

Pete has been dead now for longer than he was alive. He was a few months short of his twenty-eighth birthday when he died in a motorcycle accident on 14 June 1989, the day before my thirty-ninth birthday. I'd been away overnight, and returned to pick up an answer-machine message from Bill Drummond saying, 'Pete's dead,' and not much else. Bill's not one for sugar-coating anything. It was the first death that really affected me, and Pete's funeral was the first I ever attended. It sent shockwaves through a community and an extended Liverpool family I'd been part of for ten years. Pete was impossible not to like, and I can't think of anybody else I can say that about. And, of course, he was the best drummer in any British group during the 1980s.

I'd met Pete and the rest of the Bunnymen – Ian McCulloch, Will Sergeant and Les Pattinson – along with Bill Drummond, Dave Balfe and Julian Cope at different times during 1980. Being around them meant walking on eggshells at times for the next twenty-five years, and they crop up again and again throughout this story. There are others I'm writing about who won't remember me at all, especially from the first few years, when I was working for the corporate WEA Records. To Gary Numan, Bill Nelson, Rik Ocasek of the Cars, or the Pop Group, people I met only once or twice, I was just 'some bloke who worked for the record company'. I always wanted to be more than that and to have the opportunity to make a difference, which is why I struck out on my own after two years.

A lot of the groups I worked with during the 1980s and '90s don't feature here. Groups were independent publicists' bread and butter, and I like to think I took them all on in good faith, but the reality was that the best many of them could hope for was to make one great single that might earn them a 'Single of the Week' in one of the four inkies, or a glowing live review or initial half-page write-up in *Sounds* or *NME*, and a few plays on John Peel's show, maybe even a session. There was no magic wand that publicists, pluggers, managers or A&R men could wave, and none of us could make or break careers. Record companies often threw money at these groups, but that rarely changed anything.

The working title for this book was *Match Me, Sidney*, and for the whole time I was writing it my screensaver was a still of Burt Lancaster and Tony Curtis as J. J. Hunsecker and Sidney Falco in the film *Sweet Smell of Success*. The ruthless, cold-blooded Broadway columnist Hunsecker had the power to build or destroy the lives and careers of anybody in the entertainment industry, and Falco, the toadying publicist, would do anything for a few of Hunsecker's column inches, the least of which was hovering round J.J. to light his cigarette. He wasn't exactly a role model.

1 : FOUND A JOB

12 July 1978, Sire Records Launch, Notre Dame Hall

I'd drifted through the education system and then drifted into writing about music, and by the end of 1975 I'd established myself as a halfway decent freelance music writer. It was as if a misspent youth obsessed with pop music and with my head in the clouds during the 1960s hadn't been wasted after all. I'd been mad about pop music as a teenager. Even at the age of eight I was badgering my sister to take me to see Buddy Holly and the Crickets at the Granada in Woolwich, and sulking when she said no. Imagine that being the first gig I ever saw, instead of which it was seeing the Applejacks on a variety show in 1964, during a family holiday

Iggy Pop and Seymour and Linda Stein, flanked by Joey and Tommy (left) and Dee Dee and Johnny Ramone (right), at CBGBs in April 1976. The Ramones had just released their game-changing debut album on Sire Records (*photo: Roberta Bayley*).

in Great Yarmouth. They were a three-hit beat group whose main claim to fame was having a girl bass player called Megan Davies, a Sunday-school teacher from Solihull in the West Midlands. The first record I bought was equally inauspicious: 'Lollipop' by the Mudlarks was mind-less novelty pop that made the Top 10 in 1958. Two years later, my taste had improved after its shaky start, mostly as a result of listening to the BBC Light Programme's *Saturday Club* every week. I can hold my head up higher for the singles I remember buying in 1960: 'Cathy's Clown' by the Everly Brothers, Johnny Kidd and the Pirates' 'Shakin' All Over', the Shadows' 'Apache', Roy Orbison's 'Only the Lonely' and Jimmy Jones's 'Good Timin''. I'm still a sucker for great harmony singing, stand-out gui-tarists, big, moody ballads and falsetto voices. It was the beginning of the 1960s. There has never been a better decade to be a pop addict.

Such was the limited media of the day that you had to look under every corner to discover anything. And a little knowledge could go a long way, so you'd read every scrappy item in the music press or gleaned every morsel of information from liner notes or off the back of record sleeves. Then you could join the dots, make the connections. You'd notice recurring patterns in what different record companies put out, you'd find out where people were from, what groups they'd been in before. It was a shock to discover that nearly all the musicians in the trippy, electric San Francisco groups I loved had been in folk and bluegrass bands. Even today I remember things, and people ask, 'How do you know that?' All I can ever say is that 'I just do . . .' I've never forgotten most of what I read or heard on the radio during the 1960s, and it put me in good stead to write about music.

So at twenty-five years of age I was doing something that could hardly be described as a proper job, getting paid for it and being given entry – a foot in the door at least – into the music industry. I was wined and dined by record companies, invited to all the receptions and parties that came along almost daily, and was given all the free records and tickets I could wish for, whether I wrote anything or not. It was a cushy time for a well-meaning hack, but I never seriously considered that I might have a long-term career as a music journalist or get a job in a record company. I had little or no idea where things were leading.

The music industry was a much smaller place in the 1970s, and so much more laissez-faire than it was once the marketing men moved in a decade later. It was built on layers and layers of contacts and everybody seemed to know each other, but Dave Walters was a good friend, which was less common. Dave worked in the press department at WEA, which took its name from the flagship US labels Warner Bros, Elektra and Atlantic, and was second-in-line to department head Moira Bellas. I used to marvel at the fact that Moira was on first-name terms with everybody in the music industry. She'd worked at Pye Records in the mid-1960s, and then became part of the EMI press office just as the Beatles were releasing their final records. WEA was one of the key corporates, along with CBS, Phonogram, RCA and the British giants EMI and Decca, most of which were within walking distance of each other around Soho and the West End. Dave was about as laid-back as you could get but, like all the best PRs, gave the impression of doing very little. He was knowledge-able about music too, and not just whoever was on WEA. If anybody was a mentor to me, it was him. When sometime in May 1978 he and Moira asked me if I'd fill in for a month or so as WEA's in-house writer – the previous incumbent had been sacked for stealing – I thought, 'Why not?' Freelancing is a solitary existence, and I knew and liked everybody in the press department, but I had no intention of staying on once they'd hired somebody permanent. It was just another freelance gig, one that had come along when work seemed a little scarce, plus I'd become dis-enchanted, less about the music than the opportunities open to me as a writer. After five years, I was just treading water.

It was *Let It Rock* magazine that had given me my initial break. Founded in October 1972, *Let It Rock* was a monthly magazine that ini-tially favoured 1950s rock 'n' roll icons and the history of rhythm and blues, but also took in current trends and genres – including British folk, country and soul – that didn't usually appear under the same roof. I rang up Dave Laing, the editor, who surprised me by saying, 'Come up to the offices and have a chat.' I'd sent him stuff I'd written for a Leicester University magazine we'd produced called *Fast & Bulbous* and, while I was studying for a master's in information science, for University College of London's *Pi* magazine – pieces about the Grateful Dead, the Mothers of Invention, Kevin Ayers, Leonard Cohen and Amon Düül. I sat outside his office for a good half-hour, but as the door opened I heard him say, 'Better let the poor sod in.' That did little for my confidence, but I was commissioned to submit a feature, which ran in February 1973. It was a worthy, overlong piece about Tim Buckley that earnt me £25. It meant my name was among the distinguished list of contributors, most of whom I found unapproachable. I felt intimidated in the company of Simon Frith, Charlie Gillett, who had recently published *The Sound of the City*, and Marxist *Melody Maker* folk writer Karl Dallas. I'd sit in meetings in Dallas's Tottenham Court Road flat, envious of his wall-to-wall record collection, and say nothing.

Let It Rock was a precursor to future rock monthlies like *Q* and *Mojo*. It folded after three years, with my first and only cover story on the last of its thirty-five issues: a Q&A with Emmylou Harris, who was still torn up over the death of Gram Parsons. During that year I had become more involved in the editorial side of the magazine, which was now operating as a writers' collective, and however alienated I felt at first, I now belonged. I'd found something I wanted to do for as long as it lasted.

I felt good about writing the odd piece for rival monthly *Zigzag*, which Pete Frame had started up in 1969. *Zigzag* was the first British fanzine dedicated entirely to music, and it was inspired by American folk magazines such as *Sing Out* and *Little Sandy Review*. Its forte was lengthy Q&As and almost genealogical features, which Frame took to a logical conclusion by creating wonderful, intricate, hand-drawn family trees. With its passion for American West Coast rock and the UK underground scene, it was much more my spiritual home. *Let It Rock* was a little too knowing, whereas *Zigzag* looked at music from a fan's point of view and had been the reason why a bunch of us at Leicester University first began writing about music.

In the broader scheme of things, it was more significant that I'd started writing for *Sounds* in 1975. The newest of the four major weekly music papers, *Sounds* was often the first to pick up on trends, but its content veered from heavy metal to punk to prog and mainstream rock from one week to the next. My contributions would have been just as confusing to readers since they included pieces about artists as diverse as John Denver, Justin Hayward and John Lodge of the Moody Blues, Mike Nesmith, Queen, Led Zeppelin, Dr Feelgood and the Stranglers during 1976 and 1977. I wrote one of the first live reviews of the Stranglers after they performed at the Hope & Anchor in London, and observed that most of their bass lines were lifted straight from the first two Love albums and the keyboard sound was entirely ripped off from the Seeds. Next time I saw them at the Hope, Jean-Jacques Burnel came at me with the neck of his bass. It summed up the boorish behaviour and snotty attitude of British punk that I hated.

At twenty-six I was in danger of thinking, 'I'm too old for this,' although I was younger than two of the Stranglers. I found myself grumbling that I'd heard it all before. I'd also seen first-hand how much of punk had been a consequence of pub rock. Journalists liked the idea of watching an undemanding good-time band while propping up a bar with a pint in their hand. Groups such as Bees Make Honey, Roogalator and Brinsley Schwarz were all a little too revivalist and comfortable with their surroundings. Of course, punk swung to the other extreme; punks were more likely to gob in a journalist's beer than buy them a pint after their set. I interviewed Wilko Johnson for *Sounds* in January 1977, and was clearly not the first person to ask him about Dr Feelgood being hailed simultaneously as godfathers of punk *and* pub rock. Wilco gave me a withering stare: 'With a lot of these new wave people,' he snarled, 'it seems that as long as you can put across that aggression and excitement it doesn't matter what you fuckin' play. Or how badly you play it.'

The problem for me when UK punk exploded in the summer of 1976 was that I was always going to be a bystander. As a journalist, I had no outlet and could only watch as former *International Times* editor Mick

Farren nailed his and the *NME*'s colours to the mast in an article that ran in June headlined 'The *Titanic* Sails at Dawn'. It tore into 'materialistic and decadent superstars' like Elton John and Rod Stewart, and declared that 'the sooner the *Titanic* founders with all hands, the better'. It provoked an angry response from readers, but over the next year the music press seized every opportunity to boost circulation figures by intensively covering a phenomenon that was now less about the music and more a hollow threat to the nation's established order. The pop press were happy to conspire with Sex Pistols' manager Malcolm McLaren in his shrewd media manipulation, and soon the tabloids couldn't get enough either.

I had no platform from which to rail about punk. I now look back on an embarrassing list of people I interviewed during 1976. It included affable Welsh rock trio Budgie, who that year released an album called *If I Were Britannia I'd Waive the Rules*, Judas Priest, Peter Frampton, Rick Wakeman and the short-lived so-called supergroup Rough Diamond, which brought together a gaggle of B-list rockers in David Byron from Uriah Heap, Clem Clempson, late of Colosseum and Humble Pie, and ex-Wings drummer Geoff Britton. Much as I might chastise myself for being such a hack, record labels were no less guilty. They all wanted a piece of punk but continued to hedge their bets: it was Island Records who signed Rough Diamond in the same year they signed Eddie and the Hot Rods, a young Canvey Island R&B band smart enough to see the change ahead, even if it just meant they played faster; and it was A&M, riding high all over the world with *Frampton Comes Alive!*, who went after the Sex Pistols after they were dropped by EMI. We were all hypocrites.

I'd landed a job as the London correspondent for the US magazine *Circus*, for whom the UK punk scene didn't exist. *Circus* was little known in the UK, where it had no proper distribution. It wasn't as big and well respected as *Rolling Stone* or as countercultural as *Creem*, but it came with a monthly retainer. It focused on British hard rock, prog and metal acts for content, which opened up doors for me, if not the right ones. So I spoke to all four members of Queen for 'The Queen Tapes', to Jimmy Page, to Black Sabbath's Tony Iommi and to the pre- and post-Peter Gabriel members of

Genesis. They were all disarmingly charming fellows, but I never put their records on at home. Obliged to cover the latest personnel reshuffles in Yes or absurd offshoot solo albums by the Moody Blues, I could occasionally sneak in stories about Graham Parker, Kilburn and the High Roads or Dr Feelgood that reflected the fact that something else was happening. Even when punk gave way to new wave in the US, *Circus* played it safe. They preferred Kiss over the Ramones, Rush over Talking Heads, and Grand Funk Railroad over the Clash; new wave meant Nils Lofgren and Tom Petty.

I was soon writing regularly for *Time Out*. Working regular shifts there covering for absentee writers for the music section was as close as I came to a staff job. My then partner Cornelia was the magazine's picture editor, and although I only wrote about music I felt like a part of something that was politically and culturally significant working alongside a great pool of writers across the arts and politics, such as its then editor Richard Williams, Duncan Campbell, Chris Petit, Dave Pirie, Steve Grant, Brian Case and, not least, regular music contributor Giovanni Dadomo. *Time Out* was a competitive environment and I did some of my most satisfying work there, such as writing about Tom Waits ahead of his first UK dates at Ronnie Scott's, a cover story about Fleetwood Mac's *Rumours* tour, and a piece about DIY indie pioneers Desperate Bicycles that led to a regular column reviewing the independent singles that were proliferating in 1977. The Desperate Bicycles mantra was: 'It was easy, it was cheap – go and do it!' And there were plenty who did. In 1976 the best punk records had all come out of the US, or even Australia. The Saints' 'Stranded' was streets ahead of anything released in Britain, but by 1977 DIY labels were grabbing the initiative with genuinely classic singles as good as anything released anywhere else, anytime, like the Mekons' 'Where Were You?' or the Only Ones' 'Lovers of Today'.

It was the independent rather than the punk ethic that I bought into. I felt out of place at punk gigs but I could listen to singles from the comfort of home, and if at first labels such as Stiff and Rock On – and in their wake Beggars Banquet and the great Walthamstow-based Small Wonder – were metropolitan, it soon became clear that punk had inspired a nationwide boom of kids 'going out and doing it'. Among the first home-brewed labels were Raw Records, run out of a Cambridge record shop called Remember Those Oldies, Rabid Records in Manchester, Zoo Records in Liverpool, Good Vibrations in Belfast and Fast Product in Leeds. For all its limitations of style, punk had triggered a new crop of fascinating bands that were anything but London-centric and who were proving to be far more interesting than the movement that had inspired them. My introduction to a number of bands I was soon to work with – the Undertones, the Rezillos, the Teardrop Explodes, Echo & the Bunnymen – came via memorable independent singles that made them more widely known nationally. As it turned out, everything I later worked on was post-punk in so far as it was inspired by punk and had the energy of punk, but was then transformed into something more complex and colourful.

Punk scenes soon developed across the globe, but the key one coming out of the US had actually pre-dated British punk. It was a scene that evolved in the Bowery area of New York during 1974/5, and it centred on CBGBs, a run-down tunnel of a dive situated at 315 Bowery that had opened in late 1973 to serve up beer and folk (the initials stood for 'Country, Blue Grass and Blues'). The first I knew about it was from reading a couple of pieces in the NME in 1975 written by Nick Kent and Charles Shaar Murray, and it was Television who seemed to be the front-runners. They released the scene's first single, which arrived in the UK in October as an import. Hearing 'Little Johnny Jewel', released on their manager Terry Ork's label, Ork Records, at the end of 1975 confirmed that Kent and Murray were on to something. It was easily the most exciting single I'd heard since the Byrds' 'Eight Miles High' or the Kinks' 'You Really Got Me'.

Then, during 1976 and '77, everybody Kent and Murray had namechecked – Patti Smith, the Ramones, Talking Heads, Richard Hell, Blondie and Television – was playing these shores and had released dazzling and distinctive albums. I thought of them all as, quite simply, great 1970s American bands doing what they did far better than any UK groups, and as such they were part of a line that went back to Steely Dan or Little Feat. You couldn't say the Ramones had the same instrumental chops, but so-called American punk always had a great sense of rock history as well as a degree of art rock, compared to the one-dimensional UK model. In the US punk was more musical statement, whereas in Britain it was more social commentary. John Collis, the music editor at *Time Out*, would say British punks were 'musically illiterate'. He probably thought the same about the Ramones, but they had a strong conceptual element; their sense of black-humoured fun and pop sensibility didn't trivialise or reject classic rock 'n' roll but revelled in it. It was Giovanni Dadomo who first told me about them, and I bought an import copy of their debut album a couple of months before they made their now-historic UK debut at the Roundhouse on American Independence Day, 4 July 1976. It wasn't pretty, but it was unforgettable.

At the Roundhouse, after a false start, Dee Dee yelled, 'One–two–three–four', and the Ramones crashed straight into 'Blitzkrieg Bop', before unleashing their entire debut LP so fast you'd think the world was about to come to an end. It was hard not to make fun of the Ramones or wonder if they were actually taking the piss. Today everybody writes that they blew headliners the Flamin' Groovies off stage, but fewer than half the people there thought that. The rest of the audience mocked and jeered, or just shuffled off to the bar. Even those of us who'd heard the Ramones' album were still thinking, 'This lot can barely play.' It didn't matter. We didn't expect they'd emulate the record, but it was the sheer, uninhibited, loud relentlessness of their performance that was such a shock. What nobody could dispute was that they'd seen nothing like it before. It was a spectacle capped by Dee Dee leaking blood over the Prince Charles T-shirt he was wearing after splitting open a finger. It was shambolic and energising, but it took a while to sink in.

Everyone I knew had gone along to see the Flamin' Groovies, one of those bands who were more popular in Europe than back home, but who were on a hiding to nothing trying to follow their new Sire Records label-mates. After the primitive force of nature that was the Ramones, the Groovies were too premeditated, right down to their Cuban heels and Beatle jackets. Did I think I'd seen the future of rock 'n' roll in the Ramones? Absolutely not, no more than I could have foreseen my own future, in which, two years later, I'd be looking after press for the label that had snapped them up.

Television's first album, *Marquee Moon*, didn't appear till a year after the Ramones' debut; the Ramones' second release, *Leave Home*, had already arrived the month before. When Television made their London debut at Hammersmith Odeon at the end of May 1977, it was obvious that this was a classic ensemble rock band, whereas the Ramones had looked close to falling apart at any point. These guys knew how to play, and how to play together. This wasn't the Allman Brothers, although Television also relied upon a classic twin electric-guitar sound, but songs like 'Marquee Moon', 'Venus' and 'Friction' were so daring. Guitarists Tom Verlaine and Richard Lloyd were trading rhythmic and melodic lines that took off into free-ranging solos. They improvised, but not in the way the Grateful Dead did, and they weren't rhythmically metronomic like the Velvet Underground either. They were icy cool too, stretching certain songs to fifteen minutes of free-jazzed-up rock 'n' roll that blew away hackneyed British prog and hard rock. At Hammersmith, Television had been supported by their CBGBs peers Blondie, whose more superficial, guileless garage sound was too pop for punk and too punk for pop. They didn't look at home on a big stage, but Debbie Harry looked stunning and repeatedly had to cope with predictable shouts of 'Get 'em off'. 'Same old story the world over,' she sighed with great dignity.

If Television and the Ramones and Blondie were very different from each other in approach, then Talking Heads were different again. Their debut album, *Talking Heads: 77*, had a clipped, uptight sound and a danceability that sounded like a deliberate attempt to avoid what all the other New York bands had done on their debuts. Talking Heads had been late arrivals to the CBGBs scene, not playing there till June 1975. The album was six months away when they played the cramped Rock Garden in Covent Garden in mid-May, before continuing on a UK and European tour with the Ramones; their debut single, 'Love Goes to Building on Fire', was all that had been available. It was on Sire too, and they opened with it, David Byrne playing a twelve-string acoustic guitar, which was decidedly un-punk. They upped the volume by the close, with a first hearing for most of us there of 'Psycho Killer', the song which initially characterised the group and singer David Byrne. His distinctive prating vocals and jerky guitar may have stood out, but recent recruit Jerry Harrison added spirited 1960s garage Farfisa keyboard fills, and the surprise element was a tight rhythm section straight out of the classic Stax review. They also had a female bass player, Tina Weymouth, who everybody fancied. Megan Davies was long forgotten.

Like the Ramones, like Television, they were unpredictable and unclassifiable, and all three trashed anything that was coming out of Britain. For me, almost all the great music of the 1970s came out of the US, and it didn't stop with this trio of bands; releases by Richard Hell, the Modern Lovers, Suicide and Pere Ubu were just as revelatory. It intensified my disappointment that I was going nowhere as a writer, frustrated by not having the opportunity to write about any of them. But I was about to become part of the action.

While I was at WEA, tucked away in a small office that intermittently smelt like rotting fish, Sire Records shifted from Phonogram in the UK to WEA. The New York-based label had become the most significant label in the US in the two years since releasing the Ramones' debut album. I was beside myself with excitement, but nobody within WEA's Broadwick Street offices other than the lads in the post room had a clue what Sire Records was about. WEA had been the only major label not to sign any UK punk groups during 1976 and 1977. Suddenly they had Sire and they had Radar, a new label formed by Andrew Lauder and Jake Riviera. Lauder was one of the most forward-thinking and most desperately unassuming figures in the music business, who had nurtured the disparate likes of the Bonzo Dog Band, Man, Hawkwind, Can, Dr Feelgood and the Stranglers at Liberty/United Artists. Riviera's instant cred had come from co-founding Stiff Records in 1976, and he'd brought Elvis Costello and Nick Lowe along with him. Radar's first two albums in March 1978 were Lowe's *Jesus of Cool* and Costello's *This Year's Model*.

'Maybe I should stick around,' I thought. Moira Bellas had the same idea; she couldn't have failed to pick up on my enthusiasm for Sire and asked if I'd like to stay on as the in-house writer but also handle the press for Sire. I hadn't seen it coming because I'd never considered a job in PR and wouldn't have done so had the carrot being dangled not been Sire Records. If I had any doubts, it was because I thought I was thoroughly unsuited for the job – softly spoken and anything but outgoing, pushy and confident – all of which, it transpired, worked in my favour. In the end it was too tempting, especially the prospect of working with the Ramones and Talking Heads, who I knew had albums on the way, and within weeks I was tasked with organising a Sire Records launch party. So, on 12 July 1978, two years since seeing the Ramones at the Roundhouse, my new life began.

In truth, I merely helped Dave Walters organise the event, which was held at Notre Dame Hall, Leicester Square, where Sid Vicious had made his first appearance with the Sex Pistols. I'd never organised any sort of party, let alone one for three hundred and fifty people. The hall had a dancefloor, so we found somebody to make a huge chalk drawing of the yin/yang Sire logo in the middle. We also decided on a buffet comprising multicoloured food that was more appetising than it looked, and the main attraction was a special appearance by the Flamin' Groovies. They were in London, staying in a houseboat on Cheyne Wharf and recording their third album for Sire. I'd loved the Groovies since their classic 1971 album *Teenage Head* and a couple of singles they released for Andrew Lauder, notably a bluesy garage-rock anti-drug anthem called 'Slow Death'. They suffered from the curse of being perpetually championed by leading rock critics, but were largely ignored by the record-buying public. They were stoned and distant at the soundcheck in Notre Dame Hall, perhaps with good reason. They were homesick after several months in the UK and, having been in the right place at the right time when Sire released *Shake Some Action*, they were quickly sidelined once the label signed so many of the new Bowery bands. The group felt short-changed that their second album, *Flamin' Groovies Now*, released at the tail end of the Phonogram deal, wasn't given enough of a push. It had failed to click with fans, who felt it was weighed down by retro covers of songs by the Beatles and the Byrds. The Groovies' set that afternoon reflected this, with 'Shake Some Action' the only original song in a rusty set that included two classic 1960s Stones songs in '19th Nervous Breakdown' and 'Paint It Black', and closed with two Chuck Berry rockers from the early Stones' repertoire, 'Let It Rock' and 'Around and Around'. It was a perfect party set. These days you'd probably book a tribute band, which was more or less what the Flamin' Groovies were that afternoon.

We gave away a green vinyl promo LP that I'd helped compile and written notes for. It came in a cushioned, vile, pinkish orange PVC sleeve, on the back of which 'The Sire Story' was printed in orange text on black plastic. Only four hundred copies were made, and everyone who attended the launch party was given a copy. It featured ten tracks by Sire's finest: the Rezillos, Talking Heads, the Paley Brothers, the Flamin' Groovies, the Dead Boys, Radio Birdman, DMZ, Richard Hell and Tuff Darts. We also included the Ramones' 'Carbona Not Glue', which had been left off UK pressings of *Leave Home*. The other giveaway was a see-through plastic case stuffed with dayglow press releases and photos of the key Sire acts, retro sweets – blackjacks, flying saucers and shrimps – novelty games and a plastic mac. If there was a reason for the plastic mac, it's a mystery to me now.

I met Sire Records' boss and founder Seymour Stein for the first time at the launch. His wife Linda was there too; she was co-managing the Ramones with Danny Fields, and she paraded a forlorn-looking Joey Ramone around Notre Dame Hall like a dog on a very short leash. I met him briefly. He mumbled something like 'How ya doing?' and we shuffled around each other for a few minutes, both trying to avoid eye contact, before Linda tugged the chain and dragged him away. Seymour, far from being the vociferous character I'd expected, wasn't enjoying the celebration of his label. He was ill-tempered, and his mood was not helped when he was confronted by Scottish art-school group the Rezillos, the first UK signing direct to Sire, who were determined to give him grief.

I'd met them the week before to write a new biography and then had to supervise a photo session, where I felt as uncomfortable as half the group at being herded around, while feisty vocalists Fay Fife and Eugene Reynolds played to the camera. At the launch Eugene snared Seymour to complain about their album having been delayed for five months. It wasn't the time or the place to whine, but he did – it was Eugene's forte. Seymour gestured despairingly with his hands: 'What can I say? Believe me, it was for the best.' He found their boisterous behaviour irritating and was even less happy when they pelted him with gaudy-looking food from the buffet.

That evening, the more civilised Talking Heads played the Lyceum, a one-off UK show that was part of a third European tour. *More Songs About Buildings and Food* was released just days later. I was introduced to them that night. I tried desperately not to be overly effusive about how much I loved the band and their new album. 'Just be cool, Mick,' I said under my breath. They were slightly self-conscious too, but friendly and polite as they were presented to a bunch of WEA execs much higher up the food chain than me, including one middle-management exec who days before had described the album as 'jungle music' and said that David Byrne 'sounded like a cat being strangled, and he probably should be'.

I'd spent much of that long day on my feet and in a daze, still unsure of what I was doing but getting more and more excited about what lay ahead. I already felt part of something, in a way I never had as a journalist. The Lyceum gave me a breather, time to gather my thoughts. I just wanted to lose myself in the audience and watch Talking Heads. And they were incredible. A year on since the Rock Garden, they had stepped up beyond belief. Jerry Harrison now looked like he belonged; he was playing a lot more guitar and had switched from the Farfisa to what I was told later was a Prophet synth, which soon became integral to their sound. David Byrne was no longer tentative; he'd turned into a singularly commanding frontman and an effective but ungainly guitar hero. I'm surprised I didn't melt when I met Tina Weymouth. Her bouncy, animalistic bass lines defined Talking Heads' sound as much as anything else. It was hard not to have a crush on her. She was married to drummer Chris Frantz, and, boy, was he good too.

I can take no credit for the brilliant reviews their second album received. Talking Heads had always been a critics' band, but *More Songs About Buildings and Food* pushed them in popularity beyond a knowing clique of music-business insiders and critics. I wasn't kidding myself; I knew it had little to do with my efforts. I just happened to be the person whose name appeared at the foot of the press release when it was serviced to the British music-press cognoscenti: 'For further information contact Mick Houghton.'

2 : ROAD TO RUIN

12 July–31 December 1978

When it first moved over from Phonogram, Sire Records UK comprised only two people: Paul McNally and Andy Ferguson. Both had history with WEA. It was Paul who ran Sire day to day, and he had hired Andy as the label's radio and TV promotions man. Andy had previously been sacked by WEA's head of promotions, Bill Fowler, for stepping out of line once too often. Paul had little doubt that Linda Ronstadt, the Eagles, Jackson Browne and Fleetwood Mac would still be the priority acts within WEA, just as they had been when he was general manager for Elektra several years earlier, before moving to Phonogram. Neither he

It's not punk, it's new wave. Talking Heads began eclipsing the Ramones after *More Songs About Buildings and Food*. Jerry Harrison, David Byrne, Chris Franz and Tina Weymouth in London in 1979 (*photo: Chalkie Davies*).

nor Andy particularly relished being back, nor did they expect WEA to be overly excited at Sire coming under its umbrella.

The lack of interest in Sire had been a real eye-opener for me, even though I wasn't so naive as to believe that working for a corporate label was always going to be as much about music as business. I could never figure out what the label managers did, other than take long lunches and bark orders at their long-suffering assistants. I soon discovered that WEA's recently appointed chief marketing man, David Clipsham, had come straight from Nabisco and knew as much about music as I did about Shredded Wheat. Luckily, in my first six months at WEA I worked closely with Paul and Andy and had little interaction with anybody else there outside of the press office.

I'd never worked in any kind of office environment before, but I knew everybody in the press department and, despite my inexperience, Moira Bellas gave me a free hand. I learnt so much from just being around Moira, who never seemed to be fazed by anybody or anything. She could charm and placate the biggest egos in the business, but she was also was very protective and reassuring, and whatever the provocation I never saw her lose her temper. There's an art to taking shit from somebody and then getting them to see things your way without them realising. So from Moira I learnt that the best way to persuade anybody to do anything was to hoodwink them into thinking they'd come up with the idea themselves. It's one of the fundamentals of the PR game.

Dave Walters was Moira's back-up man, and he was happy not to have her level of responsibility and answerability. He was too easy-going for his own good, and was becoming more so now that he was doing less press, partly as a result of my arrival. He was moving towards a more vague artist-liaison role. Dave 'Monster' Jarrett was the other main press officer. He could deal with whoever or whatever was thrown at him. He could sell a veal steak to a vegetarian. Everybody liked Dave. He didn't take himself at all seriously, and journalists, far from being irritated by his nonsensical patter, liked his no-bullshit approach. We couldn't have been more different.

We sat opposite each other, and I learnt by not following his example, because I never had his effrontery. Whoever he was looking after, Dave would make the same calls, whether it was clean-cut chart duo Dollar, anti-fascist South Shields skinheads the Angelic Upstarts, punk-friendly Aussie hard-rockers AC/DC or French disco group Sheila B. Devotion. Where Dave would make the same thirty calls, it struck me pretty quickly that you needed to make only ten. 'Black Echoes will never write about the Angelic Upstarts,' I'd say, but it was never say never with Dave; he just liked chatting to people. I'd be trying to think of angles, agonising over the right thing to do or say while trying to summon up the courage to ring people I didn't know. Cold-calling never got any easier.

I took my role very seriously. I was being given the responsibility of handling one of the most important aspects of somebody's career. Coverage in the music press was the first step up the ladder once you'd made a record, effectively the first line of both defence and offence. In the first six months after I joined WEA, from July to the end of the year, I was handed four major Sire acts: the Ramones and Talking Heads, and two UK signings, the Rezillos and the Undertones. My job as I saw it was not just to get them in the press, which was never going to be difficult, but to get them the right sort of press. There is a distinction.

Being a press officer – I've always preferred 'publicist', which sounds more dignified somehow and less like working for the Gas Board – isn't a tough job. The basics are obvious, and the rest is common sense. Anybody can pick up a phone or stuff a record into a mailer; what matters is getting to know and understand the people you work with, both artists and the media. Bad publicists always saw it as a case of 'them and us'. It's not; we're all part of the same process, and that's something else that Moira and Dave instilled in me. The music business is no different to any other; it's all about supply and demand.

Music was the only common link between the four Sire groups. It was a complete culture shock, working with people from different backgrounds, classes and cultures. At times I doubted we even spoke the same language, and of course all artists mistrust record labels – or come to do so very quickly – so from the start I had to win them over. I never found it difficult talking to journalists because I never stopped thinking like one. That was to my advantage, but I still had trouble getting over the stigma of being a press officer for a record label and no longer a journalist.

Sire had been set up in 1966 by Seymour Stein and Richard Gottehrer, a writer-producer for the McCoys and a former member of the Strangeloves, a Brooklyn band that scored a hit in 1965 with 'I Want Candy'. In 1977 he produced the debut albums by Blondie and Richard Hell and the Voidoids. Seymour, a compact, shrewd, Jewish New Yorker, is one of the great old-style record men and without doubt a complete one-off. I'd certainly not met his like before – nor have I since. By day he'd be harassed and quite tetchy, but outside office hours he'd be checking out groups around the country with Paul McNally. Not many in his position would bother, and that was one of Seymour's strengths: to strike first and make a deal before the competition upped the price. He never paid huge advances. He was a hard-nosed businessman, and if you challenged him about anything, he would feign astonishment and in an exaggerated Brooklyn accent plead: 'What are you trying to do to me? Oh, you're killing me, you're killing me.' The other side of Seymour was the gregarious bon viveur who always seemed to be around when the more cultured Talking Heads were playing in London. You can't dine out with the Ramones, he'd say, 'even Italian food is too exotic for them'.

I could never resist that epicurean side of Seymour, which drew on a music-industry past in the US that went back to the late 1950s and early '60s, the real good ol' days of chart rigging, payola and crooked deals. The names alone would have me salivating: Syd Nathan at King Records, Red Bird Records and the Shangri-Las – 'Nothing I can tell you about those girls is repeatable,' he'd tease, but he never did tell – Shadow Morton, Phil Spector and Bert Berns. He also possessed a profound, encyclopaedic knowledge of all music genres and had an ability to recall just about any lyric you could name. He could give full *Billboard* chart details if asked, but never took any prompting to burst into song – usually doo-wop

27

and Brill Building classics and Broadway show tunes. With his voice, he would never have signed himself.

I'll admit to being blinkered about Seymour. He reminded me of a Damon Runyon character, but where the petty hustlers in *Guys and Dolls* hung out at Lindy's by day and then came up against a more sinister world of hit men and gangsters from Brooklyn and Harlem by night, the teenage Seymour went from high school by day into the corrupt, cut-throat music industry. He was Brooklyn-born and was brought up in an Italian and Jewish neighbourhood. He was almost as much a caricature New York Jewish record company boss as the Ramones were cartoon New York punks. He enjoyed playing and living the part of the wheeler-dealer hustler that's something of a cliché, but the entertainment indus-try was dominated by Jews, whether in television, motion pictures or music. The great songwriters whom he loved were Jewish – Irving Berlin, the Gershwins, Rodgers and Hart, and Jerome Kern – as were many of the greatest writing teams – Leiber and Stoller, Goffin and King, Barry Mann and Cynthia Weil.

When he was just fifteen and still at high school, he persuaded the edi-tors of *Billboard* to give him a part-time job, and he stayed there till after graduation. Alongside music editor Paul Ackerman, he was responsible for establishing the familiar Hot 100 format, rating singles according to their sales and airplay, and for compiling the overseas charts. Seymour noticed the hits coming out of Europe and never forgot that music from other territories was a source of revenue. Yodelling Dutch prog band Focus gave Sire a hit in 1973 with 'Hocus Pocus', and then its first gold album. He picked up the Euro-punk anthem 'Ça plane pour moi' by Plastic Bertrand from Belgium, which became a UK Top 10 hit in 1978 and was Sire's biggest-selling pre-Madonna single.

R&B was Seymour's major influence, and he saw at first hand that it was controlled by small independent companies all over the States, and that's what he wanted: his own label. It was the upsurge of Bowery bands in the mid-1970s that eventually put Sire on the map worldwide. Until 1976 it had built up a bizarre catalogue of singles and albums by such strange bedfellows as traditional folk singer Jean Ritchie, the Bob Marley-produced Martha Veléz and Sire's meat and drink, European blues rock and progressive groups such as Focus, the Climax Blues Band, Renaissance and Barclay James Harvest. Once alerted to the new punk scene in his native New York, Seymour was smitten by the Ramones' fast and off-kilter take on old-school hit-factory teenbeat. He signed them immediately, which placed him in pole position to snap up many of the other Bowery bands on his doorstep: Richard Hell and the Voidoids, Tuff Darts, the Dead Boys, DMZ and, after a year of dogged pursuit, Talking Heads.

This was the beginning of a new era for Sire. Seymour had bought out Richard Gottehrer, and once Warner Brothers agreed to worldwide distribution in 1977, he had the muscle of a major behind him. 'Seymour was definitely an arch manipulator,' says Paul McNally, 'and would try and get the meanest deal, but that's how everybody operated. He was always open about it. When he signed some of those New York bands, like the Dead Boys, Tuff Darts and DMZ, it didn't matter if they were shitty deals he was offering. Nobody else wanted to sign them, and a Sire album really gave those groups a kudos they wouldn't have got from any other label.'

Seymour was in Britain so much that he acquired a flat near Baker Street. 'He's a collector by nature,' says Paul, 'and he discovered art deco furniture in London as well. I'd be running round picking up bits of furniture; you couldn't move for the stuff piled up in his flat.' It was while checking out antiques on Portobello Road that he stumbled into the new Rough Trade Shop, which had opened in 1976, and that fed his other great love: collecting records. Collecting British DIY punk singles led to friendships and eventually deals with Geoff Travis at Rough Trade, Martin Mills at Beggars Banquet, Bill Drummond at Zoo and Daniel Miller at Mute. Primed by Paul, and with a full hand of strong calling cards, Seymour was in the box seat when it came to signing British bands. Sire's UK signings brought him some success, but it was the British groups he signed to Sire in the US during the 1980s, including

Echo & the Bunnymen, the Smiths, Depeche Mode, the Cure and the Pretenders, among others, that really increased his stock.

Seymour first set his sights on the UK when he signed the Rezillos in late 1977. He'd heard 'I Can't Stand My Baby', released on their local Edinburgh label, Sensible Records, which was run by their first manager, Lenny Love. It was Scotland's first punk single and had cost £300 to record. By the time the Rezillos' second single, 'My Baby Does Good Sculptures', was released, the group were on Sire and touring with the Ramones. They recorded their debut album in March 1978 in New York. The band had been formed in 1976 by a bunch of friends from Edinburgh who were all studying either art or architecture. From the start, DC Comics, pop art, tacky 1960s fashion, flying saucers and bug-eyed monsters were their cultural reference points. Their early repertoire consisted entirely of covers: Eddie Cochran songs, 1960s girl-group songs, Johnny and the Hurricanes instrumentals and beat-group hits. By 1977 they were playing around two hundred gigs a year. They didn't give a shit whether people liked them, but that's what drew an audience to them.

Things became more serious once they began introducing original songs, mostly written by guitarist Jo Callis. They were never punks, but the existence of the genre gave them a sense of direction outside of Edinburgh, which led them to Sire. When I inherited them, the music-press groundwork had already been firmly laid. Fay Fife was the chief visual draw, her looks, gaudy miniskirts and a wild, madcap stage manner casting her somewhere between Lulu and Poly Styrene of X-Ray Spex. Eugene Reynolds, meanwhile, commanded the stage, a solid four-square counterpoint with cool shades and a curling lip, Elvis Presley meets Gary Glitter. The Rezillos' controlled chaos and cartoon-strip fun was clever without being contrived.

They released their third single, 'Top of the Pops', and the delayed album *Can't Stand the Rezillos*, in August; both went Top 20. Although the single mocked the programme, they were duly invited to appear on *Top of the Pops*. I went along to TV Centre, where it was recorded.

It was a TV institution, and I'd never had the chance to attend before. Nobody was ever cool about being on the show for the first time. There were payphones lining the corridor by the studio, where even the most cynical of artists could be found ringing family and friends to say, 'Hey, we're on *Top of the Pops!*' I'm sure Eugene phoned home, but he hated that the Rezillos were conforming to the requirements of the record label and the music business.

The album met with near-rave reviews everywhere for its irreverent, smart pop approach. They had a hit single and a hit album, but I soon noticed there were ructions within the group about the direction they had taken since signing to Sire. It became Fay Fife and Eugene Reynolds versus the rest. Fay and Eugene wanted to return to what they saw as the original blueprint for the band, which was more sassy and derisive, but Jo Callis was worried they'd be dismissed as a novelty band. A little bit of success is always the fork in the road, and less than three months after appearing on *Top of the Pops*, and a week into a major autumn/winter tour, the Rezillos announced they were splitting up. I didn't see it coming. After all, they were signed to the coolest independent label of the day. Were they mad? In interviews Fay and Eugene blamed Sire and the people at WEA, which I guess meant me as well. Their latest Sire single, 'Destination Venus', hadn't made the Top 40; it had been remixed against their wishes, the artwork was wrong and basically the label hadn't done a good enough job.

The Rezillos called it a day in December 1978, after a handful of farewell shows; the Glasgow Apollo show was recorded and released as *Mission Accomplished . . . But the Beat Goes On* in March the following year. They continued to bicker in the music press. *Sounds* ran a feature with a wonderfully apposite headline 'Can't Stand the Other Rezillos'. The back end of the band stuck with Sire, while Fay and Eugene formed the Revillos and went back to square one. They never made the same impact without the songwriting skills of Jo Callis, who proved his worth when he joined the Human League, for whom he co-wrote the million-selling singles 'Don't You Want Me' and 'Open Your Heart'. Most groups start out as friends, but then cracks start to appear. They don't all split up with so much acrimony as the Rezillos, so they were a great group to be blooded on. I learnt a lot working with them during those brief six months, but didn't realise this wasn't a freak occurrence.

In all I had racked up over a hundred interviews in the space of three or four years as a journalist, almost all done in record-company offices or hotel rooms and suites in London. The furthest afield I'd ever travelled was to Leicestershire, to interview Black Sabbath's Tony Iommi in his lavish Georgian house. Now, less than a couple of months into my new job at WEA, I was handed my first trip to the US. It was to oversee interviews with prog relics Yes, whose restored 'classic' line-up, including Jon Anderson, Chris Squire, Rick Wakeman and Steve Howe, had sold out five nights at Madison Square Garden in just hours. I hated Yes, but I didn't care – I was going to New York. So much for my principles. Moira had set it all up, and I didn't know either of the journalists I was going to meet at Heathrow. That morning, the excitement of going to New York was replaced by severe panic. I was taking two complete strangers over there, armed with nothing but the manager's name and where he and the group were staying. What could possibly go wrong? 'Just don't go mad,' was Moira's final instruction before I left.

David Hancock of the *Evening News* cared even less for Yes than I did. A former soul-music writer for *Record Mirror*, he now wrote the Adlib gossip column for the *News*, and we immediately bonded through our indifference to Yes. John Gill from *Sounds* was a major fan. He was as quiet and studious as Hancock was camp and extrovert. I sat with Dave in the smokers' section of the plane, so we ended up several rows behind John. It was rude and unprofessional, and we all but ignored him throughout the flight, during which I quashed my growing anxiety by knocking back large vodkas.

The plan was to do the interviews with Jon Anderson the next day and see the show that evening. We would then fly back to London the day after. We arrived in New York in the late afternoon and had a quiet evening in a restaurant near our hotel, the stately Gramercy Park Hotel overlooking the park. My two charges were now getting on famously, so I went back to my room to fret. The next morning it took me several hours to get hold of Brian Lane, Yes's manager, who told me the interviews were postponed because 'Jon wasn't feeling too well'. No problem, I thought, as long as we do them the next day. 'I'll let you know later,' he said, thereby confining me to my hotel room for the rest of the day waiting for his call.

The others had no reason to hang around, so I gave them their tickets and we agreed to meet inside Madison Square Garden. I waited all day but still had no confirmed interview times, so I rather balefully joined the lengthy queue at the venue, where an attractive, spaced-out American girl sashayed over asking if anybody had any spare tickets. I said, 'Sure, you can have this one.' 'Wow, thanks,' she said, and skipped away. As the queue moved slowly forward she reappeared and thrust a tablet into my hand as a 'thank you'. I didn't really do drugs, at least not excessively. I'd never taken acid, which I figured was what I had in my hand, I didn't smoke dope because I didn't like it, and it was only speed I'd taken with any regularity. I should have just dropped the tablet on the ground, but my anxiety was rising again. 'Sod it,' I thought, and swallowed the tablet. I was now freaked out by my own stupidity.

I made my way to my seat, which was far too close to the stage for comfort, wondering why my charges weren't seated next to me, when the drug kicked in with a surging whoosh inside my head, just as Yes took to the stage to a tumultuous roar. I was pinned to my seat by waves of chest-pounding bass. Around me rows of hollering fans were passing joints, throwing frisbees and setting fire to polystyrene cups. I drifted between euphoria and paranoia. Jon Anderson was flying above the stage, singing about centaurs, elves and bright fairies, and Rick Wakeman had become a giant hovering bat. The rest of Yes were now tiny orcs on a huge revolving stage. It was just like *Sunday Night at the London Palladium*, with cardboard fairground horses bobbing up and down around the stage. I was too panicked to move. 'Please let them stop,' I repeated to myself for what seemed like hours. This was Yes, of course, so it *was* hours.

I finally caught up with Dave and John at a rather polite after-show party in one of the labyrinthine function rooms. Mercifully I'd not been introduced to Brian Lane or anybody from Atlantic Records, so nobody was any the wiser as to how hard I was concentrating on trying to behave as if I was totally together. I know I made it back to the hotel because I was awoken the next morning by Brian on the phone telling me we'd have to postpone the interviews for another twenty-four hours. 'Yes . . . but . . .' I started to say. 'Don't worry. Just change your flights,' he said, and hung up. I could barely change my socks, let alone change flights. My brain was racing with 'what ifs', all amounting to an overriding 'What if I fuck up completely and we fly back without the interviews taking place?'

As it was, they were sorted at the third attempt, although they were with Chris Squire and not Jon Anderson. He was still unwell, though he had looked fine when he was hovering above the stage the night before. We had a far more civilised extra couple of days in New York, during which I got to walk round Greenwich Village, Little Italy, Broadway and Times Square and lose myself in cavernous bookshops and funky record stores. I even made it to the Guggenheim Museum. The flight back quickly blurred into an alcoholic haze, we said our fond farewells, and I decided to head straight into the office. I didn't know what to expect; aside from all else I'd run up a massive expenses bill on my brand-new Amex card. 'I didn't expect to see you today,' said Moira cheerily, as I sheepishly stuck my head round the door to her office. 'Did you have a good time?' There was no sense of irony in the question. Everything was all right. Brian Lane had already spoken to Moira and thanked me for being so accommodating. We didn't get the cover of *Sounds*, but Dave Hancock's article duly ran in the *Evening News*, with the prosaic headline 'Yes, Please', alongside a photograph of the wrong line-up. It was a perfunctory piece that briefly touched on seeing the group in New York, followed by a handful of quotes from Chris Squire that could easily have been done over the phone in ten minutes.

What did I learn? Patience, perseverance and don't take drugs from strangers.

You should not underestimate the impact the Ramones made in Britain during 1976 and 1977. The evidence isn't in record sales or chart positions, but just about every band that formed in the late 1970s was touched by them in some way. I came on board as their new publicist just in time for the backlash targeting their fourth album in two and a half years, *Road to Ruin*. They were also arriving in Europe for their first dates since drummer Tommy Erdelyi had left. Usually considered to be the brains of the outfit, he'd played his last gig as a Ramone in May 1978, but still co-produced *Road to Ruin*. Tommy Ramone had shaped the band and created one of pop's most identifiable and prevalent signature sounds. It always struck me that the Ramones were one of the few New York bands who displayed no discernible influence of the Velvet Underground. Their songs were short, fast and highly reductive, with a lyrical New York twist that revealed a dark sense of humour. There were no hidden messages; the Ramones were simply about having fun both on record and onstage, and up until now the critics had loved them.

The group were by no means a household name in the UK, but in an alternative punk universe they were stars. I travelled on the bus with them a lot on that tour, usually with Paul McNally. I met them for the first time after a show at Bristol Locarno on 26 September 1978. They looked exhausted coming offstage but handled the meet-and-greet backstage like pros; it was obvious they weren't at all dumb. The Locarno was the worst kind of venue in which to see them play, a tacky, characterless Mecca ballroom with a low stage and so much floor space it looked empty from halfway back. Everyone was crammed up front. It was hard not to get sucked into a Ramones live show: dressed in trademark ripped jeans, tight T-shirts and leather jackets, they created their own infectious fantasy world.

I fully expected a barrage of questions from the group about why the UK press had suddenly turned against them, but they were pretty resigned to it. They'd already been primed that the British press built people up just so they could knock 'em down. I may have been green but I knew my job with the Ramones was more of a holding operation. After four albums in quick succession and a couple of UK tours there was nothing new this time around. I thought that was missing the point: Ramones fans wanted that reassurance that their group was never going to change.

I went back and listened to all the albums again, and *Road to Ruin* was clearly a departure, however subtle. It was the first Ramones album to run over thirty minutes. There were even songs that spilt over the three-minute mark, but the revelation was that it introduced acoustic guitars and a few disquieting love songs, like 'Don't Come Close' and 'Questioningly'. 'I Wanna Be Sedated' was, however, a stone-cold classic, and 'I Just Want to Have Something to Do' and 'I Wanted Everything' showed no signs of a band slacking or limiting their use of the word 'want'. What they wanted, though, was more downbeat this time around. When one journalist asked whether the Ramones wanted to be taken more seriously, Joey quipped, 'Yeah, it's our *Berlin*.'

Groups invariably think their new album is the best they've ever done, and this one was no exception. The Ramones had wanted to progress. They wanted to add medium-tempo songs alongside the usual speed-limit stuff. They wanted radio play back home. They wanted that elusive hit. Offstage they kept to themselves, although they'd insist on going for a curry before every gig, ordering the hottest thing on the menu and then perspiring profusely underneath their leathers. Paul said that when they first came to England, they hated Indian food, but our burger joints didn't pass muster, so the local Taj Mahal was the best alternative. More than once the chicken vindaloo was later vomited up onstage. Much as they liked touring over here, where they were bigger than anywhere else in the world, they despised being spat on, especially Joey. He would walk offstage covered in spittle, all over his hair and dribbling down his jacket. It was a disgusting sight.

They weren't a party band and never stayed up late. In England there was nowhere to go anyway; even the TV had shut down by the time they made it back to the hotel. They wouldn't miss breakfast, though. Johnny was usually the first one down. 'What's up?' he'd say with a penetrating look; it was less a greeting than an indication of some minor gripe or other. Otherwise they were easy-going and in interviews were lively and mildly argumentative. On the face of it they put up a united front as Ramones, so-called brothers in a band, but they were very different, and Paul said that since they'd first toured here, cracks had begun to appear.

Johnny could be particularly hard work; he'd question how many records, tickets and T-shirts they'd sold that day. Paul would arm himself with figures, more often than not made up to placate him. Joey had a shy, quiet nature compared to the others. He stayed in one spot onstage, stooped over the mic stand. It emerged later that he had serious OCD. If he sat on a coach or plane with checked seats, he'd count and count the number of squares. Paul said one time they had to drive back from Heathrow to the hotel so Joey could complete one of his ritualistic checks.

Joey and Johnny had little in common. Joey hated sports and was a liberal; Johnny was a serious Yankees baseball fan and a conservative. I witnessed a telling example of Johnny's strange logic when somebody travelling with us on the coach brought up a particularly vindictive *NME* piece written by Tony Parsons that ran a few months before the 1978 tour. Johnny laid into Parsons for wearing a hammer-and-sickle badge and said he must be a commie. 'So,' Johnny was asked, 'was everybody who wore a swastika a Nazi then?' 'Look,' he replied, 'Germany lost the war, so there's no threat right now of any Nazi thing, but there is a communist threat.'

Dee Dee was the heart and soul of the band. He was the true punk, but he wasn't stupid and with Joey shared most of the songwriting credits. He usually said the first thing that came to mind, and sometimes that was dumb or inappropriate. It was already common knowledge that Dee Dee had struggled with drug addiction for much of his life, particularly heroin. He'd been using drugs since he was a teenager and continued to use for the majority of his adult life, but I never saw any signs when I was around. Meanwhile, new drummer Marc Bell – Marky had been the drummer on Richard Hell and the Voidoids' album *Blank Generation* – had a more solid, heavier drum sound than Tommy. He was quiet and unassuming, maybe because he was the new boy. He was still trying to fit in on that 1978 UK tour. So was I and usually hung out with him in the bar back at the hotel.

Talking Heads were not native New Yorkers. David Byrne was born in Dumbarton, just outside Glasgow, though his parents moved to Canada, then Baltimore, which he thought was very similar to his place of birth: it was grey, had lots of slums and was pretty rough. There he remained, until he went to Rhode Island School of Design, where he first met Chris Frantz and Tina Weymouth, both Midwestern-born navy brats. All three were well educated and middle-class, and therefore they were branded as an upwardly mobile ersatz rock 'n' roll group. It was an impression only confirmed by Jerry Harrison delaying joining the band till he'd completed his degree in architecture at Harvard. *Rolling Stone* said they dressed like a quartet of Young Republicans, but it was John Rockwell in the *New York Times* who applied the term 'art rock' to them early on.

I only met Talking Heads a few times in 1978, but I found them readily approachable. We were more or less the same age and they were the sort of people I would likely have met in everyday life, whereas the Ramones, the Undertones and the Rezillos were not. Although David Byrne is always described as an oddball, I always liked that he would talk deeply and eloquently one moment, then make a funny comment and laugh out loud. Lee Ranaldo of Sonic Youth had seen them at CBGBs early on. 'One of the things that struck me first,' he said, 'was that they were all wearing wrist watches, which was somehow unusual and made them appear so oddly normal.' Talking Heads had always looked different to the other CBGBs groups. All four, Tina Weymouth included, had short hair, and the boys shunned leathers and ripped clothing in favour of smart leisurewear – neat slacks and open-neck shirts. One of the earliest Talking Heads interviews I saw appeared in US fanzine *Trouser*

Press, and I remember Jerry Harrison very pointedly saying there were no junkies in the group and they were always responsible and punctual.

One of the first times I met them Chris said that many groups at CBGBs were still aping the riffs and moves of the Who and the Stones, whereas they were listening to funk and even disco, and you can hear the influence of Sly and the Family Stone and Funkadelic on *More Songs About Buildings and Food*. The obvious clue is their cover of Al Green's 'Take Me to the River', but it isn't an anomaly, it's very Talking Heads. It was a US Top 30 hit thanks to heavy radio play. Seymour Stein's campaign of telling US radio programmers, 'It's not punk, it's new wave,' had benefited Talking Heads but not the Ramones, for whom *Road to Ruin* was another album that failed to make the US Top 100. Natural momentum had seen Talking Heads replace the Ramones as Sire's key band. The Ramones had helped kick-start punk in 1976, but they were stranded in time. After 1978 they would never be as popular again. By the end of the year *More Songs About Buildings and Food* had become one of the year's must-have albums. If I had any mission in 1978, it was to try and spread the word about Talking Heads beyond just the music press.

However much I struggled at times to understand the Ramones' Brooklyn accents, it took months before I could comprehend a word any of the Undertones said. They all seemed to emit an angry barking sound and it required a considerable amount of guesswork if any kind of conversation was to be had. Like Paul McNally, whom they nicknamed 'Noisy', I was quietly spoken. Conversations were difficult: they couldn't hear me, and I couldn't understand them.

The Undertones were from Derry, in Northern Ireland, and they were all on the British mainland for the first time, having been brought over in late October 1978 by Sire Records, ostensibly to appear on *Top of the Pops*. Understandably, the whole experience was a complete culture shock for them. As hard as I tried not to exploit it in any way, there was a perverse novelty value in a band from Northern Ireland that didn't sing about the Troubles. Instead, they made punk-laced pop songs. It became a standing joke, which never entirely went away, that almost every feature written about the Undertones began with the phrase 'From the war-torn streets of Derry'.

Though hardly the most successful band to come out of punk in the late 1970s, the Undertones now have a lasting fame through one of their first recordings, 'Teenage Kicks', a song that, since they split up in 1983, has taken on a life of its own, not least for being John Peel's all-time favourite record. The group hadn't wanted it as the lead track on their first EP, which was released at the end of August 1978 on the independent Belfast label Good Vibrations. Peel loved it instantly and played it incessantly. Famously, Seymour heard it while driving up the motorway – he was on his way to see the Searchers play in Southend – and began screaming, 'Stop the car, stop the car, pull over, pull over.' Paul thought his boss was having a heart attack and followed orders, while Peel obligingly played 'Teenage Kicks' again. Wary of travelling to 'war-torn' Derry, Seymour immediately dispatched Paul there to sign them, telling him, 'My name is Stein and yours is McNally, so you're going to Northern Ireland.' What Seymour instinctively appreciated was that 'Teenage Kicks' was a mixture of romantic Red Bird/Phil Spector pop and early Rolling Stones licks and attitude.

John O'Neill, the group's guitarist as well as its chief songwriter, told me years later that 'By the time we'd made the *Teenage Kicks* EP we were close to breaking up. We believed all the stuff about punk and we tried to be the real thing. It was important to be as spontaneous as possible but at least we'd made a record, something to prove that there had been a punk band in Derry. Whatever else, we'd left our mark. What happened after that was pure chance because John Peel loved the record.'

Like many groups feeling their way in 1976 and 1977, the Ramones, the Clash and the Sex Pistols had provided a blueprint for John's writing. Out went the more R&B sound they first adopted, influenced by the Rolling Stones, Eric Clapton and Dr Feelgood, and in came short, fast songs, simple chords and a simple beat. Bass player Mickey Bradley bought the Ramones' album in summer 1976 and it blew them all away, and the New Yorkers became the template for John's writing. Another friend in Derry had a record collection that exposed them to Iggy and the Stooges, the Velvet Underground and Elektra Records' garage-band compilation *Nuggets*. I was in total awe that they could play almost the entire *Nuggets* album, and occasionally they'd slip a track into the set list or a soundcheck and totally nail it.

John was the eldest of a bunch of school friends who first thought about forming a band in 1974. At that point the group consisted of John, Billy Doherty, Mickey Bradley and John's brother Damian on guitar. It was only when Feargal Sharkey joined in late 1975 that they started taking the idea seriously. Feargal was already well known in Derry for winning every Catholic-school singing competition going. Although he had been in Billy's class at school, he was outside the original circle of friends. He was also the only one who was working, so he had access to a van thanks to his job with Radio Rentals, which was handy for transporting gear.

Paul McNally duly flew to Derry to see the Undertones at the Casbah, one of the few venues in the city where they could get a gig. He met the band the next day at Feargal's house, where they signed a provisional contract that was witnessed by *Melody Maker* journalist Ian Birch. Two weeks later the deal was clinched and 'Teenage Kicks' was released by Sire on 13 October 1978. Three days later they recorded their first session for John Peel, and on 25 October they performed 'Teenage Kicks' on *Top of the Pops*. That's where I first met them, with Feargal having to rush back home for work the next day. 'Teenage Kicks' eventually peaked at a lowly no. 31 during a six-week chart run.

The Undertones lived up to their ungainly 'boy-next-door' image, with half-mast trousers and the sort of Christmas jumpers you'd never actually wear. Whatever clothes they put on in the morning they later wore onstage or on TV. It was important to them that they could go back to Derry and no one would have a go at them for trying to be a pop star. Most bands would have killed to be on *Top of the Pops*, but half of the Undertones didn't want to be there. That attitude would never change. Aside from Feargal and nineteen-year-old Damian, the others were always homesick. They were a remarkable group. The *Teenage Kicks* EP was a little too raw and crude for my taste, but once I saw them play live it was obvious that being a punk band was something of a facade. The Undertones would have been a great group in any era because of the strength of their songs, and there were far better songs than those on the EP in their set. And they could really play, tight but never slick, and Feargal was an incredible frontman. Annoyingly self-deprecating, they didn't know just how good they were. They thought every other band they liked was better than them, especially the Clash and Buzzcocks. At *Top of the Pops* they went round collecting autographs, including that of Elvis Costello, who was quick to point out that they were higher in the charts than him.

Towards the end of the year the Cars, from Boston, MA, arrived in London ahead of a series of European dates and a sold-out gig at the Lyceum. Ric Ocasek and Benjamin Orr had been songwriting and performing partners for almost ten years, mostly leaning towards a close-harmony, Crosby, Stills and Nash style. They epitomised the distilled version of new wave and fooled nobody by wearing mirror shades. Their surprise UK no. 3 hit 'My Best Friend's Girl' was basically a result of a new marketing ploy: it was the first-ever picture-disc single. Their self-titled debut album followed swiftly and was produced by Queen's regular producer Roy Thomas Baker, which didn't win them too much new-wave cred in the UK, and none at all with me. I was being asked to look after a group whose music did nothing for me. I didn't warm to them either; they were too standoffish. I confronted the manager when I insisted he didn't sit in on an interview with the *NME*'s Max Bell. Word of this spread among journalists and did my reputation no harm whatsoever.

Todd Rundgren did me no favours either. I was a massive fan of his solo work, and *Hermit of Mink Hollow*, released just before I took the job at WEA, had made some amends for his awful, overblown prog vehicle Utopia. He was in London producing Tom Robinson's *TRB2* at Pye Studios just before Christmas, which he combined with a series of shows at the Venue in Victoria. The shows were great and he wore an odd, onesie-type get-up which was so tight it left nothing to the imagination. For some reason the front of the stage at the Venue was lined with mounds of potatoes: the ongoing joke was that he'd stuffed a couple of King Edwards down his pants. While he was over he agreed to do one interview a day at noon. Each day I would turn up at the palatial rented house in Mayfair where he was staying, but he never managed to get up in time to do any of them.

It had been quite a start to my unlikely career as a press officer. At the end of the year I was completely taken aback when the *NME* voted me their 'golden phones PR of the year'. It was just a line in its gossipy inside-back-page section T-Zers but, after only six months in the job, it was a kind of validation. I'd already made more of an impression as a publicist than I ever had as a journalist.

3 : BEYOND GOOD AND EVIL

January 1979–August 1980

In the space of twelve months WEA had switched from a policy where almost everything was provided by the three American parent companies to going on a shopping spree for home-grown artists, mostly signed through a series of UK-based labels. These included Real Records, soon

The Undertones could do no wrong in 1980, landing their only Top 10 single, 'My Perfect Cousin', and Top 10 album, *Hypnotised*. Both were characteristically self-deprecating, dumb entertainment.

almost solely identified with the Pretenders, Beggars Banquet, Automatic and Korova, as well as direct signings such as cheesy Scottish pop singer-songwriter B. A. Robertson and politically charged skinhead punks the Angelic Upstarts. When Dave Jarrett was on holiday I took Charles Shaar Murray to the F Club in Leeds to review the Angelic Upstarts for the *NME*. It was a real eye-opener for a naive closeted southerner. We took a cab from the hotel to the gig. The driver had an accent as thick as Mackintosh's celebrated toffee, warning us that 'Thou'll be like a spot on a domino in there.' I had no idea what he meant till we walked into the wrong bar of a segregated pub. The gig was wall-to-wall skinheads. I cowered at the back with Charlie and watched in awe as Pennie Smith grabbed her camera and strode purposefully into the throng, which made way for her. It was like the parting of the Red Sea in *The Ten Commandments*.

I took journalists away on such trips every week and travelled to every major UK city and European capital, as well as enjoying half a dozen more New York jaunts during my stint at WEA. Mostly overnighters, it was frustrating going to so many fantastic places where all you experienced was the hotel and the venue, and the journey in between. After a while my role as a glorified travel agent's rep became second nature, but this was how I got to know the groups and, more importantly, how I built up relationships with journalists and photographers. There were very few I'd make sure never to go away with again, but I never came to blows with anybody. I just grew an extra layer of skin.

Six months into the job I surprised myself at how much I was enjoying being part of a corporate machine, and I began looking after artists from all the different labels. I felt like I could take anything in my stride: overseeing interviews with AC/DC's Angus Young following the death of the group's singer, Bon Scott; looking after a demanding Etta James, here to play popular London dive Dingwalls ahead of the Montreux Festival, or a subdued Steve Martin, who was over to do the *Parkinson* show. Another time I had to supervise a Chuck Berry press conference held during the Capital Jazz Festival at Alexandra Palace in July 1979. The tour manager took me to one side, saying Chuck wouldn't take questions about his recent incarceration for tax evasion. I made this known to the assembled journalists, all happy just to breathe the same air as the great man. Come question time, though, one journalist broke ranks. Mike Nichols from *Record Mirror* was renowned for not doing what he was told, so he raised his hand, as I knew he would, and that was the end of it. Chuck exited the press conference almost as speedily as he did at the end of the gig a few hours later, having played for exactly the allotted time he was booked for, and which famously was generally paid for in cash. I didn't care; it's not every day you get to meet one of the great rock 'n' rollers. I even got to add another tick to my Bowery group checklist. Tom Verlaine's self-titled debut album had been released in September 1979 by Elektra Records. I'd done my share of interviews that were like picking eggshells out of a garbage bin, notably with Lou Reed and Ray Davies, but Verlaine proved no less challenging for the journalists I'd lined up. They all left shaking their heads despairingly. His album came out a year after Television split up, which was all anybody wanted to ask about, but it wasn't on his agenda. At least he didn't walk out.

The Undertones were the first group with whom I felt confident that I could make a difference. Andy Ferguson had become their manager. Even before their self-titled debut album was released he was telling me about the tensions already manifesting themselves within the group. Yet the Undertones appeared to be enjoying a charmed life since recording 'Teenage Kicks', and in the eighteen-month period following the start of 1979 they had hit after hit and were perceived almost universally as purveyors of perfect pop. The only blip was that their second single, 'Get Over You', flopped. It was one of their best, a New York Dolls-influenced song that I much preferred to the irritating 'Jimmy Jimmy', which saw them break through into the Top 20 in April. The following month *The Undertones* reached no. 13. Press reaction to their debut album had been nothing short of wholesale approbation, the band being lauded with superlatives: 'More perfect pop', 'Teenage Dreamland', while *Melody Maker* ridiculously claimed that it was 'A competitor for Abba's *Greatest Hits*'.

The album's black-and-white cover shot was taken in front of a wall opposite the O'Neill brothers' house. All five Undertones were still living with their parents when the second album, *Hypnotised*, came out a year later. It did even better, landing at no. 6. *Hypnotised* was another feast of great songs, including their first Top 10 hit, 'My Perfect Cousin'. It sealed their fate as an innocent pop-punk act. The video, shot by Julien Temple, was filmed at the O'Neills' house, with the band miming and pretending to play their instruments in the back garden and playing Subbuteo in the front room. Yet *Hypnotised* was far more imaginative and there was an obvious maturity and sensitivity on songs like 'Wednesday Week', 'Tearproof' and 'The Way Girls Talk'. The album's opener was Damian's tongue-in-cheek 'More Songs About Chocolate and Girls', which set out their stall perfectly, inviting listeners to settle down and enjoy some dumb entertainment. It was typically self-deprecating, and the backlash the group expected never came.

The Undertones were defined by the music press in 1979. They disarmed even the most hardened critics. No one could ever quite come to grips with their apparent innocence and naivety. They weren't at all naive, but that's how they were portrayed, and that would ultimately prevent their later work from being taken as seriously as it deserved. The perpetual teenagers played up to the image. The cover of *Hypnotised* was a silly snapshot of Mickey and Billy, both with cheesy grins and wearing oversized paper bibs with lobsters printed on them. The photo was taken in Patrissy's in Little Italy, Seymour's favourite Italian restaurant, during the group's first visit to New York. It was a jolly affair, with Seymour footing the bill and being Mr Congeniality. However, he'd left his wallet behind, and one of the girls from his office had to do the honours.

John O'Neill never took the plaudits showered upon the Undertones seriously and genuinely believed it was because English journalists felt sorry for them coming from Derry. Feargal and Damian aside, they were far from ambitious. If anything, they'd already achieved their ambition once the first album was released. They had their own set of rules, which were inspired by punk attitudes and were against anything intrinsically 'rock', and would question playing somewhere that was too big. They would pull me up for saying 'gig', or 'album' instead of 'LP'. And only hippies took drugs, which were strictly taboo for the group.

They didn't care about chart positions, even when the odd single flopped. Instead, success brought tours and commitments that took them away from Derry, and Billy and John in particular were so home-sick that tours were often kept short, or else they'd fly home on days off. John, Billy and Feargal all married in the summer and autumn of 1980, while Mickey married the following May, leaving only Damian hanker-ing after a more rock 'n' roll lifestyle. If half the band weren't flying back and forth to see their wives, then the wives would come on tour. 'British Airways made more money out of The Undertones than we did,' com-plained Damian.

Feargal would get riled because he knew you had to put in the hours and do the tours. He was the frontman, and with that came extra respon-sibilities. He handled most of the interviews and was always singled out for photos. Cover stories, which for a while came thick and fast, usually featured a picture of Feargal on the front page. Resentment built, the others would let him do the talking, but then often disagreed with what he said. Feargal was definitely the main man onstage. Bare-chested and skinny like Iggy Pop, he would crouch down every three or four songs in a seemingly choreographed James Brown-type move, but the real reason was that he smoked too much and needed a breather. He chain-smoked for the whole band. Damian reckoned the energy he had onstage came from living on a diet of coke (the sugary drink variety) and Mars bars. That's all he ever saw him eat.

Not that the Undertones weren't fun to hang out with on tour; you just had to be well behaved. They had a brilliant tour manager called Martin Cole, who always kept an avuncular eye on them and accepted there was never going to be any rock 'n' roll misconduct. Being in a successful band didn't go to their heads. By then, just being around successful bands was going to mine; my moral compass was certainly beginning to deviate. Not so the Undertones. When we all checked in to the Taft Hotel in New

York, the first thing they asked at reception was where could they find the nearest Catholic church? I don't think that was uppermost in anybody else's mind, but there's nothing wrong with being good Catholic boys or getting married. In one classic interview Tony Wilson brought up the fact that four of the group were married, and almost in disbelief simply asked, 'Why?'

I spent a lot of time touring with them. They were a phenomenal live band, truly exciting, and with a connection to the audience that I never saw bettered. I wasn't going to miss out on their first US tour in 1979, which just so happened was supporting the Clash from 14 September to 2 October. I arrived in time for two shows at the Palladium in New York, with Sam and Dave the added attraction. The soul duo hadn't spoken in years and really did come onstage separately, Sam from the right, Dave from the left. Things between John and Feargal had not deteriorated that much yet. It was at the Palladium that the Clash's Paul Simonon smashed his Fender bass into the stage and Pennie Smith captured the classic shot that would make the cover of *London Calling*.

The Undertones had to open, with the hall all but empty still. After two or three songs, instead of crouching down Feargal sang the next couple from row six of the auditorium. 'I always wanted to see how good we were,' he said, on returning to the stage. The Clash were very welcoming, and although John was too respectful to even speak to them during the tour, by the end the others were attacking them in the dressing room with water pistols. It was during that tour that the ongoing saga of Billy's pigeon ran in the *NME*'s T-Zers section. It summed up the Undertones' innocence in a nutshell. After that first Palladium show, Billy Doherty found a wounded pigeon in the street and took it back to the hotel. 'Are you fuckin' crazy?' the guy at reception said, when Billy asked him if he had a cardboard box. 'You can't bring that thing in here.' So Billy carried the pigeon up to his room cradled in his jacket, and it joined the tour party for the next few days. When I left for home, the wounded bird was still alive, six flights up, outside Billy's hotel-room window. The next morning it was gone from its resting place, its fate open to question.

*

In 1979 there was no doubting that the extreme work ethic and spirit of adventure that had characterised Talking Heads for the last eighteen months was paying off in spades. The year began with three months on the road in the States, before making their third album, *Fear of Music*, in May, with producer Brian Eno in charge for the second time. It was recorded in a mobile studio dragged up to Chris and Tina Frantz's Long Island loft, where the band rehearsed for ten days; it was then completed in under two weeks, before the group went back on the road to Australia, New Zealand and Japan, with a brief stopover in Europe, but no UK dates. A month ahead of the release of *Fear of Music*, this was an unmissable opportunity, enabling me to organise a trip to Paris with Max Bell and Pennie Smith for an *NME* cover story.

The Paris show was in the ultra-chic Théâtre le Palace, after which the promoter threw a party for them in a massive mansion on the Left Bank that was utterly bourgeois, obscenely luxurious and the height of bacchanalia. Max Bell set the scene: 'Room after room reveals the splendours of a lifestyle which may not have changed one jot since the demise of the Sun King. Everything is renaissance, Louisian, rich and tasteful.' It was almost humbling, until the vintage wines and champagnes got me attuned to the surroundings – along with the generous lines of coke being chopped out on priceless antique glass-topped tables.

At one point I stepped out for air and sat on a small garden wall with Pennie Smith, necking disdainfully from a fine bottle of Château Lafite Rothschild. Then, stage left, a slightly sozzled David Byrne ambled by carrying a plate of food, before tripping and falling headlong into some shrubbery, food flying everywhere. You couldn't but feel for him as various onlookers tried to help him. I glanced at Pennie, who was almost as shocked as David, her camera still on her lap. His embarrassment was thus only witnessed by a few onlookers.

The next day another party was thrown for the band, this time at the very 'in' underground disco Les Bains Douches, which was formerly public baths. But I'd had enough of the Parisian high life and had grown tired of feeling shabby beside the super-stylish, well-heeled Parisian set and so, like David Byrne, whom I'd seen scurrying off earlier, I made an early retreat. The next day I took Max along to David's hotel room, where he produced what appeared to be a small briefcase that opened out to become a top-of-the-range cassette player with separate speakers. He politely asked if we'd like to listen to the imminent new album, *Fear of Music*. Either to save his or our discomfort at listening to it in the presence of its creator, he excused himself and left. I still think it's Talking Heads' best album, which has nothing to do with the privileged circumstances in which I heard it for the first time. Max and I sat there, rendered speechless as 'I Zimbra' soared out of the speakers, its combination of African rhythms and lush effects and textures topped by David's jabbering vocal. From there on it was as if the music had developed by itself, serious, complex, weird, absurd and unexpected by turns, leaving me and Max to marvel that Talking Heads had succeeded in reinventing themselves again.

In September they shared headline slots with Van Morrison and the Chieftains at the Edinburgh Rock Festival, where an apprehensive David asked me to join him while he had afternoon tea in the Caledonian Hotel with a brace of elderly Scottish aunts down for the day. I always found him so easy to get along with, and never more so than that afternoon eating cake and sipping tea out of fine china tea cups with him and his inquisitive relations. After Edinburgh Talking Heads continued on their European trek, which ended with three major London shows in a week. I was smitten by the band, who, for all the rigours of a lengthy touring schedule, were happy to hang out. Max and I caught up with the Frantzes at the Portobello Hotel, where it wasn't long before they began grumbling about the focus of the group shifting increasingly towards David, and how it was undermining the group. Much of Tina's ire was directed towards Brian Eno and his and David's inseparability. 'They are starting to look alike,' she joked. I was shocked when she told us that when Talking Heads got their contract with Sire, she had to audition for the group again. 'And that wasn't his idea,' she added, pointing at Chris, who was absent-mindedly rolling another joint. Her congenial husband would always play down the differences between his wife and David, but I'd arranged interviews for the group that week, and David had requested doing his separately. It wasn't for me to ask why, but I was told he felt uncomfortable and inhibited when the others were around.

The year ended with *Fear of Music* being named as the best album of 1979 by the *NME* and *Melody Maker*, and with yet another accolade in the form of a *South Bank Show* special, which aired two days before Christmas. I was happy to bask in the glory of Talking Heads' mounting critical success while the group returned home for an extended break, amid quiet speculation that Chris and Tina were considering leaving the group or that David was going solo.

Instead, they all went off and did their own thing for a while. David immediately began a new collaboration with Eno, exploring the possibilities that 'I Zimbra' presented and following the same principle of no prearranged music. *My Life in the Bush of Ghosts* featured everything from Algerian chants to politicians and evangelist preachers, but it was held up over rights issues. Jerry Harrison was working with Nona Hendryx, who would soon be brought into an extended Talking Heads line-up. Only Chris and Tina took a lengthy holiday, going to the Caribbean, where they observed voodoo rituals in Haiti and got to hang out with prolific rhythm section and sought-after producers Sly and Robbie in Jamaica. At the end of their break they moved into an apartment above Compass Point Studios in Nassau, where they'd recorded *More Songs About Buildings and Food*. In the spring David and Jerry joined them, and they began the familiar pre-recording instrumental sessions ahead of a fourth album.

The Ramones didn't tour Europe in 1979, but June saw the release of *It's Alive*, a double LP that has every right to stand beside the four studio albums that preceded it. Recorded at London's Rainbow Theatre at the end of 1977, with the original line-up that had played over a hundred and fifty shows that year, its twenty-eight songs in fifty-eight and a half minutes were essentially drawn from their initial classic triumvirate of studio albums. It's one of the great, overlooked live albums and proof that however limited a guitarist Johnny Ramone was, nobody could play faster. Its release afforded me the opportunity to pitch taking journalists to CBGBs, where the Ramones were playing their spiritual home for the last time in a benefit gig to raise money for bulletproof vests for the NYPD.

The 10 April show was electric, with none of the now-trademark choreographed set pieces possible on such a small stage. It kicked off with Joey barking, 'We're the Ramones,' going straight into 'Loudmouth,' 'Rockaway Beach' and 'Blitzkrieg Bop'. CBGBs was everything I wanted it to be, although on the face of it, it was just another small, dingy club. Back in the day the Ramones would play to just a handful of people, but now it was as suffocating as the Tube at rush hour. The entire history of the Bowery scene that spawned the Ramones was all around you on the posters, flyers and stickers peeling off the walls.

The Ramones were awaiting the opening of the film *Rock 'n' Roll High School*. The soundtrack included a remix by Phil Spector of the title track. He reportedly spent ten hours listening to its opening chord, which might have given Sire and the group food for thought about the imminent prospect of making an album with him. On paper, like the impending collaboration with Spector, the film was a perfect vehicle for the Ramones. It was produced by 'King of the Bs' Roger Corman's New World Pictures and should have been so much more than a throwaway teen rock flick. The day after CBGBs Johnny had been put forward to do interviews. He talked about Corman's Edgar Allan Poe and biker movies and films like *Attack of the Crab Monsters*, but *Rock 'n' Roll High School* wasn't in that league, and Johnny's lack of enthusiasm reflected that. They hadn't enjoyed making the film: 'Long hours and too much time doing nothing. We had to be on set whether we did anything or not,' I overheard him saying. He admitted they hadn't wanted to do it but were coerced by Sire.

Using every cliché from those corny old teen rock musicals, the premise was that the students of Vince Lombardi High would stop at nothing to see their idols, the Ramones. The ending, in which the kids blow up the school but carry on dancing to the Ramones, was hardly up there with Lindsay Anderson's *If*, and there were general murmurs that it was another nail in punk's coffin.

When the Ramones' wall of noise eventually met Phil Spector's wall of sound, it was a fraught affair all round that took six months to complete. Sire then had to prise the masters out of Spector's hands via a legal threat. He had wanted to produce the band for two years, making a pitch along the lines of 'Do you want to make a good album by yourselves or a great one with me?' Spector's services didn't come cheap either. The album came in at $200,000, almost twice the cost of all four previous albums combined, and Spector's name hadn't done any favours for albums he'd produced for Leonard Cohen, Cher and Dion in recent times. *End of the Century* did become the Ramones' best-selling US album, but it failed to cross over substantially or convince the diehards. They cancelled each other out: it was neither a great Spector album nor a great Ramones album.

Press interest in the Ramones had seriously waned, and the advance tapes of *End of the Century* weren't turning that around. Usually very open in interviews, they were reticent when it came to talking about Spector. Marky was always my main confidant, and he told me how tough it had been on Johnny, because Spector wanted a certain guitar sound and Johnny couldn't get it right. He'd make him do take after take, only for his efforts to be replaced or lost in the mix. Spector had never worked with a rock band before and mostly used his regular session guys. Johnny didn't speak out of turn until years later, when he said it was the Ramones' worst album. Nobody cared for the front-cover image either, the first one in colour. Gone were the leather jackets, replaced by a cheesy family group shot. Johnny hated that too, but was outvoted by Joey and Dee Dee. 'I wasn't asked what I thought,' said Marky.

Years later, after Dee Dee left the Ramones I met him on a plane back from New York and we sat together. It was great. I'd not seen him in ten years or more and was surprised he remembered me. The long flight passed in no time. He told me that Phil Spector had been impossible to work with because you never knew what to expect from one day to the next. 'He was always a little crazy, and some days he was just mental. And he was never satisfied, so we'd be doing the same shit again and again.' They had just come off making *Rock 'n' Roll High School*. 'That was a mistake, and I was so out of it the whole time we were making that,' said Dee Dee, 'so I never got any songs written for the Spector record. It was hard on us all, but he had it in for Johnny.'

The tours in 1980 drew the fans, but it was a much more subdued Ramones, who were bewildered by the greater success back home of so many British bands, like Dire Straits and the Police, and bitter that old Bowery contemporaries like Blondie and Talking Heads had forged so far ahead of them. When the Ramones returned to Europe in the autumn, I travelled to Belfast, where they played at Queen's Hall. The audience went crazy. We were all staying at the infamous Europa Hotel, which had a reputation for having been bombed more times than any other hotel in Northern Ireland. Everyone bought 'I Survived the Europa' badges, and outside the hotel I managed to talk us out of being arrested when Dee Dee tried to persuade a bunch of on-duty soldiers to take some photos with them, and could he maybe hold one of their rifles? 'Who are they?' one of the squaddies asked when things calmed down. 'They're the Ramones,' I said to blank stares.

Andrew Lauder was the first person I met in the music industry, when I was still at university. He was also the first person to send me an album for review, and was highly amused when I asked where I should return it to. Since it was Can's *Soundtracks* I was pleased to hang on to it. Although I wrote for a student rag, he said to call in the next time I was in London. He was head of A&R at United Artists, but in an otherwise typical corporate setting he'd installed western-saloon-style swing doors in his office in homage to the Red Dog Saloon, arguably the place where the San Francisco music scene began. He had shelf after shelf full of albums, singles, unreleased reel-to-reel tapes of concerts and vintage magazines. The walls were covered in original Avalon and Fillmore ballroom psychedelic posters by Rick Griffin and Stanley Mouse. I finally got to work with him at Radar in 1979, and over the next year I looked after much of Radar's output, including the debut albums by the Yachts, the Inmates and Bram Tchaikovsky.

Radar's roster paid too much lip service to Stiff's skinny-tie pop and pub rock. The Yachts' self-titled debut, recorded in New York City with Sire's Richard Gottehrer, and Bram Tchaikovsky's *Strange Man, Changed Man* were released in early summer 1979, and both aimed for the bright, tuneful, British power-pop style that was prevalent. It was an antidote to punk but was too lightweight to be classed as new wave. Neither group found great favour among journalists or the wider public. It was hard on the Liverpool-based Yachts, whose witty, tuneful, bright pop songs were made for the charts but never came close. But even a hit record would not have prolonged their lifespan.

I took Paul Du Noyer to Germany for an *NME* feature with Bram Tchaikovsky. The future editor of *Q* and *Mojo* was just starting out and was taking on the stories nobody else wanted to do. Paul was shy and as softly spoken as I was. We both despaired and gritted our teeth at being on the road with a group who thought it was hilarious to pose with their arses pointing towards the arrow of a traffic sign that said 'Ausfahrt'. They were touring with Suzi Quatro and had managed to break into her dressing room and steal a pair of her knickers. Neither of us found it easy to join in such merriment. 'What's his problem?' one of them asked, indicating Paul. I just bit my tongue, but we were both relieved when the job was done and we could head home. Paul's page-filler piece ran a couple of weeks later, but was of no consequence to anybody.

Radar had too many groups who were never going to break through in any meaningful way and released too many records. It racked up fifty singles during 1978/9 and twenty-five albums, but only Elvis Costello and Nick Lowe sold. Too many of its artists, such as former Deaf School singer Bette Bright or R&B group the Inmates, were stranded in an era that was rapidly waning. The Inmates emerged in the late 1970s as spiritual heirs of Dr Feelgood but ended up shipwrecked on an indifferent WEA alongside the Yachts and Bram Tchaikovsky when Radar closed down.

Andrew's boldest signing, one that did look to the future, was the Pop Group, who announced themselves with a startling debut single, 'She Is Beyond Good and Evil', in March 1979, their album *Y* following six weeks later. Getting coverage in the music press was never going to be difficult: they had been on the cover of the *NME* before they even had a record out. The Pop Group comprised five Bristol teenagers fresh from finishing their A-levels, whose uncompromising music went beyond three-chord punk to embrace funk, dub reggae and feral free-jazz blowing. Their strong anti-capitalist stance was always going to set them on a collision course with WEA. 'She Is Beyond Good and Evil' was a remarkable statement of intent. Singer Mark Stewart waged war on everything, and unsurprisingly the Pop Group were derided within WEA, with head of promotions Bill Fowler describing their songs as jungle music (as he had once dismissed Talking Heads).

I went with *Melody Maker*'s Richard Williams to Portsmouth, where the group were supporting Alternative TV, only for the stage to be invaded by belligerent punks shouting 'Anarchy'. The group were shaken; they'd invited the audience to participate, but it had backfired. Williams's piece mentions a 'WEA employee' who is fretting about the lack of support within WEA and is unsure of what he can do. To the group, though, I was just another insignificant cog in the corporate machine they looked down upon. The album sold poorly, but the band already had their exit plan in place. They had never signed a contract with Radar and duly walked across to Rough Trade. I'd done little but fret.

The only time the Pop Group gave me the time of day was when I managed to get them into the after-show party at the London Palladium for Tom Waits. Having interviewed Waits for *Time Out* in 1976, I went to every show when he first played at Ronnie Scott's during that long hot summer. I just about remember one lengthy pub crawl around Soho, on which I showed him where all the famous jazz, blues and folk clubs used to be. My time at WEA coincided with the release of *Blue Valentine* and *Heartattack and Vine*, a show at the London Palladium and a fantastic few days taking jazz writer Brian Case and photographer Tom Sheehan from *Melody Maker* to an intimate jazz club in the old city quarter of Copenhagen, where Waits was playing with his hot jazz trio. It was an interesting time: his contract with Asylum was up and *Heartattack and Vine* was a bridge to the rebranding that came when he moved to Island Records. We talked about movies a lot, and I tried to engage him in a game of 'Name That Noir', based on describing classic noir films till somebody guessed the title. He was sceptical about the credibility of British crime B-movie actors like Ballard Berkeley, who often played posh policemen, or the charmingly villainous Ferdy Mayne. 'Ferdy Mayne,' Waits growled. 'What kind of name is that?'

Doll by Doll were the only significant band on the Automatic label, which had been set up by Nick Mobbs, the man who had signed the Sex Pistols to EMI. Doll by Doll weren't punks, but they formed in 1977 and rode in on a punk ticket. It was early in 1979 when I first met Jackie Leven and Jo Shaw from the group in my smelly WEA office. Both of them were tripping out of their brains. I blathered on about all the obvious music-press targets and was met with silence, so I asked them what they wanted, to which Jackie responded, 'I'd like to meet a man in a castle.' I couldn't oblige, but later in the afternoon I took them along to meet Robin Denselow, who was interviewing them for the *Guardian*.

I saw Doll by Doll play a few days later at the claustrophobic Rock Garden, where they were deliberately intimidating, always on the edge of violence and emotionally cranked up to the max. Onstage Jackie Leven had a mesmerising presence that dared you to look away. The music was unforgiving and their set always rose to a blinding crescendo of white noise and strobe lights with the epic 'Palace of Love'. They polarised opinion. They were either reviled or they cast an almost evangelical spell over people. Jackie liked stirring the pot and created considerable controversy within the press. Features on the band rarely touched on the music, sinking into intellectual discourse over his confrontational lyrics. They performed benefits and donated money to contentious psychiatrist R. D. Laing's Philadelphia Association. It seemed fitting that Doll by Doll would address mental illness, since they cultivated a sense that collectively they were psychotic.

The group lived in an infamous squat in Maida Vale, where Nick Kent interviewed them for an *NME* cover story. He described it as 'a chilling, harsh environment frequented mostly by human debris. Drug abuse is so rife that even the police have virtually ceased patrolling the vicinity, choosing merely to let the beleaguered inhabitants get on with the business of living out their zombie existence.' I'd left Kent in their company on a Friday afternoon to do his interview, and thought no more of it. On Monday *NME* editor Neil Spencer called to ask if I had any idea where Nick might be.

My line on the group was, 'So what if they're a bunch of hard-drinking, drug-taking, borderline psychotics? They've still made a great record.' It didn't work, and they always managed to alienate more people than they won over by distributing inflammatory statements and images, notably of the tortured Antonin Artaud (one of the first victims of ECT), whom they regularly used in their artwork. Despite my efforts at appeasement, it was not enough just to like Doll by Doll's music; you had to accept the philosophy behind it. I liked Jackie, a big, imposing man, but I was never going to become a disciple.

I was always guilty of being too much in thrall to Seymour Stein, and Beggars Banquet's bosses Martin Mills and Nick Austin couldn't possibly compete. Taking their cue from Rough Trade and Chiswick, they founded their label in the punk era, running it out of their Earl's Court record shop, and began with two great singles by the Lurkers, 'Shadow' and 'Freak Show', both released in 1977. The Lurkers were inspired by the Ramones, and true to the concept could hardly play at all. It was the Doll's 'Desire Me' that marked the start of the label's liaison with WEA at the beginning of 1979, in a deal struck by head of A&R Dave Dee (the same Dave Dee who fronted Dozy, Beaky, Mick and Tich). 'Desire Me' reached a respectable no. 28 in the charts but wasn't the smash Dee predicted, and further success never followed, although singer Marion Valentine briefly became a punk-pop sex symbol. Neither the Doll nor the Lurkers generated much press interest, and I found it hard to take Beggars Banquet seriously. I thought the label was directionless and sometimes in poor taste. I remembered reviewing Johnny G's 'Call Me Bwana' back in my *Time Out* days. The less said, the better.

The £100,000 advance from WEA kept Beggars Banquet afloat and enabled Mills and Austin to buy a Korg synthesizer for Gary Numan, the third act on the label and, ironically, the one WEA thought had least potential. Mills backed his hunch that 'Are "Friends" Electric?' from Numan's second Tubeway Army album *Replicas* should be its first single. He couldn't believe his luck when Dave Dee offered to make it WEA's second picture disc, which nudged 'Are "Friends" Electric?' into the lower reaches of the charts. Six weeks after its release on 4 May it made it to no. 1, with *Replicas* reaching the top of the album chart simultaneously. The music press had been resistant, but increasing radio play and Numan's appearances on *Top of the Pops* and *The Old Grey Whistle Test* had created genuine momentum. The press had been caught napping and I was dismissed for defending an *NME* piece about Gary Numan written by Paul Morley that Mills thought was character assassination.

I met Numan only a couple of times. He was quiet and unassuming and didn't like doing interviews. With two albums making it to no. 1 during 1979, he had to deal with the pressures of fame and stardom to a greater extent than anybody I would ever work with. A year later he was talking about retreating out of the limelight altogether. I remember watching him on Saturday-morning children's TV show *Swap Shop*, where he was quizzed by fans during a phone-in session. He fidgeted nervously and was completely flummoxed when one young girl asked why he never smiled, to which he answered that sometimes he did, but his expression couldn't help but suggest otherwise.

Sometime in August 1979 Paul McNally mentioned that Seymour Stein had seen Echo & the Bunnymen and wanted to sign them. He took a shine to singer Ian McCulloch's looks and a voice that reminded him of Del Shannon. I'd already read about the group and bought their only single, 'Pictures on My Wall', when it was released in May. It came out on Liverpool's independent label Zoo Records, which had also released two singles by the Teardrop Explodes, 'Sleeping Gas' and 'Bouncing Babies'. I'd bought those as well; there was something unique in the way both groups were eschewing the prevailing trends.

Both were managed by Dave Balfe and Bill Drummond, who also ran Zoo Records. They met when Balfe joined Big in Japan, one of the first punk bands to emerge in Liverpool, and the pair launched the label with Big in Japan's valedictory EP *From Y to Z and Never Again*. Nowadays Big in Japan are remembered because everyone in the group subsequently became famous: Holly Johnson, Jayne Casey, Ian Broudie and Siouxsie and the Banshees' drummer Budgie.

Bill Drummond had an unusually high music-press profile and was often name-checked in the group's interviews. He and Dave Balfe were the subject of a two-page feature in *Sounds* in 1979, when Lori and the Chameleons' 'Touch' was released by Zoo. The catchy pop confection featured a deadpan spoken vocal by blonde teenage art student Lori, but it was masterminded by Drummond and Balfe under the name they adopted as producers, the Chameleons. 'Touch' was a small-budget but somehow grand-scale production, in keeping with Zoo's aim to make great-sounding records and not the usual scratchy indie fare, but a straight-faced Drummond raised a few eyebrows when he declared, 'We're very much into musicals and as much as you may find *The Sound of Music* or *West Side Story* corny, they send shivers down your back.'

Taken alongside the similar success being enjoyed in Manchester by Joy Division and the Fall, the music press were positing that 'the North will rise again', but the Bunnymen were quick to pour scorn on the idea of a new Merseybeat. Liverpool had long been in the shadow of the Beatles, but something was happening there again, and it centred on Eric's, on Mathew Street (opposite the site of the Cavern). The Liverpool groups steered clear of the usual punk imitations, and Eric's was far more cosmopolitan. The club was a magnet for an extraordinary collection of local chancers and characters who constantly shifted in and out of different groups. Some would play there only once and then split up. Both Echo & the Bunnymen and the Teardrop Explodes had debuted there on 15 November 1978.

Deaf School had been the only Liverpool group to emerge in pre-Eric's Liverpool. Formed at Liverpool Art College in 1973, they offered up a show-band Roxy Music-style pastiche and made three albums for Warner Brothers between 1976 and 1978 that did them little justice. The group, which included Bette Bright and future producer Clive Langer, played their last shows in Liverpool in April 1978. A month later, on 5 May, the Clash played Eric's, with Ian McCulloch, Will Sergeant, Les Pattinson, Julian Cope and Pete Wylie all in attendance. Sergeant is said to have met McCulloch there and asked what he was doing. 'I'm waiting for the gift of vision,' was McCulloch's reply. And so the myth-making started, except they had already met outside the ladies toilets of the less trendy wine bar Kirklands. Will had already been told about Mac by his old school friend Paul Simpson, the first keyboard player in the Teardrop Explodes. It wasn't long before they decided to form a band, Will inviting another school friend, Les Pattinson, to complete the trio on bass. Will and Les were both twenty and had day jobs; Mac was a year younger and didn't. Les was born in Ormskirk, a market town a dozen or so miles north of Liverpool; the others were Liverpool-born and proud of it. They chose the name Echo & the Bunnymen because it was funny, meaningless and would get noticed.

Great bands are not made, they just happen, and a month after Seymour saw them play, the trio brought in a drummer, frustrated that the drum machine they had been using was restraining them. It was a Mini Pops Junior, painted green, and it had only two beats: Rock 1 and Rock 2. It had conked out once too often. It was typical Bunnymen that they didn't even try anyone other than seventeen-year-old Pete de Freitas, whom Balfe had suggested. His brother had recommended Pete; the two were at school together, and Pete was waiting to take up a place at Oxford University. 'It was like "he'll do",' said Will, but according to Bill,

'He was everything the rest of the Bunnymen were not. He was southern, public-school educated, had A-levels, spoke politely. By the end of that afternoon's rehearsals the Bunnymen were a thousand times better than they had been that morning. Even Will, Mac and Les had to recognise this. He was also given the name Taff for no apparent reason.' Taff, in the meantime, thought of them as the Three Stooges, one of whom had thought Goring, in Oxfordshire, where they believed his family lived, was in Wales.

Seymour had signed too many artists when he promised the Bunnymen a deal at the end of 1979, so instead they were signed to Korova – named after the milk bar in *A Clockwork Orange* – which was partly funded by Sire and partly by Warner Music through a deal with Rob Dickins, who ran Warner's publishing arm. Dickins already had a history with Liverpool, having been instrumental in signing Deaf School and even producing some sides with Big in Japan; he also did a deal with Drummond and Balfe to create Zoo Music under the Warner umbrella. Bill didn't tell the Bunnymen they weren't going to be on Sire till the deal was done.

The Bunnymen's first single for Korova was 'Rescue', released in May and produced by Ian Broudie. Their forthcoming album, *Crocodiles*, already recorded, had been produced by the Chameleons. It followed two months later. The Bunnymen had never visited their London-based record company – nor would they for several years – but I wanted to meet them before we started doing any interviews. Dickins suggested I ring Bill to sort something out, but we ended up talking at cross purposes: he thought I was either the WEA rep who sold advertising space or that I worked at the pressing plant, and he put the phone down on me when I mumbled about arranging to meet the band. Bill continued to be something of a mystery to me. I met him at Sire's offices, but he rarely seemed to be around the group whenever I was there. I found him blunt and intimidatingly tall. He always had somewhere else to go and was already running late.

My first meeting with the Bunnymen eventually took place in May 1980, when I oversaw an interview for the *NME*. The timing was unfortunate: just as the Teardrop Explodes appeared on the paper's cover, despite having nothing new to promote. I was oblivious to any rivalry between the two groups. I took the train to Liverpool with journalist Paul Morley and a lanky Dutch photographer called Anton Corbijn, who had recently started working for the paper. The Bunnymen met us at the train station and we drove in their rusty transit van to nearby Southport, a sleepy off-season resort town that was home to an old fourth-division football team.

I'd no idea what they'd been told about me. So as far as they knew I was a company man through and through, clearly a middle-class Londoner and completely superfluous to proceedings. It was my first experience of the north–south divide. They were so unwelcoming that it felt like Hadrian's Wall stood between us. 'So what are you doing here then?' were pretty much the only words Will said to me that afternoon. Not that Morley fared much better. We adjourned to a café to do the interview, where I sat two tables away, pretending I wasn't there. A cloak of invisibility is one of the prerequisites for any publicist. They were all sat round a small table, and because they were so uncommunicative the effect was one of silent collective bullying.

Morley wasn't as fazed as I was, but it was still painful to observe from underneath my cloak. His piece described the mounting torpor of the encounter. As the interview was wrapping up, Mac finally got on a conversational roll, concluding that 'our egos aren't big enough to disregard self-criticism'. He declared he needed a piss and left the table. In the gaping silence that followed, Morley asked Will if he agreed. 'What you were talking about earlier is a load of crap,' he snarled back. It was a gruelling afternoon, only occasionally lightened when polite Pete forgot himself, remembered his social graces and thanked me for getting the teas in, only to be glared at by the others.

The Bunnymen's interview technique in those days was simple but effective: they were taciturn and surly. An encounter with Deanne Pearson for *The Face* in a crummy Sheffield hotel bedroom during the Bunnymen's first national tour actually went down in music-press history.

She described Mac as arrogant and negative. I'd marked him down as shy and introverted and figured this was his defence mechanism. 'Form your own opinions,' he said between yawns, 'make it up.' As for Will, '[He] is hidden behind a copy of a *Star Trek* comic, curled up on a bed in a dark corner of the room. He says nothing during the entire meeting, no hello, no goodbye.' Once again, only Pete broke ranks.

I remember asking Bill about their hostility, because I thought it was holding them back. 'It's the only way they know how to deal with it right now,' he said gruffly, as if it was none of my business. Between the group and its management I wondered why I was bothering, but there was something about them. For all their frostiness, what had come across in what I'd read about them was a strong belief in the notion of 'Echo & the Bunnymen'. Mac would talk about 'the mission' and how he saw the group becoming crusaders like the Velvet Underground. The Bunnymen only did things the way they wanted, which Bill later described as 'spiritual correctness'. Mac's arrogance was tempered by Will's pessimism, while Les held the balance. Stubbornness was something they all shared, along with an avoidance of anything they found embarrassing – or too 'cherry on', as Will was fond of saying.

It was infuriating, yet I couldn't help but be drawn to them. I'd heard the album too. It was quite stunning, but they'd never believe me if I said so. I remember telling Will I thought 'Simple Stuff', one of their B-sides, sounded like the 13th Floor Elevators. He just gave me a 'What the fuck do you know?' glare, as if I'd said it reminded me of Gerry and the Pacemakers. *Crocodiles* presented a near-perfect sequence of songs, from the rousing 'Going Up' to the romantic imagery of 'Stars Are Stars', the darker, almost degenerate 'Villiers Terrace' and the rage and power of 'Crocodiles' itself.

While the Bunnymen continued to give the press the silent treatment mostly, journalists did nothing but eulogise about *Crocodiles*, hailing it as the year's best debut album. There was a sense of mystery and wonder about their music, and Mac's lyrics – like Lou Reed's or Dylan's – conjured up rhymes and phrases that lingered long in the memory.

He would never explain the words and insisted that they were not to be printed on the album sleeve. The obvious interpretation of 'Villiers Terrace', with people crawling round on carpets mixing up the medicine, branded the Bunnymen as psychedelic, which they hated as much as the idea of being part of 'the new Merseybeat'. 'People always said the LP seems druggy,' said Mac. 'I think three pints would get us rocking in those days.' *Crocodiles* was praised to the hilt, and rightly so, and overnight the Bunnymen became the fastest-rising cult group in the land.

By August, when I had decided I was going to leave WEA and set up independently, I knew I would be able to hold on to the Sire label and to the Undertones, who were soon to jump ship, but I wouldn't have bet on the Bunnymen coming with me. I didn't feel I had made any great impression on the group or Bill, but I knew that Rob Dickins had struggled to gain their acceptance. He was keen to retain me, so maybe I was simply the devil they knew. That was good enough for me. They were special, but as individuals they were caught between self-doubt and self-belief. They just needed to hold on to the latter. Years later I heard that Bill had once suggested a moratorium, whereby they set a date by which time the Bunnymen would have to break up, not if they hadn't made it, but if by mutual consent they were no longer interesting. That, of course, made them even more interesting.

4 : DO IT CLEAN

25 June–December 1980

After two years I was beginning to feel I no longer belonged at WEA. I'd always felt distant from the people in A&R, marketing and sales, but I was beginning to feel less at home in the press office as well. There was nowhere

Julian Cope, a picture of innocence at home in his Liverpool 8 flat in September 1980, just as I began working with the Teardrop Explodes (*photo: Kevin Cummins*).

for me to go and I didn't want to stay there and climb the greasy pole. I never wanted to be a permanent part of the machine. I felt closer to most of the artists and was always at home around journalists. I also believed I could achieve more for whoever I was working with if I set out on my own.

I wanted to get more involved with the groups, and the opportunity was there because I now had a strong relationship with the music press, which was broadening beyond the dominance of the four weeklies since the arrival of *Smash Hits*, founded in 1978, and *The Face*, which started two years later. *The Face* was essentially a glossy, monthly variant on the *NME* in those days, but *Smash Hits* was a very different breed of pop magazine. It was smart enough to encroach upon weekly-music-press territory. A lot of its writers were refugees from the weeklies, and it covered the kind of groups I worked with – the Undertones, Echo & the Bunnymen and the Teardrop Explodes – as much as Duran Duran or Spandau Ballet.

The industry was also changing, and just as I was about to leave at the end of August 1980 it was dealt a body blow by Granada TV's investigative *World in Action* series, when 'The Chart Busters' aired on the 18th. It probed the practice of chart-rigging and made WEA its chief target, although the finger could have been pointed at any of the majors. *World in Action* alleged that records by the Pretenders, Elvis Costello, B. A. Robertson, the Undertones, Gary Numan and others had all been subjected to chart-hype attempts – basically, inducements and free gifts offered to shops reporting to the British Market Research Bureau.

The exposure of a practice that had been going on for years rocked the industry, and it would never be the same again. The laissez-faire attitude under managing director Derek Taylor that still lingered at the end of the 1970s was now replaced by hard-line strategic marketing. Taylor once arrived at the office and decided it was such a lovely day he'd shut the place down and take the entire staff to the park for a picnic. WEA was no longer run by genial chaps who smoked dope and cared about music but by more brusque business types who didn't do either. Under the new regime, WEA was also going to seriously limit expenses. I discovered that in my final year my expenses were second only to John Fruin, the soon-to-depart managing director. It was the right time to leave.

My departure was very low key. I left on the Friday but knew I'd be back there the following week, since my 'clients' – as they had become overnight – were still largely in the WEA basket. I now needed a name for my new venture. I chose Brassneck Publicity. It had nothing to do with the character in the *Dandy* but was a phrase I'd heard the Undertones use. Billy Doherty used to call himself Billy Brassneck when he was hassling for gigs, reviews and radio sessions early on. I moved into a room below Undertones manager Andy Ferguson's office at 132 Liverpool Road, Islington, sandwiched between a newsagent and a launderette, and with a decent pub diagonally opposite. I didn't need to put up much of a front. This was going to fulfil my private-eye fantasy, which was straight out of Raymond Chandler's *The Big Sleep*. 'You can't make much money in this trade, if you're honest,' says Bogart's Philip Marlowe to Bacall's Vivian Sternwood in Howard Hawks's richly plotted film version. 'If you have a front, you're making money – or expecting to.' So I was Philip Marlowe, PR man, in a one-room office, with a desk, a typewriter, a phone and a filing cabinet. I never went as far as keeping a bottle of rye, two dusty glasses and a .38 Special locked away in the desk drawer. The dowdy office was lined with sacking on the walls and had cheap carpet tiles on the floor and the sort of blinds that created film noir shadows. In bright sunlight you could see the dust in the air. I had my own assistant too. Geraldine Oakley had worked with Paul McNally at Sire, swapping their plush Covent Garden suite for my down-at-heel joint. I began working out of Liverpool Road in late September.

To my astonishment, after having told Bill Drummond I was leaving to set up as an independent, he asked if I wanted to look after the other Zoo group, the Teardrop Explodes. My relationship with Bill changed after I struck out on my own and I began to feel part of an expanding Zoo team. I was still very conscious that I was an outsider, but I figured I just had to bide my time. I always wanted to do the best possible job, even when I was working at WEA, but sometimes all I could achieve there was the basics. I wanted the challenge of finding out if I was good enough to take a group to the next level. That was the real motivation. I'd watched too many Howard Hawks movies where the flawed lead character comes good in the end. Now, as an independent PR man, I could totally commit to the things I believed in. Echo & the Bunnymen had a major tour coming up, the debut album by the Teardrop Explodes and the fourth Talking Heads album were due in October, and another Korova band, the Sound, were releasing their debut the same month.

Mr Pickwick's on Fraser Street in Liverpool was where the first-ever Beatles Convention took place in October 1977, and the Fall recorded a live album there a year later, but none of that mattered. On 25 June 1980, on what was my second visit to Liverpool, it was where I first saw Echo & the Bunnymen play live – and in their own backyard. Everybody that had once crammed into the basement at Eric's was probably at Pickwick's that night, every local luminary from every local band. 'There's a lot of great bands up here,' boasted Pete Wylie, whose group, Wah! Heat, was one of them and had released two cracking singles – 'Better Scream' and 'Seven Minutes to Midnight'. Wylie was holding court, well within earshot of Les and Will from the Bunnymen. 'So it's a pity you've come up to see this lot.' He gestured to Les and Will and smirked. He liked nothing better than to stir things up.

It was the first time I met Dave Balfe. We chatted about *Crocodiles*, which was due to be released the following week. Seven years younger than Bill, the wide-eyed Balfey looked barely old enough to have left school. 'I was such a hustler,' he told me years later. 'I asked Bill what he was going to do after Big in Japan. I'd only been in the band two months, but when he said he was thinking of starting a record label, I asked if I could do it with him. We started by putting out an EP of Big in Japan demos to try to pay off the band's bank overdraft. So we learnt how to run a label by just doing it.'

Zoo's offices were in Chicago Buildings, right next to key record shop Probe Records, near Eric's and close by Brian Epstein's NEMS (North

East Music Stores) offices. Zoo was never meant to be just a record label, but now that Drummond and Balfe were managing, publishing and producing the Bunnymen and the Teardrops, there wasn't time for Bill's wider ambitions of making films, publishing books or putting on a revival of *The Sound of Music.*

Although I was just hanging out, waiting for the Bunnymen to play, Balfey was as serious as hell, asking if I'd got wind of any reviews yet and quizzing me about working with Talking Heads. At one point he looked me firmly in the eye and said, 'This is important to us. Are you going to do a good job? This is make or break time – for our label, Zoo, and for both our bands' careers.'

His intensity was astonishing and it threw me a little. 'So what's happening with the Teardrop Explodes then?' I asked in return. He and Bill had recorded their album during April, back to back with the Bunnymen's. They'd had two weeks to record and mix each one. 'Nobody wants to sign us,' he said, 'so we're going to find the money somehow to finish the album and release it through Zoo.'

Balfey wandered off towards the mixing desk. I hadn't come up to Liverpool with anybody, so I was sidling towards the back, feeling paranoid that somebody had affixed a label to my back that said, 'This man's from London and works for a big record company.' Then, out of nowhere, a tall, beaming but commanding figure in a heavy dark coat came bounding towards me. 'You're the legendary Mick Houghton,' he said, which stopped me in my tracks. I've replayed the conversation plenty of times since, and in my mind I came back with: 'And you must be the legendary Julian Cope.' I wasn't that quick-witted. So why was I such a legend in Liverpool? Months later Julian said that Les had told him I was the only person from London who used the word 'shag'. 'Whatever gets you noticed,' I thought. I knew it from a speech bubble that was drawn on a photo on the wall behind Moira's desk at WEA. It showed Derek Taylor whispering something to John Lennon, with the bubble reading, 'Fancy a shag, John?' Years later Julian wrote that it was Rob Dickins who told him about me, not Les. His later contention that

I was also responsible for introducing the phrase 'skin up' to London was even more unlikely. One of my most consistent failings in life is the complete inability to roll a decent joint.

Echo & the Bunnymen were known to be 'hit and miss' live. Even Rob said they could be a bit dull. After a year and a half they'd still never played more than three gigs consecutively, but that night at Pickwick's they were on one. A few days later in London I saw the tense and uneasy Bunnymen play at the Y Club off Tottenham Court Road, where they were having technical problems and looked like they just wanted the stage to swallow them up. Not so in Pickwick's ballroom, where they had a real swagger. 'Going Up' bled into 'Do It Clean', which wasn't on the album and powered up out of a great opening riff that said, 'Here is a great British rock band in the making.' I loved *Crocodiles* for all its mystery and grace – it's such a beguiling record – but I hadn't expected that they could rock. They played every song from it – probably every song they knew – including a new brooding slow-burner called 'Over the Wall', with lyrics that made no sense but played to all their enigmatic strengths.

I couldn't take my eyes off the stage. Will Sergeant was staking a claim as the original shoegazing guitarist. He never looked up but was capable of playing with the tension of Tom Verlaine, while Ian McCulloch had everything: pop-star looks, Jim Morrison's casual sexuality and an impassioned, soaring voice. I was swept along by an atmosphere of anticipation, not just on my part, but on that of a crowd of onlookers, half of whom were urging them on, the other half hoping they'd fall flat on their faces. In my mind, Bill came up afterwards and said, 'They were shit.' Maybe he did? I knew that was how he motivated them. I was already buzzing.

Three months later I was handling their publicity independently. I had got to know them better by persistently turning up for no apparent reason. They were still hard work, but I knew I'd got good results around the album release. How much of that was down to me, who can say, but if nothing else they now knew what I did. They'd grown in confidence in the months after *Crocodiles* was released. They still gave journalists grief but the critical success of the album and sufficient sales to make the Top 20 definitely saw them up their game live. I went along when they played at Futurama in Leeds in September, and they were the best group on show, amid a host of other independent outfits, including Swell Maps, Clock DVA, Wasted Youth and Altered Images. Mac later dismissed them collectively as '(in)detritus', a sign of the caustic wit to come once he'd found his interview legs. They closed with a lengthy 'Crocodiles', now with a trademark middle passage where they took the music down, allowing Mac to find his inner Iggy and his inner Jimbo (Jim Morrison). 'That's so psychedelic,' he purred, causing Will to look up from the floor in disgust and then down again, before pummelling his guitar. The Bunnymen were beginning to believe. At the end of 'Crocodiles' Mac saluted the audience, and as a parting shot rightly boasted about 'that touch of class'.

The next time I saw them was during the full UK tour that followed in October. Things had changed. Now they were dressed in army combat fatigues and khaki headbands and were swathed in a backdrop of camouflage netting draped from the PA downwards that covered all the group's back line. The whole effect was enhanced by red, green and blue lighting filtered through a constant haze of smoke that filled the stage, turning the group into shadows and silhouettes. It was dubbed '*Apocalypse Now* chic' or 'camo chic' and formed an empowering setting that enabled them to overcome any remaining self-consciousness onstage.

Julian Cope has always asserted that it was his idea to use army surplus scrim netting to drape across the stage, only for Bill to steal it for his rivals. Bill's justification was that the Teardrop Explodes didn't need such trappings, but he had to come up with something to make the Bunnymen less boring. Much credit must still go to Bill for building a production team able to execute this vision. They were from a theatrical rather than a rock background and brought a more extravagant panache to the stage sets and lighting that distinguished the Bunnymen from every other group treading the boards. Bill's first recruit was Bill Butt, a close friend from when they were in the same class at Northampton School of Art, and the two revolutionised the stage sets and lighting. Butt lived in Bristol, in a large house known as the Palace, and over the next few months brought in some of his friends and housemates from the Bristol Old Vic.

The Bunnymen cult grew substantially by the end of the year, and it was largely generated through the music press. They finally made the cover of the *NME* in November, and *Crocodiles* was no. 4 in the paper's Albums of the Year chart, with a similar showing in *Sounds*. The Bunnymen were shifting albums and selling out bigger and bigger venues, and they were tipped as the band most likely to break big in 1981. It didn't matter that they were yet to have a hit record. If anything, that lessened the pressure and kept them focused on what mattered.

At the close of this momentous year Echo & the Bunnymen played London's Rainbow Theatre, which should have been a triumphant moment, their biggest London show so far. I remember the audience's reaction, not to the Bunnymen's entrance but to the smoky, doomy, North Vietnamese jungle that was revealed as the curtains folded back. It got the biggest reaction of the entire night. This did not go unnoticed by the group or by certain reviewers who were disappointed that the Bunnymen hadn't moved on. They were sluggish that night, and they knew it. Julian smirked at the reviews: 'I knew it wouldn't be long before journalists realised they were just the new Uriah Heap.' Three months was a long time in those days; there was no standing still. Bar one final outing, the camo was packed away for good. 'We had to kill off Ziggy,' said Mac.

Julian Cope must have stood out in Liverpool like Rik Mayall's posh punk from *The Young Ones* calling people 'shitheads' in a refined middle-class accent. Julian wasn't much of a punk. 'I didn't want everything to sound the same,' he once explained. 'I never lost the social graces and I was never bored.' Born in Deri, South Wales, in October 1957 and brought up in Tamworth in the West Midlands, Julian's mother taught English and his father worked in insurance – at the Pru. In September

1976 Julian had gone to C. F. Mott Teacher Training College on the out-skirts of Liverpool. A passionate music fanatic with his eye on the prize, he began to discover what that was among a group of freakish strangers, arty misfits and ne'er-do-wells at Eric's, some of whom became princi-pal characters in his life. 'I was really forged in Liverpool from 1977 to 1980. Those were my fundamental roots, the first people to accept me as a weirdo who was capable of something and not just a weirdo.'

First among his cast of characters is Gary Dwyer, the drummer and Julian's only constant comrade throughout the entire life of the Teardrop Explodes. Gary was the soul of the Teardrops, and without him they might never have gone beyond talking tactics and fancifully dreaming about what might have been. The pair couldn't have been more different, and they couldn't have been closer. I can't recall too many conversations with Gary that went much further than a good-natured 'All right, Mick?', 'Skin up, la" or, when it came to doing interviews, 'Nah . . . they only ever want to talk to Copey.'

Others came and went during the band's four-year history, but with-out doubt the most significant was Dave Balfe. His influence was as meaningful when he was out of the band as when he was in it. Balfey was the only person who could and would stand up to Julian. If Gary was the rock, Balfey was the wall Julian would beat his head against. It was always his belief that the songs needed to be more modern and arranged, which created a constant battle of wills between the two of them. It was a clash between head and heart. Julian never forgave him for putting trumpets on 'Happy Death Men', the final song on *Crocodiles*. The Bunnymen didn't forgive him for that either, but for Julian it was another betrayal by a friend and fellow band member who had given away one of his soon-to-be-signature ideas.

During the first eighteen months that the Bunnymen and Teardrops co-existed any neutral observer would have expected the Teardrops to make it long before their rivals. Prior to 'Rescue', the Teardrops had released three singles to the Bunnymen's one, the third of these, 'Treason', selling an impressive twenty-five thousand copies. It was the Teardrops who had been the first to get a music-press front cover, in *Sounds*, but *Crocodiles* proved to be a game-changer. Getting their album out first saw the pendulum swing towards the Bunnymen.

The problem was that nobody wanted to sign the Teardrop Explodes, largely because the prevailing view, which might seem ludicrous now, was that Julian wasn't a good enough frontman. He didn't have the looks and he couldn't sing. It was like the famous Fred Astaire screen-test rejection, but at least Astaire could dance a little. It had been a bitter blow for Julian when Seymour Stein signed the Bunnymen after seeing them at the YMCA on a bill with his group and Joy Division, and word immediately reached Julian that Seymour liked Mac's looks as much as his voice. There was even talk of bringing in another singer after interest from United Artists, A&M and CBS came to nothing. The prognosis was that Julian wouldn't be able to cut it.

So, with no deal on the table, and unbeknownst to his wife, Bill put his mortgage on the line to pay for the recording of a Teardrops album on which the group shifted from their original minimalist feel towards a classier pop vibe. It was still defined by Julian's lyrics, but with tunefulness and more expansive arrangements replacing the earlier experimentalism. The Teardrops had been as much guitarist Mick Finkler's group. Most of the early songs were co-writes with Julian, and Finkler had played on the album they'd recorded at Rockfield, which was to be called *Everybody Wants to Shag the Teardrop Explodes*. Then in early summer Finkler was sacked. The blame was laid at Julian's door, even though he always claimed Gary and Balfey had been equally conspiratorial. There were plenty in Liverpool who were outraged, and many still reckon it destroyed the definitive line-up. Finkler was replaced by Alan Gill, who like Balfey was from the Wirral. The two had played together in Radio Blank, the Wirral's only punk band, and then in Dalek I Love You, whose debut album had already been out for a couple of months when Gill joined the Teardrops.

Dalek I had been signed to Phonogram by Dave Bates, a rapidly up-and-coming A&R man who had brought Def Leppard to the label, and against all odds the Sheffield group were now at the forefront of a new wave of British heavy-metal bands. Bates was earning a reputation for backing his own judgement over others', and one such opinion was that Julian Cope was going to be a star. He may have been the only person in the world who believed that. Even Julian may have begun to doubt it, until, buoyed by finally signing a major record deal, he began a transformation from ugly duckling to swan as his voice, looks, image and confidence blossomed. His group was back on a par with the Bunnymen again.

With Bates's backing, the Teardrops returned to Rockfield to re-record some of Julian's vocals and Finkler's guitar parts. Gill's most enduring contribution, though, was in turning Julian on to smoking pot for the first time. He was the last in the group to take drugs. Julian wanted to be like Frank Zappa or Captain Beefheart, who said they had no need to take drugs. Bill also urged Julian not to take them; he was psychedelic enough already. Julian had never even smoked a cigarette before Gill persuaded him dope would loosen him up, so he skinned up a pure grass joint and the die was cast. His first acid trip followed soon after, thanks to Balfey, who should have known better. It was the major turning point in Julian's life. Within a couple of months he'd say he'd gone from 'drug puritan to acid king'. The conversion was completed just as I came on board.

I'd been told that Dave Bates was a browbeater, so I was a little anxious about meeting him. I was half expecting to be vetted before becoming the Teardrops' publicist, but instead Bates sat behind his desk, chain-smoking and ranting about all the music he liked. Unlike the A&R men I'd encountered at WEA, he was as passionate about music as I was. When the Teardrops signed to Phonogram, Julian wanted to be on Mercury because it had been the label the New York Dolls were on. Bates knew things like that mattered. He was full of bluster about how Phonogram meant business, and he had no doubt that the Teardrop Explodes were going to be huge. So it wasn't the moment for me to voice my opinion that the first single he was releasing, 'When I Dream', was completely the wrong choice.

While the Bunnymen were allowed to evolve without undue pressure to have a hit record, Phonogram were chasing one from the get-go. 'When I Dream' was a new song and as much Julian's choice as anybody's, but it was an unashamed pop love song that lacked the wit and artifice of 'Bouncing Babies' and 'Treason'. Before long they were on *Swap Shop*. Julian was dressed in his image-making leather flying jacket, hippy headbands abounded, and Julian pouted and played to the camera with ease. 'When I Dream' stalled at no. 47.

The album, now called *Kilimanjaro*, was heavily panned and over-scrutinised on its release in October. It immediately came under fire because five of its eleven tracks were already available in one form or another. I was staggered that the reviews were so hard on Julian personally. Coming in cold I hadn't been prepared for the fact that so many music journalists wanted to pull him down a peg or two. The general consensus among critics, though, was that the Teardrops were too clever for their own good.

I loved the album and hadn't seen the backlash coming. Bill had given me an advance cassette of the original Rockfield recordings, and I played it to death. It was so audacious and adventurous in every department. The Teardrops sounded like nothing else around, and they still don't. 'We were always reaching but never arriving,' Julian said to me in a more sombre moment soon after the *Kilimanjaro* reviews appeared. 'We fell behind in the race with the Bunnymen.'

I got on famously with Julian. Whenever we hung out we mostly prattled on about music. He loved that I'd seen so many of the people he was into. I was seven years older and had been going to gigs since 1966. Among the first were the Creation at a school dance and the Who at Eltham Baths; thirty years later I read that Viv Prince of the Pretty Things had been deputising for Keith Moon that night because he was ill. I'd seen the Doors at the Roundhouse with Jefferson Airplane, both Tim Buckley's late 1960s London shows, Captain Beefheart, the Mothers of Invention at the Royal Albert Hall, Love's first tour in 1970, and both Lou Reed and the Tots and Iggy and the Stooges (with James Williamson) at the Scala in 1972. 'I couldn't believe how bad the Stooges were,' I told Julian. 'They were wearing white clown face paint and sounded like they were making it up as they went along and had never rehearsed in their lives. And Iggy terrified the audience. He was so menacing that nobody wanted to be near the front of the stage and people kept inching further and further back.' Julian simply grinned. He'd have loved it.

We'd struck up an immediate friendship. It was partly a class thing. Julian was a well brought up, nicely spoken middle-class lad, and although my roots may have been as working class as the Bunnymen's, I could no longer kid myself that I was anything but middle class myself. At the time I thought of Julian as an innocent and far too open for his own good. I felt I'd let him and the group down with the lousy reviews, whereas nothing could stop the Bunnymen moving seamlessly from strength to strength.

It was tough on Julian because the Teardrops too often came off second best to their Zoo rivals, and what worked for one didn't necessarily work for the other. I was beginning to wonder if that included having the same publicist, but it certainly backfired when they used the same photographer to shoot both groups' album sleeves. It had been Rob Dickins's suggestion that art photographer Brian Griffin should shoot the cover photo for *Crocodiles*, and he came up with a brilliant concept by photographing the Bunnymen in a small glade in Rickmansworth that was often used by film companies. It was beautifully lit, capturing the band's sense of gloomy allure, with all but Mac looking at the camera. The *Kilimanjaro* sleeve was a mess, a collage of studio shots in which Julian is unrecognisable on what he calls 'the ugly tripping fools' front cover; on the back his face is deliberately blurred. Unintentionally, though, it reflected the constant turmoil within the group. The following year the cover was changed to the now more familiar *National Geographic* zebra image.

The two bands had not toured together since they played the Lyceum in March 1980, but after Bill invested in a Zoo PA system they alternated tour schedules. This continued to the end of 1980, during which time they also shared the same road crew. Both groups had major tours lined up during the autumn and winter, the Bunnymen taking to the road first. With momentum on their side, their 'Crocodiles' tour was a total triumph. It ended in Liverpool on 17 October, and four days later the same entourage had to pull together the Teardrop Explodes' 'In Daktari' tour at Nottingham Poly. It took its name from a dodgy American television series about a vet working in east Africa, the star of which was Clarence the friendly cross-eyed lion. In many respects the Teardrops' set differed only in detail. In the space of four days the Ho Chi Minh trail had changed into an African neon jungle. In front of a black-and-white zebra-striped backdrop, the group appeared in dishevelled battle dress, with Julian in leathers and Balfey grinning nervously beneath a tin hat like a petrified American GI at Omaha beach. Four spots spraying up from the floor ejected changing combinations of coloured light through the same storms of swirling, billowing smoke.

Where the Bunnymen had been touring for a couple of months with a tried and tested set list and a ready rapport with the crew, the Teardrops had neither of those factors on their side. So they were by contrast gloriously erratic and unpredictable, and the set pieces often misfired. Ultimately, the group's ambitiousness and freedom was their undoing, with Julian an idiosyncratic ringmaster who was never quite in control of proceedings and appeared to revel in the chaos. They had never played live with Alan Gill and had a brass section that rarely managed to come in when it was meant to.

I saw four shows in all, but the disarray at the first date in Nottingham was nothing compared to the penultimate show at Leicester University, where they were arguing before, during and afterwards, with Julian returning to the stage to explain courteously that 'We can't do an encore because we're splitting up tonight.' I took my time before going backstage afterwards, where an unusually flustered Bill Butt told me they'd already left. 'Have they split up then?' I asked. 'Only till tomorrow,' said Bill knowingly. The final show in London proved to be the last by that particular line-up. Only Julian and Gary were still talking. Gill left because he hated touring, and soon after Julian sacked Dave Balfe. They'd had another major clash over the new songs Julian was writing. Bill tried to persuade Julian otherwise, but he was having none of it. At least before he left Gill had gifted the band the bones of a song called 'Reward'.

On tour they smoked a little dope. Acid wasn't yet mandatory, but they were inhaling pulse-racing amyl nitrate heavily. I was in the van with them once on the way to record the *Old Grey Whistle Test*. At some point the van jolted and the bottle of amyl spilled over; everybody's hearts were racing, while Bob Proctor at the wheel was careering all over the road. They thought it was hysterical. I thought I was going to die. I never liked driving in cars or vans. I couldn't drive myself and used to joke with Julian that I was a 'dangerous passenger', so I was freaking out. The performance that night was ragged beyond belief. It was no way to introduce the wider world to 'Reward', a song that everyone who'd heard it thought was a smash.

Gill was quickly replaced by Troy Tate, recommended to Bill by Paul McNally, and within weeks they'd auditioned and recruited a new keyboard player, Jeff Hammer, and bassist, Alfie Algius. Julian no longer wanted to play bass. The old line-up had already completed a fired-up version of 'Reward'. I hate pop videos, almost without exception, but the one they made for 'Reward' was a wonderfully fast-paced romp that captured a moment in time, after which it was never the same again for the cast of characters who had started out together at Eric's two years earlier. Although the rift was most publicly personified as being between Julian and Mac, Bill and Dave Balfe were caught in the crossfire. Julian had always expressed an almost irrational animosity, even hatred towards Balfey, who until he was sacked had been in the invidious position of playing in a band he was also co-managing, as well as co-managing their closest rivals. Bill was equally compromised, caught in the middle between Julian and Balfey, but particularly between Julian and the Bunnymen. Whatever bond Bill and Julian once shared was becoming increasingly tenuous. I did my best not to get drawn into the tussle between the lot of them and spent the next twenty-five years trying to remain impartial.

Julian had petulantly barred Balfey from taking part in the video for 'Reward', which was filmed at the docks by Bill Butt. Mac opted out, but otherwise the cast included all their mates, including the rest of the Bunnymen, original keyboardist Paul Simpson, the shared crew, the new recruits to the band, as well as Pam Young, now running Zoo with Bill and Balfey. Julian's wife Kath was there too – they had married in August 1979, much to everybody's surprise and concern. New guitarist Troy Tate and Les Pattinson braved the heights and mimed the trumpets atop a two-hundred-foot-high wobbly platform.

'Reward' was released in early January 1980 and went to no. 41 on its first week. They missed out on *Top of the Pops*. The single then dropped to no. 45, before bouncing back to no. 41. This time they were offered *Top of the Pops*, just as the new five-piece line-up was about to head off for a tour of the US East Coast. En route to London Julian had a change of heart and a belated pang of loyalty; they drove past Balfey's house and invited him along to mime the trumpets. They were all off their heads on acid, aside from new boys Alfie and Jeff, who must have wondered what on earth they were getting into.

5 : CRISIS OF MINE

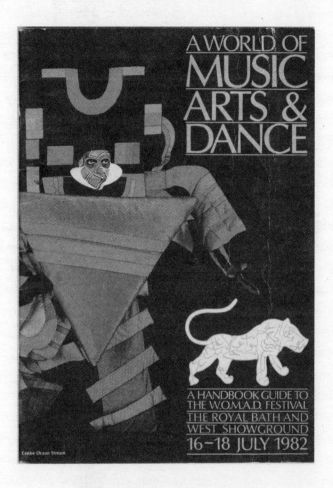

September 1980–December 1982

Andy Ferguson had been counting down the days until Sire failed to pick up the option on the Undertones' contract and had no second thoughts about leaving the label. I thought it was a mistake and

A lack of publicity was certainly in part responsible for the poor attendance at the first WOMAD festival. After two years as an independent publicist, it felt as if everything was crumbling around me.

it would have been better to renegotiate with Seymour Stein, as both the Ramones and Talking Heads had done. Instead, rubbing salt in the wound, the Undertones toured in December, calling it 'The See No More Tour'. They played Hammersmith Palais, where the audience kept them onstage for nine encores. Four months later they announced that they were setting up their own label, Ardeck, and had signed a worldwide licensing deal with EMI, and on 5 May 1981 their third album, *Positive Touch*, was released.

The record they delivered to EMI was more ambitious and experimental but, as usual, a great pop record, and the move from Sire didn't change the tenor of the reviews. In the eyes of the press, having found the formula for perfect pop they were right to stick with it, but as Damian ruefully observed later, things had changed: 'We were influenced by Love, Blues Magoos, and particularly the Stones' *Aftermath*; it was more 1966 than 1981, which was out of sync with the likes of Duran Duran, but was also out of sync with what we were doing a year earlier.'

The group desperately wanted to move on and drop 'My Perfect Cousin' and even 'Teenage Kicks' from the set. The new songs reflected a progression from the verse–chorus–hook model to something more sophisticated, but people wouldn't let go, musically or image-wise. *Positive Touch* was the first time that the group tackled political issues. Damian and John, the most Republican members of the group, had friends who'd been in internment. John's song 'Crisis of Mine' was about his inability to address his concerns, but at the same time he didn't want to exploit political questions in the way others – Stiff Little Fingers in particular – had. Damian said his song 'It's Going to Happen', the first single taken from the album, with its refrain, 'It's gonna happen till you change your mind', targeted the British government and Margaret Thatcher. This was news to co-writer Mickey Bradley, who didn't see it that way at all. By coincidence, they appeared on *Top of the Pops* the day hunger-striker Bobby Sands died. Damian wore a black armband. The gesture went completely unnoticed, but they argued about it afterwards and, like all the problems within the group, this one went unresolved.

Positive Touch crashed out of the Top 20 after just one week, and although they undertook their biggest UK and European tour ever, they never regained ground. They released the sublime 'Julie Ocean' in the summer, the first of two singles re-recorded with Dave Balfe and Hugh Jones. They appeared on *Top of the Pops* for what would be the last time, but the single reached only no. 41, the absolute worst chart position in an era when the grail of a Top 40 single was all record companies sought. Cracking the Top 40 was so fundamental to record labels and whatever marketing and promotional ideas they employed that if you didn't make it, they soon gave up. There was never a plan B. When in February the following year the next single, 'Beautiful Friend', failed to make even the Top 75, EMI immediately cooled on the group.

Already the Undertones were finding that EMI interfered more than Sire over the way they looked and dressed. 'This was the first time we all had proper haircuts,' said Mickey, 'proper London hairdressers rather than your mum cutting it. It was alien to us to talk about what we were going to wear onstage, but we'd have looked just as ridiculous looking the way we used to.' I knew my days were numbered once EMI began looking to cut costs. We'd had the usual press accolades for *Positive Touch*, but just recording an album of great songs was no longer enough. The Undertones were never going to change – or be allowed to – and were never going to resurrect a career that they had decided among themselves was already on the skids. EMI demanded more of a say in song selection, which the group didn't have the will to challenge. The fact that I was ousted in favour of an in-house EMI press officer was the least of their worries.

I still cared. The Undertones meant a lot to me, and I knew I had contributed to their success. The group were struggling to find or agree upon the new direction required of them. There was a two-year gap before they released their fourth and final album, *The Sin of Pride*, in March 1983. Not only had making it been a desultory experience, it was then greeted with public and critical indifference for the first time in their careers. There was no chart placing at all, and within four months they'd played their final show.

I'd see them in the office and was well aware that the relationship between John and Feargal had long since reached breaking point. Now nobody was speaking to Feargal. He was the one who eventually said he was leaving, but they all wanted out. 'Feargal got more and more frustrated by my easy-going approach,' explained John. 'When he said he was leaving, it was a big relief. The fun had been sucked out of it. It was always meant to be fun. The Ramones always said that, but they carried on for years not speaking to each other. I'm glad we stopped when we did.'

The news that the Undertones had disbanded ran in the music press on 11 June 1983. They issued a silly press statement saying the reason for breaking up was the fact that the group was on the verge of international superstardom, and that wasn't what they wanted. It was typical Undertones, underselling themselves right to the end. Like so many groups, they made one album too many, but given the group's tangle of personalities and insecurities it's a wonder it didn't all end after 'Teenage Kicks'.

The album Talking Heads had begun rehearsing in Nassau in the spring was *Remain in Light*, again produced by Brian Eno and released at the beginning of October. My immediate reaction was that it was overly complex and lacked the warmth of their earlier recordings. Did it uphold Tina's fears that David Byrne was working too closely with Eno? That appeared to be so when on the first pressings of *Remain in Light* the songs were credited only to Byrne and Eno. David took the blame for this, and on future pressings the credits were duly shared equally among the participants.

Tina's gripes now appeared in print, backed by Chris and Jerry. In the first interview I set up, which ran in the *NME* in November, she said, 'Brian wanted to say it was his record. David wanted to say it was his record. They both thought it was the greatest venture of their lives ... but [it was] the collective influences that created the result. No one could put an individual claim to it.' David wasn't happy about the compromise, which he later agreed was sometimes completely fair, although not in every case. I had shared enough good times with everybody in the group not to be saddened by the state of affairs, and by now realised that all the Sire bands I'd cut my PR teeth on were riddled with internal squabbles and resentments.

David hadn't expected to tour in support of *Remain in Light* but agreed to the idea of an expanded line-up, including the likes of guitarist Adrian Belew, bassist Busta Jones and keyboardist Bernie Worrell, the P-Funk music director who played on Jerry Harrison's ongoing solo album, *The Red and the Black*. The initial shows went so well that they decided to take a nine-piece band on a full world tour. It began in October and reached London in early December. However disappointed I was with the album, I wasn't about to miss out on seeing two shows (on 2 and 3 November 1980) at New York's fabulous art deco Radio City Music Hall. I'd long wanted to see somebody play there and offered the exclusive to *Melody Maker*.

I thought I'd finally managed to kill a journalist when the *Melody Maker* writer couldn't be raised the morning after some serious late-night partying. Seymour Stein and Sire had arranged a bash at Patrissy's for the assembled media, and we'd been properly wined and dined. There'd been plenty of what Americans rather contrarily call blow (and which we used to call beak), which the writer wasn't used to. By midday, after incessant calls and repeated hammering on the door, I persuaded the hotel chambermaid to let me into his room, where he was dead to the world, though not actually dead. He wasn't in great shape at all ahead of the scheduled interview with David only an hour later, and I broke my usual rule and sat in the room in case he nodded off or worse. He came through it with minimal prompting but did later fall asleep throughout much of the show.

David was still doing his interviews separately. We spoke to him first at the Berkshire Hotel, which was within easy walking distance of Radio City Music Hall. As we arrived there, Chris and Tina were being photographed under the marquee displaying the group's name. 'This building is so amazing,' said Chris warmly. 'It really is something to play here.' I asked Tina what it was like now with nine people onstage. 'What's great is that nobody is grandstanding and there's plenty of space and enough holes for us all to fit in.'

A few hours later I thought the nine-piece touring band was so packed together onstage that it shone the spotlight even more on David. The original four-piece, with the addition of Belew, began by playing the early favourites – 'Psycho Killer', 'Warning Sign' and 'Stay Hungry' – before being joined one by one by the other musicians. After seven songs the full ensemble launched into 'Once in a Lifetime', from *Remain in Light*, which dominated the rest of the set. With performers doubling on keyboards, percussion, guitars and vocals, the endless musical ideas and textures brought the recorded version to life.

After completing the expanded-group tour in Japan in February, it would be solo projects and other distractions that further undermined Talking Heads as a recording unit. There was a three-year gap before the next studio album. During that time I sent out the various individual albums and set up occasional interviews, but solo albums are never a substitute. The delayed Byrne/Eno collaboration *My Life in the Bush of Ghosts*, which had fleshed out many of the ideas on *Remain in Light*, was finally released in February 1981. Chris and Tina's venture the Tom Tom Club's self-titled debut followed in September and was the first of three albums in as many years. They pointedly described it as 'a musical, anti-snob record' to deflect from the seriousness and artiness surrounding Talking Heads. Recorded for Island Records, *The Tom Tom Club* sold around twice as many copies as any Talking Heads album.

After a year in which four extracurricular albums were released – the other two were *The Catherine Wheel*, Byrne's collaboration with choreographer Twyla Tharp, and Harrison's *The Red and the Black*, both in November and neither particularly well received – the gap in the group's release schedule was filled by *The Name of This Band is Talking Heads*, a perplexingly patchy two-album live set released in March 1982, drawn from concerts between 1977 and 1980. It was the last Talking Heads album I worked on, but what people wanted was a new album by the more collaborative core group. *Speaking in Tongues*, released in June 1983, was just that. It was still on Sire, but in the UK it went through EMI. I'd always got on well with the group but I never made a pitch to carry on working with them. In the time since *Remain in Light* I'd had little direct contact and I got lost in the shuffle.

To have worked with Talking Heads, particularly during 1979 and 1980, is a real highlight for me. I don't pretend anything I did was crucial. I thought they were the best group in the world. The last time I saw them was when they played two shows at Wembley Arena in July 1982, with Tom Tom Club supporting. They never played in the UK again, and after a disastrous festival-headlining show in New Zealand in February 1984 Talking Heads never played anywhere again. I loved the band, and *More Songs About Buildings and Food* and *Fear of Music* rank as two of the greatest albums of all time. I wouldn't trade having worked with them for anything, and for a few years being able to share a little of their hedonism made for some great times. We'll always have Paris.

Talking Heads were always moving forward, to the point where they always seemed to be a group in transition. The Ramones, on the other hand, were perpetually in limbo after *End of the Century*. Sire brought in another 'name' producer for the next one, which turned out to be my last with them too. 1981's *Pleasant Dreams* was given over to 10cc man Graham Gouldman to produce. It was an odd choice; there was nothing in Gouldman's background to suggest it was a sound move. The group wanted Steve Lillywhite and felt coerced into using Gouldman, the aim once again being to steer the Ramones towards a more radio-friendly sound. It negated all their strengths on what was a considerably better set of songs than on the misfiring Phil Spector album.

When the Ramones arrived in Europe in October 1981 to promote *Pleasant Dreams*, it had been a little over five years since they had played the Roundhouse. After six albums the only press we were getting was for old times' sake. The Ramones no longer meant anything. I saw them play a late-night show at the Venue in Victoria, where they looked tired and jaded. They didn't tour the UK and Europe again until 1984. I wasn't alone in losing interest in the Ramones after *Pleasant Dreams*, and the limitations of their style became even more apparent with a succession of lacklustre 1980s albums.

In the three years I worked with them they kept their secrets well, and few knew that their onstage facade masked a growing rift between Joey and Johnny. Once Dee Dee left in 1989, they were the last remaining original members. What held the Ramones together was also what divided them, and now everybody was aware they were bitter enemies. 'We were always broke, so we just had to keep touring,' Dee Dee told me in mid-flight over the Atlantic in the mid-1990s. 'I'd just had enough after fifteen years of increasingly getting nowhere. We were doing the same show every night and nobody was getting on any more or talking to each other.'

My involvement with Sire was completely over by the end of 1982. Seymour's greatest coup had come earlier that year, when he signed Madonna. Sometime in 1983, around the initial release of 'Holiday', I was in the WEA office and was invited along to an early-evening PA Madonna was giving at Le Beat Route in Soho. My only recollection is that she mimed to a couple of songs in front of a meagre audience almost entirely made up of WEA employees. I left wondering what on earth had possessed Seymour to sign her.

There were those who always thought my reputation was based entirely on the great groups I worked with. They were correct. It would have been hard for anybody to have fucked up with Talking Heads, nor could anybody have done anything to reverse the Ramones' declining fortunes after 1979. As for the Undertones, inner tensions and fans who wanted to wrap them up and preserve them as a perfect pop band were ultimately their undoing.

As an independent publicist with a good reputation I was operating within a certain cultish niche, but despite having left WEA nothing had changed. I was working on too many projects that were over within the usual three-month lifespan of an album. Although I'd hardly distinguished myself with the Teardrops, Dave Bates kept offering me work. He was very persuasive, and whether out of inexperience or a fear that I now had bills to pay I took on a couple of Phonogram signings I should have at least questioned doing. I had yet to appreciate that if you have to think twice, don't do it.

Taking on Tom Robinson's Sector 27 in November 1980 was certainly rash. When the Tom Robinson Band broke up in 1979 following a critical drubbing for *TRB2*, he formed a new group. The idea was for a musically freer, guitar-based line-up that eschewed Robinson's trademark political directness. The problem with the self-titled album was Robinson's aggressively shouted vocals, not its 1980s post-punk sound. It had the hard-hitting drum sound and ringing guitars that were fast becoming the hallmarks of a record produced by Steve Lillywhite. That same year he produced the Psychedelic Furs' debut, Peter Gabriel's third album and U2's *Boy*. *Sector 27* was at least spared the mauling *TRB2* had suffered, not through my skills but simply because nobody in the press really cared either way.

Bill Nelson was another who was out in the cold as far as press interest went. He had been recording since 1970, and his most recent recordings under the name Red Noise were met with indifference. Bates was as bullish as ever: 'We just want to get him in the *NME*,' he said. Nelson's album did have something I could work with, but it was all done by remote control. I never even met the West Yorkshire-based Nelson. *Quit Dreaming and Get on the Beam* was originally earmarked as a Red Noise album, until they were dropped by EMI. Nelson sent Bates a cassette, and he bought the rights for Mercury to release it as a Bill Nelson album. The other smart move was attaching a bonus album of home recordings and musical sketches, *Sounding the Ritual Echo*. His new experimental electronic style was in keeping with a new vogue for electronic keyboards, synths and drum machines, and *Quit Dreaming* met with considerable approval. The marketing ploy boosted it straight into the Top 10 in May 1981, making it statistically at least the most successful album in Nelson's career.

It set a pattern he's followed to this day of esoteric releases coming along with staggering frequency. In the 1980s alone Nelson released a further twenty albums, but none that called upon my services. But Dave Bates continued to offer me work. In autumn 1981 I travelled with him to see his latest signing, Tears for Fears, play in Brighton. I didn't get their brooding synth pop and knew it would be a tough ask getting the press onside. At least I was right about that. My turning somebody down was usually like handing them a passport to worldwide success. If you wanted to be doomed to cult success and credibility, then I was your man. Over the years I've wondered if this said more about me than the artists. The world will never know what Tears for Fears' fate would have been had I taken on their press. As it was they went on to achieve the level of success Bates had always expected of the Teardrop Explodes.

Although Rob Dickins released a steady flow of singles on Korova in the early 1980s, the label had become almost synonymous with Echo & the Bunnymen. The only other group to make any impression was the Sound. It's fair to say they were cut from very similar cloth to the Bunnymen, but they presented a very different face to the world. The Sound were led by guitarist and songwriter Adrian Borland, and they recorded their debut album, *Jeopardy*, for £700 at Elephant Studios in Wapping. It was raw and edgy and bore the admitted influence of James Williamson of the Stooges on Borland's playing. The Sound toured with the Bunnymen when *Jeopardy* was released in October 1980. Journalists who hated the Bunnymen or thought they were overrated loved the Sound, and vice versa. It said something about the contrasting images and musical content of each group, and was an interesting PR conundrum. The Sound were more bleak and uncompromising and were often tagged as south London's answer to Joy Division. Richard Williams described them in *The Times* as the most thoughtful of the recent gang of British doomsday rockers. They had a deliberate lack of visual style compared to the Bunnymen, and Adrian was a stocky figure who was serious and cerebral, but plenty of journalists preferred that to Mac's droll Scouse arrogance.

A year later they recorded the richer and more refined *From the Lions Mouth*, produced by Hugh Jones, who was fresh from finishing the second Bunnymen album. It's regarded as their most commercial album, with more uplifting songs such as 'Sense of Purpose' and 'Winning'. Reviews were again ecstatic, but a chart peak of a lowly no. 164 signified that it was not commercial enough. Shunted over to WEA, the Sound were dropped after a third album, *All Fall Down*, having deliberately pursued a more experimental path because the record company had demanded the opposite. 'Good on them,' I thought.

I bumped into Adrian seven or eight years after the Sound had split up in 1987, and he was back recording in Wapping. I never found him anything other than bright and talkative, and he was always appreciative of my past efforts and results. I had no idea that he was prone to melancholy and serious depression till I read that he'd taken his own life in April 1999. I later worked with others, like Lawrence from Felt and Guy Chadwick from the House of Love, and they said how much they liked Adrian's guitar-playing and his highly personal, idealistic lyrics.

Paul McNally had left Sire not long after I left WEA, and in 1981 he set up his own label, Why-Fi, in a deal with RCA. We were friends and had worked together successfully, so I was his first choice to look after his label, and I was never going to say no. It didn't work out well for either of us. Even Paul wasn't sure that Sparks' *Whomp That Sucker*, released in June 1981, was the best way to launch Why-Fi. Ron and Russell Mael had finished the album and were looking for a deal, while Paul wanted something he could put out quickly. *Whomp That Sucker* tried to revive Sparks' 1970s heyday with its return to the loopy concoctions of old, but nobody wanted to know. As the publicist, when that happens there is little you can do except pray, if you are that way inclined. You get an awful feeling of desperation and guilt when the record company or the manager thinks you should be able to pull something out of the hat. You can't, and of course I felt I'd really let Paul down.

Why-Fi soldiered on, although RCA had stopped funding the label after less than a year. Paul released several singles by Troy Tate, but being the guitarist in the Teardrop Explodes wasn't enough and nothing could disguise the fact that Troy was a gifted sideman but not a frontman. I thought Why-Fi's best shot at making a mark was with Virginia Astley, the classically trained daughter of British film and TV composer Edwin Astley. She released two singles for the label, but her lingering, pastoral English salon music had no identifiable context in 1981. At the beginning of 1982 she toured with the Teardrops as part of the trio the Ravishing Beauties – a kind of conservatoire Bananarama – but the album she'd begun recording for Why-Fi, *From Gardens Where We Feel Secure*, ended up on Rough Trade. It was a neoclassical antecedent of the KLF's *Chill Out* and quite brilliant. I wish I could have seen it through.

I found the adjustment to independence tough during the first couple of years. Sometimes I was clutching at straws where there were none; other times I'd done a decent job but to no effect. One of my first independent jobs had been looking after New York-based power-pop group the dB's, whose debut album, *Stand for Decibels*, was released in January 1981. They were part of a London showcase for a new wave of New York groups, held under the banner of 'Taking Liberties'. Albion Records flew me and a bunch of journalists over to cover the alleged new scene, which also involved the Bongos, the Fleshtones, the Bush Tetras and the Raybeats. Despite good advance coverage of the New York trip in *Time Out*, *NME* and *Sounds*, the cavernous Rainbow Theatre sold so few tickets that management refused to turn on the heating. It was cold and empty, the PA was inadequate and none of the groups came out of it well. I didn't see it as a failure on my part, but it was a reminder that readers of the music weeklies had minds of their own.

Nor did I feel responsible for the poor attendance at the first WOMAD festival in July 1982, which Echo & the Bunnymen headlined on the Saturday. It was the first and last time I looked after a festival. WOMAD's

94

lofty ambitions for a multicultural international music festival were ahead of their time and media interest lagged behind; the phrase 'world music' had yet to become a catch-all term. Festival culture was also undeveloped in 1982, when even Glastonbury had yet to be firmly established as an annual event. A lack of publicity was partly blamed for the disappointing turnout at WOMAD, but the Shepton Mallet Showground in Somerset was quite a schlep and ongoing British Rail strikes and severe disruptions that weekend were highly damaging.

WOMAD shook me and I did ask myself if I could have done more. The recurring question of whether I was good enough never went away. After two years out on my own I was beginning to doubt myself. I'd made some poor decisions and nothing new I'd taken on had worked out or had any longevity. I was never complacent but I knew I'd let Sire slip away. I was in a precarious position and becoming increasingly dependent on the perilous fates of the Teardrop Explodes and Echo & the Bunnymen.

6 : CHRIST VS WARHOL

1981-2

After a two-year spell at Northampton School of Art that ended in July 1972 Bill Drummond enrolled at Liverpool School of Art, but quit the fine art course after a year. Over the next two years he had a variety of jobs, including spells as a ward orderly in a mental hospital, a steel worker, a milkman and an apprentice trawlerman in Aberdeen, and a stint in the carpentry workshop of the Belgrade Theatre in Coventry. He returned to Liverpool in September 1975, where he was hired as a master carpenter at the Everyman Theatre, until it closed for refurbishment in June 1976. He found a new job almost immediately, designing and building clever and disorientating sets for Ken Campbell's staging of the *Illuminatus!* trilogy at Liverpool's School of Language, Music, Dream

Ian McCulloch, Les Pattinson, Will Sergeant and Pete de Freitas. By the end of 1981 the Bunnymen were the biggest cult group in the land. It was theirs to lose (*photo: Peter Noble*).

and Pun. Theatre director, actor, improviser, experimental writer and all round oddball Campbell made a huge impression on Bill. He took Campbell's inspirational guidelines to heart in all his endeavours thereafter, not least that any idea you have can be achieved or turned to your advantage. The irrepressible Campbell wasn't one for half measures; you had to think heroically and go for the big risk too, a mindset Bill was now applying as manager of two aspiring groups who were both very much on the up at the start of 1981.

The first time Bill outlined a specific plan to me proved to be the final outing for the Bunnymen's camo look, when they played a mystery show at the end of January. Fans were required to apply to the Zoo offices for a free pass to the event, and coaches were laid on, picking up in London, Liverpool, Manchester, Leeds and Sheffield. The tickets declared 'Destination Gomorrah' – in reality, the Pavilion Gardens, Buxton. The show was to be filmed, and the film would have a theatrical release, even if initially it was shown only at the ICA in London in August. What became *Shine So Hard* was small in scale, but it aimed to elevate the Bunnymen to something greater, and it was the first of many such ideas that kept raising the stakes.

Shine So Hard was filmed by Bill Butt and captured the 'camo chic' era for posterity. He also set out to capture the four distinct personalities in Echo & the Bunnymen. Butt filmed vignettes of each member of the group on the afternoon of the show, which took up a third of the final thirty-two-minute film. They were embarrassed having a camera following them around as it captured Will wandering through the gardens, Les sailing a remote-control boat, Pete having dinner and Mac gazing into mirrors. They also had to contend with the presence of *Melody Maker*, there to do a cover story for the first time. On top of which nobody was speaking to Pete, who had shaved his head the night before as a kind of protest against Bunnymen protocols. Shaved heads are common enough today, but in 1981 they were associated only with skinheads. Pete looked marginally less devilishly handsome, but he'd broken the rules – the Bunnymen didn't do shaved heads. With too much going on the group weren't at their best at Buxton and there wasn't enough mystery for the event to be memorable. The logistics of getting the coaches back in time, leaving London fans stranded, further soured the project, even though a four-song EP of live performances, released in April, finally broke the Top 40 barrier.

The stage set they unveiled when they next toured in April was visually barren. There was no drum riser at the back either; instead Pete was to one side, in a line with the others, all of them casting long shadows against a white backdrop. They wore civvies, not combat fatigues, and proved they could wow audiences without gimmicks. They also had a new album in tow. In June 1981 *Heaven Up Here* was Echo & the Bunnymen's second album in the space of twelve months. Recording it was the most enjoyable experience they ever had in a recording studio, and it shows, even though one reviewer described it as a glossy celebration of existential sadness. The odd doomy moment aside, I found the music totally uplifting and exhilarating, from the furious opening 'Heaven Up Here' to the thrilling conclusion of 'All I Want'. The group was evolving naturally and quickly, nowhere better illustrated than by Pete's spontaneous tom-tom drum mantra for 'All My Colours' that set up Mac's soaring voice. Like the rest of *Heaven Up Here*, it was, as Mac once told me, 'nothing to do with anyone other than ourselves. Those sessions turned into songs out of nothing, and we knew instinctively what we were doing.' *Heaven Up Here* impressed the critics even more than *Crocodiles*. The only slight hiccup was, once again, a flop single. 'A Promise' stalled outside the Top 40. It didn't bother the group, but WEA were now aware of what they had in the Bunnymen and would soon be pressing harder for that elusive hit.

The Bunnymen knew they were on a roll. There was such a strong camaraderie within the group and among a solid extended family. We all believed they could do no wrong. I thought the only band around that could touch them, musically at least, was Talking Heads. The Bunnymen definitely felt a kinship with them and had been influenced by *More Songs About Buildings and Food* and *Fear of Music*. They all had those albums and played them to death, and you can hear it in the choppy, funky rhythms and percussive touches on *Heaven Up Here*.

I'd grab every opportunity to take journalists out on the road with the Bunnymen. It was just fun to be part of, and a curiously innocent fun at that. Travelling with them on the coach around Europe was like a rolling summer camp. There was a certain amount of bevvying but nothing excessive. They were still an essentially drug-free band; only Pete smoked pot and he'd taken LSD with members of the Teardrops. The touring entourage was the reverse of the rock 'n' roll norm: the bourgeois contingent made up the crew, not the group that took to the stage, with the exception of the drummer. I remember sitting in Pete's room with Mac and guitar tech Jake Brockman (another of the Bristol Old Vic contingent), and they'd been given a bottle of Mezcal. Tequila was the tipple of the day, but none of us had drunk Mezcal before. It made me want to choke and nobody wanted to eat the worm that gravitated to the bottom of the bottle. We sat around looking at it in disgust, till Pete just picked it up and swallowed it. He smiled, saying, 'Let me know if anything weird happens.'

All four Bunnymen were a little strange, some more than others. Will could be dour but had the driest and drollest sense of humour, totally off the wall. He was always drawing cartoons – usually blokes with big noses. Les was never less than amiable but prone to mad episodes, and in the mornings would recount his colourful dreams of being chased by bears in a supermarket or being whisked into outer space. They were a unique double act and perfect foils, each attuned to the other's mad world. They'd take their push bikes on tour and would ride off and explore wherever the tour bus had landed, while the others slept in. They'd find weird shops that sold bizarre things, buying them and then proudly exhibiting them like trophies. Mac and Pete had an odd relationship. Both liked to party but rarely did so together. Pete had struck up a strong friendship with Jake Brockman and they became as inseparable as Will and Les. Mac became engaged in 1981 to Warrington girl Lorraine; he was already becoming a little distant from the others.

Inevitably Mac was perceived as the star, but the Bunnnymen were a singular bunch and you could not have taken any one of them away without shattering the dynamic. Les would shrug off his importance, even when people praised the Bunnymen's powerful rhythm section, saying that 80 per cent of it was Pete, and he just locked into him. I spent more time with Mac, who was now taking the lion's share of the interviews and photo sessions. As they were getting more and more cover stories, it was becoming harder to maintain a policy of photographing only the whole group. The others increasingly stood back to let Mac do it, so we'd end up hanging out with the journalists I'd brought along. Mac liked a new audience. What I cherish most about him in those days is his snickering laugh. The release valve to Mac's serious side back then was his capacity to shift from the silly to the absurd.

They could all be completely daft and laugh at each other. Pete less so. He sometimes thought the others were from another planet. A few years later their eccentricities would be the very things that began to turn them against each other, but in 1981 there was genuine comradeship. I never experienced anything like it elsewhere. Nothing seemed to matter outside of the group itself, and that bond cocooned them from all the aspects of the music industry they disliked.

They trusted that the journalists I took along were going to fit in and they welcomed the interlopers. There was no fear that a writer was going to stitch them up afterwards. Their openness generated a feeling of mutual trust. I went on some great trips that summer: Oslo, where they played in the narrowest club anybody had ever seen, Club Underground; the next day they turned up at the small open-air Smog Rock Festival, on what was no more than a village green – some of the posters billed them as Rebecca & the Funnymen. The Renaissance city of Florence in June was another highlight: they played in bright sunlight in the Uffizi piazza, surrounded by its stunning statues and sculptures, with the show being promoted by the local Communist Party. When they played Amsterdam, where Mac proposed to his girlfriend Lorraine, I was even trusted with accompanying his fiancée on the train.

At the end of the year they began a short final tour with a newly formed Liverpool group called the Wild Swans. I made it to Glasgow and Leicester, during a week when a severe winter freeze kicked in. At Glasgow's Apollo it was so cold their breath was billowing onstage like the smoky haze of old. That year they played 113 shows in a 169-day period, covering the UK and US twice, Europe, Australia and New Zealand. They were the biggest cult group in Britain. Only the Jam's slavish followers kept them from being voted best group in the *NME*, but *Heaven Up Here* was its Album of the Year and featured high on most critics' lists. It had been extraordinary to watch them grow and satisfying to feel in some way part of that. It was theirs to lose.

January 1981 was the month that shaped Julian Cope's life. During a two-week tour of the US East Coast he met Dorian Beslity at the first show in Albany and fell head over heels in love; in Boston a few days later he heard that 'Reward' was at no. 6 in the charts back home. The repercussions of these isolated events were far-reaching.

1980 hadn't ended well for the Teardrop Explodes and few disagreed that they'd failed to live up to the high expectations everyone had for them at the start of the year. For Julian, anything less than greatness was a failure. Since then 'Reward' had become the hit that Phonogram had so desperately wanted. If it hadn't been a hit, I think I'd have been out on my ear as the first sacrificial lamb. Instead, I had a bona fide pop star on my hands, but I didn't have the expertise and experience to rein in the press as it homed in on the often unstable Julian, who was loving aspects of what was happening but was simultaneously tormented. I was as guilty as anybody in exploiting the superficial pop success that Julian was ambivalent about. 'Do you mind what people are saying about you?' I asked him, when Paul Morley described him as the noble nitwit. 'Doesn't that piss you off?' 'It doesn't bother me,' he said. 'What I appear to want and what I actually want are two totally different things. I know I can be self-destructive. When things are going too well, like having a Top 10 single, I just want to put an end to it.'

Julian was rarely off the covers of the rock and pop press during 1981. He was as much a cover star of *Smash Hits* or *Jackie* as he was of the *NME*, *Melody Maker* or *Sounds*. You'd be mistaken for thinking the Teardrops were as massive as multi-hit groups such as Adam and the Ants or Duran Duran. One of Duran Duran said he thought the Teardrops were their only competition, although the caveat was the killer punch: assuming 'Julian Cope can keep it together'. We all cracked up at that. The press were going crazy over Julian, and he hit all bases. The rock weeklies embraced him because he wasn't an obvious teen idol; Julian was one of their own in a way that Sting or Simon Le Bon could never be. And he was the epitome of the charismatic frontman and chief protagonist of his group's outrageously wild exploits and its insatiable appetite for drugs. His articulate exuberance was disarmingly infectious, and his passion and commitment to the music he loved knew no bounds. He was a good-looking bastard as well, and the camera loved him more than anybody else I ever worked with.

For much of 1981 everybody wanted a piece of Julian Cope. I was shocked by an old interview schedule I found from February that year. I don't know what is more surprising: that Julian was so obliging in lowering his sights or that I was asking him to.

3.00 p.m. *Photolove*
3.30 p.m. *Oh Boy*
4.00 p.m. *Loving*
4.30 p.m. *Love Affair*
5.00 p.m. *Mates*

The next day he had *Jackie*, *Patches*, *Blue Jeans*, *My Guy* and *Flexipop*.

After meeting and falling in love with Dorian, Julian arrived back in London but didn't want to return home to Liverpool. Rather than facing his wife Kath, he stayed at Dave Bates's flat in Lisson Grove or at the Columbia Hotel. It was only after his parents brought her to Bearshank Lodge in Northampton in April, where the group were rehearsing and demoing new songs, that he finally told Kath the marriage was over. It had lasted less than two years, although there were plenty who muttered, 'I told you so.' It alienated him further from people back in Liverpool who still blamed him for sacking Mick Finkler and who thought he was becoming a megalomaniac.

None of it mattered to Julian. The Teardrops were heading back to the US and he would see Dorian again. New bassist Alfie Agius and keyboardist Jeff Hammer never fitted in. Even the official programme notes written by Julian make that obvious:

Alfie: 'Maltese. Emotionally unstable. Heterosexual in everything he does. His otherwise flawless vocabulary is marred by such words as "boilers" and "funk".'

Jeff: 'Christian and incorrigibly tolerant. Easily abusable.'

They were never more than hired hands, but what distanced them the most was that they didn't share everybody else's appetite for drugs and alcohol. It must have been hell for them at times trying to find refuge from the spiteful madness surrounding them. Julian had wanted musicians who simply played what they were told, but when they didn't add anything he felt even more antagonistic towards them. He grew to hate them and then felt guilty for doing so.

Julian and Gary still roomed together; they were a modern-day Don Quixote and Sancho Panza, on a valiant quest to take whatever drugs were thrown at them. Troy did his best to keep up. Julian had liked him instantly, but Troy would slip away and get pissed when the drugs got too much. He was able to contribute ideas but couldn't bring what Balfey brought to the Teardrops. He knew his place and where to draw the line. Despite their regular clashes, Julian respected Balfe's forthrightness. 'Balfey's the only person who says no to me,' he once told me. 'Bill doesn't. He'll do things behind my back, and then we deal with it later. Balfey's always up front, and sometimes I want to be challenged.'

The press had really kicked in ahead of the UK tour in June. It was the first opportunity for the new teeny-bopper fans to see their latest pin-up in the flesh. Touring the US as a drug-crazed cult outfit completely off their rockers was a far cry from stuffy provincial con-cert halls, outside which the screaming girls who accosted Julian in the street were immediately spurned by him. He was too well brought up to be a total asshole, but only just. He was troubled by it onstage and off; the answer was, of course, to take more drugs and try to lose touch with reality.

It was a bizarre tour, during which I never saw anything other than a facade of best behaviour onstage. The band was tight, and the audiences, teeny-boppers included, were just as enraptured by epic new songs like 'The Great Dominions' and 'The Culture Bunker' as they were by the two hits. There were surprising concessions towards the prevailing new romanticism, with Julian in leather jodhpurs and Troy in a large cape striking exaggerated poses on the guitar. Jeff was totally anonymous, but the flamboyant Alfie, bouncing up and down as he plucked away at a high-slung bass, could have stepped straight out of Kajagoogoo.

The extent of Julian's popularity was brought home to me when I had a call from a West End theatrical company asking if he'd be interested in auditioning for the part of Frederic, the dashing young apprentice pirate in *The Pirates of Penzance*. I tried not to laugh as I said I'd check it out. I knew he would never be up for it, but I couldn't wait to tell him. I only wish I could have told him face to face. Over the phone he was reduced to an unusual momentary silence, and I could imagine the idiotic grin that followed. I said he could be the new Tommy Steele. I should have said the new Peter Noone, as Julian had joked about turning into the blond, smiley, squeaky-clean singer with Herman's Hermits. Not long after, it was none other than Peter Noone who began a three-year run playing Frederic on Broadway and at London's Drury Lane Theatre.

The flawed line-up did at least record the new single, 'Passionate Friend'. I went up to Generic Studios near Reading with Bill to hear it. Julian was on a high; he was there with Dorian and producers Clive Langer and Alan Winstanley, who'd recorded 'Reward' and 'Treason', and it was one of those rare moments when we were all blown away. I can't remember Bill ever being so hyped up. We were all convinced it would be a massive hit, and this wasn't any drugs talking. We all rejoiced, despite the problems Julian was already having with life as a pop star. That one night, the consequences of another hit possibly derailing Julian didn't matter to any of us. 'Passionate Friend' was about a 'thing' Julian had with Mac's sister, Julie. 'Everybody used to think it was our rivalry,' Julian told *NME* writer Gavin Martin, 'but that's why I ended up having a big argument with Mac. Julie was the bone of contention, which is what the song's about.' Released at the end of August, 'Passionate Friend' immediately landed in the Top 30, then moved up incrementally by one place over the course of next three weeks before stalling at no. 25. This was despite two appearances on *Top of the Pops*, between which Julian sacked Jeff and Alfie and invited Dave Balfe back. The new four-piece Teardrop Explodes, with Balfey miming bass, made their debut on the band's second appearance on the show. Balfey appeared on *Top of the Pops* four times with the Teardrops, each time miming a different instrument.

Julian knew he had the songs for the new album, most of them well bedded-in from touring, but he needed the conflict Balfey would bring to make them special. Balfey was thrilled to be back and knew he had to prepare for the battle ahead. He thought the song arrangements were too West Coast laid-back and he persuaded Julian to buy a Prophet-5 synth, as used by Talking Heads on *Remain in Light*, which was the sound he thought they needed. His input radically and significantly changed a collection of songs that were mostly about the break-up of Julian's marriage, the guilt he felt and his reflections on success and his new love, Dorian. 'The Culture Bunker' was aimed directly at Mac and the Liverpool scene he had left behind.

The relative failure of 'Passionate Friend' coincided with the release of *Fire Escape in the Sky: The Godlike Genius of Scott Walker*, compiled by Julian from Walker's four post-Walker Brothers solo albums, which few remembered. Bill and Balfey had resurrected Zoo Records to release it. It sparked a revival of interest in Scott Walker, who'd long since been dismissed as a dodgy 1960s MOR icon. Julian's compilation, which came in a plain, grey sleeve with no image of Walker, had unearthed the buried treasure of Walker's own songs, and the cult of Scott Walker began. Julian also brought the phrase 'godlike genius' into the language, and the success of *Fire Escape in the Sky* confirmed his unique standing. It wasn't just teenage girls who idolised him but also serious music fans and critics. Nobody else could have persuaded them to get into Scott Walker. So where were all these people three months later, when the new Teardrops album, *Wilder*, was released? Why, for no apparent reason, did interest in Julian and the group dissipate?

Wilder was a fantastic artistic achievement and staggeringly original. It was also Phonogram's big Christmas record that year, and was released on 20 November 1981 to far better reviews than *Kilimanjaro* had received. I remember arguing with Dave Bates that they should have released a different single in advance, because they went down the 'Reward' route again with the big and brassy 'Colours Fly Away'. They shot an expensive, fast-moving, 'Reward'-style video, with Julian and the band being pursued around a chemical plant near Bristol. The budget even stretched to a helicopter sweeping in and out of shot. But 'Colours' flew away and stuck at no. 54, just as the album reached the record stores.

Instead of the usual tour around *Wilder*'s release, Bill came up with the idea of focusing more on the Teardrop Explodes as a group. They'd made a great album but they needed to be perceived as something other than just the Julian Cope show. Balfey was back and they had a cool new bass player in Ronnie François. On paper it made sense. The Teardrop Explodes would play two sets a day, three days a week over the three weeks before Christmas. Adopting the name Club Zoo, they took over a small back-alley club called the Pyramid in Liverpool. Bill's comment to the press was that the Teardrops 'are going to be great again'; privately he thought they'd get so bored doing the same show each night that they'd eventually get good by default.

The venue had a capacity of four hundred but throughout its three-week run Club Zoo was rarely more than half full, and for the first few shows only around fifty people showed up. Worse, by the time Club Zoo opened, *Wilder* had flopped. It shipped over a hundred thousand copies, but half of them were returned. It peaked at no. 29 in the album charts and disappeared during the Christmas holiday. Julian's reaction was to turn the upper floor of the Pyramid into his personal bunker, which gradually became a refuge, even from the rest of the Teardrops. The group were in good shape, but as each evening wore on the shows became increasingly erratic because of Julian's antics and deranged behaviour. One time he did a lengthy solo barking like a dog; another time he covered his face with a towel for the whole of 'Sleeping Gas' and made spooky gabbling noises throughout. He regularly berated the sparse crowd and took on the familiar faces who were heckling him.

I was completely caught up in the craziness of it all. Everything was falling apart, but I didn't want to miss a single show. Nor did I. I became Mick 'Never Sleeps' Houghton. Obsessed with the idea that whatever was going down, I was going to be thoroughly professional, I decided not only to attend every show but to make it back to my office every day. The drawback was that it was in London. Overnight we'd all stay at the nearby New Manx Hotel on Hope Street, a refuge for has-been repertory actors and down-at-heel comics, and my routine was to get the train back to London at 6.40 in the morning to be in the office by 10.30, and then catch the train back to Liverpool at around 5.30 latest. The only way I could keep this up was by taking vast amounts of speed. So I made it into the office every morning, where I was good for nothing. It didn't matter because I had nothing to do. I was making a point, but only to myself. There was no respite: in the week that Club Zoo took a break I went to three Bunnymen shows instead.

For the first couple of weeks we invited all the press we could muster, with Julian doing interviews in his bunker, where he'd decided he was now in an alternative universe and had become Kevin Stapleton. He constructed a complete world where the Bunnymen had gone the way of Buddy Holly and everybody had alternative names: Balfey was Milk, Gary was Buff Manilla, Troy was Old and, for reasons lost in time and too many drugs, I was the Big Engine. The Teardrops were now called

Whopper, and *Wilder* became *Ten Belters from Whopper*. That was the backdrop to all the interviews. The now-distinguished Mark Ellen was covering it, and although he was hardly a drug fiend, he often reminds me that he's never taken drugs since the experience of trying to keep up with Julian in full fantastical flow as he masqueraded as Kevin Stapleton in the bunker at Club Zoo.

During the third week of Club Zoo I had to accept my own reward: for the third year running I won a Leslie Perrin Publicist of the Year Award. I'd won two while at WEA, but this time it was as an independent. It meant little in real terms, but I appreciated the fact that for the last three years *Record Business* magazine had presented me with this award. I knew full well they basically rounded up a random bunch of journalists, who made the decision over a few drinks by voting for the PRs they disliked the least. The award was going to be presented over a lunch, but I overslept and missed the early train to London. I was in a shocking state after days of prolonged excess, and after catching a later train rushed from the station to get to the bash. It was bitterly cold and I'd borrowed a Polish police officer's leather jacket from Julian that had never been worn. It was three-quarter length and weighed a ton; it was probably bulletproof. The arms of the jacket were so thick they wouldn't bend, so I plodded along like a leather-clad Egyptian mummy. I more or less collapsed on arrival, in a state of severe dehydration after snorting a massive line of speed before I got off the train. I made it through the lunch, guzzling gallons of water and gabbling nonsensically. I'd set a fine example of representing the cream of my profession and never won again. The following year the award shifted to *Music Week* and it became self-important and bureaucratic. Thereafter PR companies had to submit campaigns with evidence of their achievements. That wasn't for me.

By Christmas it was all over, and with understandable repercussions on my relationship back home. Exhausted, I slept through Christmas. *Wilder* had flopped, Club Zoo had been a disaster and there was no way to turn it around. Come the new year, Dave Bates gave up on the Teardrops. Phonogram didn't even bother to release a second single from *Wilder*, even though the group toured the UK and then Europe throughout January and February. Club Zoo had been Bill's last attempt at salvaging a working relationship with Julian. He brought in an amiable chap called Colin Butler to look after the Teardrops on a day-to-day basis. He was a lovely man but had no experience whatsoever as a tour manager; it really was like leaving the lunatics in charge of the asylum, while giving the chief lunatic the keys to the drug cabinet. By default, Colin was soon effectively managing the group. Unlike everybody else, he hadn't given up; he just hadn't a clue what he was doing.

He was the ideal man to lead the group across Australia and the US during March and April. For everybody else it was simply out of sight, out of mind. And the Teardrops were definitely out of their minds. By the time they returned in May Julian no longer wanted to tour and no longer wanted to be in his own band. While they were in Australia, Bill sold the management on to Paul King at Outlaw, a successful booking agency and management company, even though it seemed obvious that the Teardrops wouldn't last out the year.

When they returned, Julian stayed with his parents in Tamworth, before finding a house nearby where he and Dorian could live together. He knew that he no longer belonged in Liverpool, and as a group they no longer belonged anywhere. The two final tours had become a descent into total drug mania, with the group refuelling regularly on acid and whatever psychedelics they could lay their hands on. They'd also amassed an £80,000 debt, before an additional tax bill raised it to £120,000. Julian, to his credit, took on the liability and agreed to do three massive open-air shows with Queen to help alleviate the band's financial problems.

I hardly saw Julian during 1982, but at some point in the weeks before the Queen dates he and I spent an evening together, known only as the '2.43 Evening'. It was a one-off throwback to Club Zoo behaviour. I can't remember where the '2.43 Evening' began, but we sat around and did a lot of speed and some coke. Julian soon ran out of pot, which kept him together, so we did more lines of speed instead. Julian was desperate to get some pot, so at 2.43 a.m. we turned up unannounced at Max Bell's house on Albion Road in Stoke Newington and got him out of bed. He didn't protest too much. We loaded him up with speed and, as Julian later described it, 'skinned up like hooligans and carried on into the next day'. I don't remember much else. I found out later that Julian went back home to Dorian and told her it was over, and she should go back to the US because life was no longer real. 'What did you take?' she asked when I called up the next day. She told me what he'd said. I was horrified, but she was laughing at the same time. 'I talked him out of it after a couple of hours,' she said. 'He gets like that if he takes coke and speed without dope.' The '2.43 Evening' was immortalised in the song 'Out of My Mind on Dope and Speed'. He tried to get the Teardrops to record it, but Balfey said it was too silly.

The three mega Queen dates in Edinburgh, Leeds and Milton Keynes at the end of May were the ultimate sacrifice for Julian, during which he perilously presented himself as a moving target for Queen fans armed with cans and bottles, deliberately baiting them by trying to out-camp Freddie Mercury. For the five-piece group that had begun life in Club Zoo this was the end of the line. Troy Tate and Ronnie François had to be let go. Julian, Gary and Balfey returned to Rockfield to record a third Teardrop Explodes album that only Balfey had any interest in making. Within weeks the sessions were abandoned by a dispirited Julian, who felt his songs were being swallowed up by a jumble of loops and synthesizers. Whereas *Wilder* benefited from the two-way creative association with Balfey, Julian was so disinterested in the new record he just gave Balfey free rein and then wanted nothing to do with the songs as they now sounded. Around half the album was more or less finished; other songs had only guide vocals.

A UK tour that nobody wanted to do had been booked in early October, and it had to go ahead or else there would be a risk of bankruptcy for Paul King and further debts for Julian. The testy trio bolstered a predominantly synth- and keyboard-based sound with backing tapes. I only witnessed the final show in Manchester, during which the tapes broke down during 'The Culture Bunker', Julian finally snapping along with the tapes and attempting to dismantle the boxing ring-like stage before disrobing and throwing his clothes into the crowd, who continued booing with sustained hostility for the best part of an hour. It was the final act by the Teardrop Explodes.

I sent out a press release on 18 November 1982 announcing that they had split up. Rather unimaginatively headlined 'The Teardrop Explodes for the Last Time', Julian's statement regarding the split began with an offhand comment that left him wide open to a critical backlash in the future: 'I regard what I do next as the opportunity for gross self-indulgence.' Balfey simply commented that 'It wasn't working any more. Copey wanted to split up, so we did.'

What began at Eric's on 15 November 1978 officially ended four years later, and Julian began his exile in middle England.

The Zoo empire had, however, moved to offices on Liverpool Road, on the floor beneath me. The idea had been for me to become a partner in Zoo Records with Bill and Dave Balfe, but effectively I just continued in my usual role as publicist. In February 1982 Zoo released its second album, *To the Shores of Lake Placid*, a compilation by me and Bill drawn mostly from the Zoo archives, plus the label's only twelve-inch single, 'Revolutionary Spirit', by the Wild Swans. It had been funded and produced by Pete de Freitas, under his middle names, Louis Vincent. The lyrical Blakean wonder of 'Revolutionary Spirit' was sung over gentle guitar, rococo keyboard rushes and Pete's dramatic drumming. Bill would declare it was the best thing Zoo ever released. The Wild Swans had formed in 1980 and were fronted by singer and first Teardrops keyboardist Paul Simpson. I was so taken with them when they supported the Bunnymen on that cold winter's tour in December 1981 that I offered to manage them, on the basis of 'Let's see what I can do to get you a deal, and we'll take it from there.' Simon Potts, the head of A&R at Arista, was keen to sign them immediately and he brought the band down to London, where I joined them all for a meeting at the lethal cocktail bar Trader Vic's. When I next rang Paul to ask how things were going, he said the group had split after he'd rejected the potential deal without consulting them. It was a lucky escape for me. I'd seen at first hand that management was far too all-consuming and I never considered it again. My record-company days ended just as abruptly. Zoo Records limped along with no further releases and ran out of money before the year was out.

After the highs of 1981, Echo & the Bunnymen were now struggling to write and record their third album. Bill's usual fail-safe ploy of booking a new John Peel radio session and giving them a couple of days to come up with four new songs failed to galvanise the band. They could muster only three songs, written on the journey down, all of which were slow dirges, including one called 'Taking Advantage'. It was the best of an indifferent bunch, but with new lyrics and a faster tempo they had something at long last. Someone (they still argue as to who) suggested adding intermittent cellos to give it a lift. Now called 'The Back of Love' and produced by Ian Broudie under the baffling name Kingbird, it propelled them into the Top 20 at long last.

It was their only release in 1982, and the third album, scheduled for June under the title *The Happy Loss*, had to be shelved, along with two British tours. Rob Dickins had dismissed the album as flat and boring. After months at each other's throats in the studio, the group weren't surprised or disappointed. Rob handled the Bunnymen very cleverly. He rarely put his foot down when he disagreed with them over anything. He'd stand his ground, but his attitude was 'on your own heads be it', and they'd either be proved right or would come round to thinking he had a point. It was a good balance. You could never tell the Bunnymen anything, but their strength was to recognise that they could sometimes be wrong. In the end half the existing songs were revamped and rearranged to give the whole thing some life and deflect from its lyrical pessimism. The album was good to go by the end of the year.

Nothing was going to stop me tagging along when the Bunnymen travelled to Iceland, where the photo shoot for the new album, now called *Porcupine*, took place. I even paid for my own flights and hotel accommodation. Why Iceland? Brian Griffin had been hired to shoot his third Bunnymen cover, and the concept demanded snow and ice to make for a cold, bleak, isolated image. Will's theory was that Bill always sent them off on weird tours because they were to places he'd been to before and wanted to revisit. Bill had travelled to Iceland when he was seventeen and originally wanted to film *Shine So Hard* there, but the budget would only stretch as far as Derbyshire.

Ten of us made the trip to Iceland, and we all made it back. Arriving to see the aurora borealis on the drive from the airport was an auspicious start. The next morning we drove the fifty miles to the Gullfoss waterfall located in south-west Iceland. I was stupidly wearing exactly what I would wear during a normal English winter; even taking gloves had been an afterthought. A hat or hood of any description never occurred to me. Nor decent boots. I'd never been so cold in my life, so I layered on absolutely everything I had with me.

A waterfall a quarter of a mile wide that was completely frozen over gives some idea of how cold it was, yet Mac wore nothing but a flimsy sleeveless T-shirt beneath his northern greatcoat. He also wore a pair of strange shoes that were as flimsy as suede slippers and had no soles. I took refuge in the vehicle while they trudged through the snow. The main shot for the cover was a result of them inching their way across a ledge on the frozen waterfall; one slip and there was nothing below them for hundreds of feet. 'I was scared,' admitted Mac afterwards, 'although it was empowering to be standing up there as part of that landscape.'

We did a final shot of the entire party, arms aloft, before we headed back, only to be caught in a blizzard. One vehicle broke down halfway back, and for a while we had to contemplate the idea of half the party travelling on ahead and then returning for the others. It was too cold to even think just how ridiculous that was. Short straws would have to be drawn. One, maybe two of us would have to do the decent thing. I knew I was fucked because I didn't have an album out six weeks later. But then, at last, the second vehicle juddered into life again.

7 : THE HAPPY LOSS

IT WAS A PLEASURE
BY WILLIAM SHAKESPEARE

PERSONS REPRESENTED

BEN ELTON, a clownish man of the masses

JOANNA STEPHENSON, a sweet songbird

WILL SERGEANT, a woodsman

McCULLOCH, Duke of Norris Green

SIR THOMAS LESLIE, a Knight with a mission

JAKE DRAKE BROCKMAN, the travellers guide

ADAM, a minstrel boy

LOUIS DE FREITAS, the traveller

HUGH LAURIE, Hamlet the Pretender

PRIESTS, SAILORS, OFFICERS and other ATTENDANTS

SCENE – On the riverbanks of the Avon near Stratford, England
late 1983

Act 1

SCENE 1 – A damp night in an open field.

Enter Ben Elton.

Ben.   Friends Romans Bunnymen, lend me your ears.

1983-5

There were rumours after the initial recordings had been rejected in the summer that WEA were having doubts about retaining the Bunnymen's services. Unbeknownst to the group, it came to a head when Rob Dickins

Programme sheet for Echo & the Bunnymen's appearance at the Royal Shakespeare Theatre, Stratford-upon-Avon, in October 1983. 'We're bigger than Henry V,' declared Ian McCulloch.

refused to put out their original mix of what was to be the next single, 'The Cutter'. This time there was no stand-off; the band had no idea what was going on behind their backs. Rob compelled Bill to remix the track, and the group didn't find out till too late that he'd added the synth-simulated trumpet sounds at the end. Will summed up the group's feelings when he told me, '*Porcupine* was so horrible to make that by then we just wanted it out.'

Porcupine had seen the Bunnymen come close to breaking point. It was the first time they questioned what they were doing, almost to the point of wondering why they were doing it at all. That tension is what makes it such a great album, even though I'd probably need a gun to my head to listen to it again. It's a suffocating experience, and *Porcupine* suffered at the hands of the critics – the first time there had been concerted adverse comments. It hurt even more because the group agreed with most of them. *Porcupine* is arguably Mac's most profound and honest body of lyrics; he's often said as much himself. It's a chilling portrait of a band in transition and of four individuals growing apart but tied together by some invisible bond.

The Bunnymen were a very grumpy bunch at the start of 1983, despite 'The Cutter' giving them their highest-ever placing in the singles chart; it reached no. 8, while *Porcupine* crashed straight in at no. 3. The fallout carried over into a UK tour, where they found the songs they'd agonised over in the studio were just as hard to play live. I arrived in Sheffield near the beginning of the tour, only to find that Mac and Les weren't speaking to each other, other than through a third party. Something had gone down that nobody would divulge. I'd gone there with Steve Sutherland from *Melody Maker*, not the group's greatest supporter. The show was terrible and Mac was contrite onstage: 'Nobody wants to be this miserable, you know.' Shut out of the dressing room, I told Steve we'd meet them back at the hotel, only to discover the group had checked out already. A terse interview eventually took place in London at the third attempt.

Tempers remained frayed after another bust-up at *Top of the Pops*, where the Musicians' Union stipulated that you had to re-record your song and mime to the new version on the show. The usual practice was for somebody to switch the tapes beforehand – everybody did it. Even the BBC turned a blind eye, but that afternoon the Musicians' Union sent a rep along so the switch couldn't take place. The backing track sounded awful and renowned instrumentalist and composer L. Shankar's violin intro, which gave 'The Cutter' its memorable hook, was pathetically mirrored by a weedy synth. Mac also had to hurriedly redo his vocal. To deflect from the debacle on the night, halfway through the song he started to pull down his loose-fitting top, which was only pinned together at the shoulders, teasing the watching world with a glimpse of nipple before eventually stripping to the waist while the others looked at him aghast. They had a furious argument afterwards, although the next day Mac, who'd been seriously bevvied, claimed he didn't remember doing it. Fans still talk about it and Mac still gets asked about it, but the single leapt up the charts to no. 11. If Mac needed further vindication, they also leapfrogged U2, who had been on the same show performing 'New Year's Day'.

A new threat to their solidarity as a group was soon rearing its head: they had to face up to their singer becoming one of the pop-media sensations of the mid-1980s. Mac had always looked the part. He had the same androgynous looks of his boyhood hero David Bowie and an arrogance born out of the fact that he firmly believed he was the greatest singer in the best group in the world. While the others now left most of the interviews to him, he'd shifted gears from monosyllabic Mac to assertive Mac the Mouth. Everybody was fair game, and depending on how his mood swung he could shift between 'serious' and 'good-humoured'. He had a quote about anything and a scathing jibe for anyone. He saved the best for his closest early-1980s rivals – U2, Simple Minds and Paul Weller – but he never went too far, at least not until a few years later, when he often strayed beyond borderline offensiveness. What began as droll, punning, funny one-liners now gave rise to a stream of not-so-tongue-in-cheek put-downs of his peers.

In April Mac took another step away from the others when he became the first Bunnyman to get married, tying the knot with his long-standing girlfriend Lorraine. The couple moved into a large house on the north side of Sefton Park, but a more surprising twist came when Will and Les moved into a house with Pete and Jake Brockman the same month. It was a big, bohemian, Victorian mansion typical of the grand houses along Aigburth Drive, at the south end of the park. Jake's close friendship with Pete mirrored the relationship between Will and Les. Both sets of friends roomed together on tour and went on holiday together. If there was a danger of Mac becoming more isolated, then that was held in check, at least for the time being, when he and Will started writing songs together again on acoustic guitars, hitting a rich vein of ideas. And that summer they embarked upon a strangely configured tour. It was dreamt up by Bill Drummond, with Ken Campbell's 'Is it heroic?' mantra firmly in mind.

Bill's strength was in jolting the Bunnymen out of their natural lethargy. They needed motivation from outside, and that's what Bill's left-field scheming provided. He came up with a 'Northern Hemispheres' tour, which effectively began with warm-up dates in New York at the end of June and would commence with a show in Reykjavik, Iceland, taking a sidestep to play the Roskilde Festival in Denmark, before they travelled to the Hebridean isles of Skye and Lewis. The tour would then wend its way south to London, via a trajectory that followed ley lines. I knew the media would lap it up and trusted Bill to put the right spin on his ideas. He was bored with the usual socio-economic account of Liverpudlian music that was trotted out. 'I made a jokey comment to a journalist, and next thing it was being quoted as the reason for the tour. It was a load of bullshit about ley lines that started in Iceland and then came through space and bisected Mathew Street, where Eric's stood, and the Cavern before it.'

I was ever the pragmatist and knew this was better coming from Bill than from the group. I kept it at a level of it being ironic, and it was definitely not the sort of thing U2 or Simple Minds would have put their names to. It stood Echo & the Bunnymen apart, and the media happily laughed along with the Bunnymen, not at them. The fine-tuning had a lot more to do with the group than is often credited. Will and Les embraced every wild scheme, and the compliant Pete was happy to go along with it all, but Mac wasn't always so amused. He may have grumbled about playing in the middle of nowhere and some of Bill's mythologising explanations, but like the rest of us who went along to the Hebridean isles, he enjoyed a wonderful three days there.

I took the night train to Inverness with Max Bell and joined the other journalists, fans and the group on the ferry to Skye. It was magical: the sky was clear and bright blue and the sea was calm. Jonathan Ashby, a journalist from the *Standard* whom I'd never met before, was amazed by how the group welcomed him. 'It was more like a holiday than a rock tour,' he said. 'They didn't know me from Adam but trusted me, and most bands have every right to be wary of journalists.' The Gathering Hall in Portree, where they played, was a lovely old building with a wooden balcony, like a school assembly hall. Four hundred people turned up, the hardcore fans arriving early and spreading out on the green, still dressed in camo. 'It felt like an invading army,' said Will, 'but it was also very *Wicker Man*.' A few days later the local paper reported how 'a rock group and their cult followers delayed a concert until after a church service at the Free Church next door where they were inducting a new minister'.

The 'Northern Hemispheres' tour coincided with a rush-released new single, 'Never Stop'. For my part, it was a salutary experience. Off the back of the tour and the substantial press done in the islands, we had three simultaneous front covers the week after the Royal Albert Hall shows. 'Never Stop' had shot to no. 15, but then immediately dropped out of the charts. There'd been no radio, no *Top of the Pops*; with nothing to cross it over beyond hardcore fans, the advance press meant those devotees had snapped the single up more quickly and it disappeared even faster.

The Skye/Lewis jaunt was a complete success and the Royal Albert Hall shows an absolute triumph. Nowadays groups play the Albert Hall all the time; in 1983 no rock band had played there in over a decade. I had a vague recollection that the last to do so had been Mott the Hoople, so I ran with it, everybody repeated it and nobody challenged it. Mac said, 'No other group in the history of the world could have created that magic that night. I really believe that.' I did too.

When three months later the Bunnymen became the first rock group to play the Royal Shakespeare Theatre in Stratford-upon-Avon, there were fewer magical moments. They'd been invited by the RSC to close a fortnight of 'youth-related' events, and it was the fastest-selling production at the RSC, so a matinee show was added. Mac declared the Bunnymen were 'bigger than Henry V'. The shows were lacklustre by comparison to the Royal Albert Hall, but fascinating for unveiling a stream of new songs: almost the entire, as-yet-unrecorded new album.

I had the idea of an actor coming on in the middle section of 'Villiers Terrace' and reciting the lyrics in the style of a Shakespearean soliloquy – as Peter Sellers had done with his Richard III reading of 'A Hard Day's Night'. Will was the only one who knew what I was talking about, but they went for it. The jobbing actor in tights, reading the lines skull in hand, was Hugh Laurie. Earlier Ben Elton came on dressed as a minstrel and introduced proceedings with the inevitable 'Friends, Romans, Bunnymen, lend me your ears.' He returned the favour in series two of *The Young Ones*. When Rick says he'll complain to his MP, Neil responds by saying, 'You haven't got an MP. You're an anarchist.' To which Rick comes back with, 'Oh. Well then, I shall write to the lead singer of Echo & the Bunnymen!'

Musically, the Bunnymen sound was evolving in a more acoustic direction. 'The Killing Moon' was recorded in Bath's Crescent Studios just after the RSC shows. One morning Mac had woken up with the line 'Fate up against your will . . .' in his head. He sat bolt upright and the rest of the song came to him naturally. But it wasn't just Mac's song; it's perhaps the best example of a team effort on what is arguably their greatest artistic achievement, certainly in seven-inch form – the ultimate Bunnymen encapsulation of mystery, melody and drama. Mac, however, hadn't been happy with what they'd come up with in Bath. Then, as he later told me, 'Pete rang up, and I remember saying I thought it was the best thing I'd ever written, and he said he wanted to redo the drums, so would I sing it? It was just the two of us, at Amazon Studios. And Pete suggested using brushes, which he'd not tried before. I still had a bit of a cold, but it was brilliant. The vocal just happened. Best thing we'd ever done. It's got everything we're about: the words, the chords, Will's guitar, Pete's drumming and my voice all combined to create something more than just a song.'

'The Killing Moon' was released in January 1984 and it rightly became one of their biggest and best-remembered hits. *Ocean Rain* followed on 4 May and was heralded in advance as 'The Greatest Album Ever Made' in all the press ads and posters. Mac wasn't the culprit – or at least only indirectly, when he said, 'It's the greatest album we've ever made,' down the phone to Rob Dickins from Paris, where it was recorded. It was in fact Rob who used the line for the campaign.

I loved its simplicity and the minimalism behind the orchestration and the way it highlighted Will's 1960s psychedelic flourishes. Pete's brush-style percussion across much of the album was inspired. 'The Greatest Album Ever Made' claim definitely impacted on reviews. Critics saw the comment as sarcastic rather than ironic, and some derided the album's embroidered lushness and pomp. I thought Biba Kopf's conclusion in the *NME* was hidden praise: 'Like the orchestra he [McCulloch] is wasted on one of contemporary rock's more worthless quests: to relocate The Chord which The Moody Blues lost a decade ago. Sad to report Echo & the Bunnymen have found it.' The Moody Blues' *Days of Future Past* was a sterling attempt to work with an orchestra. They weren't pilfering classical-sounding music or rocking up the classics. The likes of Deep Purple, ELP, Rick Wakeman and the Nice were all guilty of hamming it up, but *Ocean Rain* overcame this with gloriously original arrangements and delightful, natural-sounding strings.

The unanimous critical acclaim we expected for the album was eventually ignited by the audacious 'A Crystal Day' event on 12 May 1984, which proved to be Bill Drummond's parting gift to the group. 'A Crystal Day' was 'a day's worth of happenings in Liverpool'. Some of the 'happenings' were pure Will and Les: breakfast at Brian's (the local greasy spoon by the rehearsal studio where they'd regularly eat breakfast, with chips and gravy a speciality) and a bicycle rally that was loosely mapped out in the shape of the so-called 'rabbit God' creature on the 'Pictures on My Wall' sleeve. Will and Les dutifully completed the cycle ride together, both claiming to have arrived at the finish line first.

The day's events also included a choir recital at the Anglican cathedral and an all-inclusive 44p return ticket for a ferry ride across the Mersey (the 2.15 to Seacombe). The Bunnymen's performance at St George's Hall, Lime Street, was something of an anticlimax at the end of a very long day; it almost couldn't live up to expectations, but they played three sets and twenty-five songs.

Afterwards Will, Les, Pete and the others went up to the roof to hear the last post being sounded, but Mac was sat with Lorraine in the dressing room, tucking into a bowl of Kentucky Fried Chicken and being quizzed by Neil McCormick, who was reporting for *Hot Press*. It was one of those touching moments. Mac was exhausted and could have asked Neil to leave, but he wanted to talk, and what he said was not the usual bluster. The gist of it was that all he wanted was for Echo & the Bunnymen to be the best. 'We'll never be the biggest band,' he said wearily. 'We'll never even be big 'cause we can't make the concessions and we'll never pander to audiences; well that's not us. Our audience is discerning. I'm always amazed when a single doesn't do well but I'm just as amazed when something like "The Cutter" does, or when "The Killling Moon" went Top 10. I know we can never maintain that. No other band could have pulled this off today. I don't know why some things do better than others . . . and I don't really care that much. I just like doing it.'

I was moved by what he said, and he was right that no other group could have made an event like 'A Crystal Day' work, even though he hadn't joined in the cycle ride or gone to Brian's – that wasn't his thing. Mac always kept you hanging around and he could be a pain, but that conversation has always stuck with me, as has that parting comment: 'I just like doing it.'

The scale of the tour that followed in the autumn was huge. They played five London shows: two each at Hammersmith Odeon and

Hammersmith Palais, and Brixton Academy in late October. In Britain, where events such as 'A Crystal Day' caught the imagination, the Bunnymen were no longer a cult band, but they weren't a U2 or Simple Minds either. As Mac said after 'A Crystal Day', the Bunnymen were never going to be that big. They always seemed to exist in their own moment. And alas, 1984 was also the year when the Smiths seized the Bunnymen's cult crown, and they never got it back. The rise of the Smiths was far more damaging than U2's global success, and they dented the Bunnymen's position more than any other group. They came from nowhere in 1983, and in Morrissey had a spokesperson who was as quotable and controversial as Mac.

Once the touring was over, Bill announced he'd decided it was time to cease managing them. He called the band into a meeting in a function room in the Adelphi Hotel and invited me along. He said *Ocean Rain* was their ultimate artistic triumph and they should now stop making records and just become a touring band like the Grateful Dead. It was Bill at his most preposterous. They all thought it was a totally ridiculous idea, especially Will, who said, 'But making records is the only part of it I enjoy doing.' But the real revelation was that Bill was taking a job at WEA. He would still be able to keep a watchful eye on the Bunnymen in his new A&R role at Korova. They'd have a spy in the enemy camp. 'They are the band I always wanted to be in,' Bill told me back in London, 'that's why I was always hard on them when they were bad. I know you thought I was too hard on them, but they needed it sometimes.' I couldn't see how it could ever get any better for Echo & the Bunnymen after that summer of 1984. And I thought Bill's departure more or less ensured that that was how it would pan out.

I remember it differently, but the group claim there was never any great announcement that they were taking a year out in 1985. The year began with considerable relief for three of the four Bunnymen. Mac had released a one-off solo single in December, a rather unconvincing, Sinatra-crooned version of 'September Song'. Somebody described it as sounding like he was getting impatient waiting for opening time; I was in the studio when the B-side was recorded, a Small Faces knees-up version of 'Cockles and Mussels', and that was definitely the sound of people after closing time. 'September Song' wasn't right for the Christmas market, nor for the Bunnymen's loyal following. It was a flop and a sharp reminder that Echo & the Bunnymen were always greater than any individual. Will was convinced it was Mac testing the water as to whether he could leave the group and pursue a solo career, but the Bunnymen were too close to Mac's heart. 'I don't know how long a break we're taking,' he told me, 'but I know that the Bunnymen will still be there.'

In the five months since they ceased touring back in October none of them had been at all productive. Mac talked about further singles, about wanting to work with Benny and Björn from Abba and going into acting, but nothing came of it. Les finally bought the 27-foot motor boat he'd always wanted. Pete travelled around Spain and France on his Ducati motorbike, while Will admitted he'd sat around too much and got bored. Before long they drifted back together, because being in the Bunnymen was the only life they knew. So they went back out on the road in April, but deliberately under the radar, playing only small dives throughout Scandinavia.

They played two sets a night. The second was a regular Bunnymen set, but the first was a blinding series of covers that totally fired them up. They just used practice amps and had a laugh. It was like they always used to tour, playing small halls, often with no stage. They played songs by the Doors, three Velvets classics, songs by Television, the Modern Lovers and Talking Heads, a searing garage-punk obscurity, 'Action Woman' by the Litter, and a swaggering 'Paint It Black'. Will loved it, and years later said it was the last time they were really a band. He'd clearly had a major hand in the set list. He was the only fervent record collector in the group, whether it was garage-punk singles, 1960s British psychedelia, Residents albums or krautrock. We discovered that we'd both given disastrous talks at school about the Velvet Underground. Will came a cropper when the teacher picked up the album jacket from his desk and realised that he was simply reading what he'd copied from the sleeve notes off the back. My own experience ended curtly. I played 'I'll Be Your Mirror', which the teacher somehow related to nineteenth-century romantic German art song, but I followed it with 'Heroin'. With my classmates wincing at the screeching viola, the teacher suddenly realised what the song was about and dragged the arm across the record with a dismissive harrumph, saying, 'You can return to your seat now.'

With one album still to go on their original contract, new manager Mick Hancock was tasked with renegotiating a better deal. The choice of Hancock had been the easy option. He was the tour manager they knew and most of the group trusted him, although Will saw him as Mac's man. They agreed a new, financially more rewarding deal and the band duly signed directly to WEA for a further four albums. I always suspected that there was a hidden caveat that in future the band would have to be more compliant. It certainly seemed that way when they consented to Rob Dickins's choice of producer for a new single. 'Bring on the Dancing Horses' was produced by Laurie Latham, whose most recent credits included the Stranglers and Paul Young's string of major hits. The track took over a month to record and was a surprising departure in style. Its textured mix of programmed beats, loops, Linn drums and very little guitar wasn't my thing at all. It's by far my least favourite Bunnymen single. Others loved it, not least Rob and most sectors of the press, who all thought it would be a massive hit. It had been almost eighteen months since the last single, but it stalled at a below-par no. 21.

It should have been a wake-up call, but the year ended with another compromise: a Bunnymen singles compilation called *Songs to Learn and Sing*, which became their best- and fastest-selling album. Aware that the relationships between the four Bunnymen were becoming strained again, we agreed that all the interviews around *Songs to Learn and Sing* and the short UK tour that followed would be conducted by everybody together, and not just Mac. One idea was for them to assess each other's good and bad points. It was conducted for *No. 1* magazine, where instead of Mac slagging off his usual targets, they all ended up slagging off each other. The tone of the confessionals was meant to be light-hearted, but it became surprisingly personal. Interviewed separately, they all mentioned

Pete's excessive drinking, Mac going so far as to say he'd changed since 'becoming an alcoholic'; also singled out was Will's rudeness and bitterness, and Mac's egocentricity, and particularly his tardiness. Les calculated that in the seven years since the band formed they'd spent about four months waiting around for him. What lay ahead for Echo & the Bunnymen in 1986 was the prospect of recording a fifth album, with only a couple of mediocre songs in the bag. They had lost sight of their mission again. I wasn't sure whether they had the desire to get back on course for any other reason other than that they'd signed a new deal with WEA and contractually owed them an album.

In the early 1980s, if you were out of the limelight for more than a few months, you were in danger of being forgotten and discarded. So in April 1983 Julian Cope did a major interview for *NME*, for which he was photographed by Anton Corbijn up to his waist in a lake, literally freezing his bollocks off, only to be rewarded by a caption stating that he was 'paddling through that twilight between reality and pure strangeness', facing life without the Teardrops but 'keeping his "dickhead factor" intact'. That last was Julian's own assessment. Keeping his 'dickhead factor' intact never ceased to be important to him.

He had bought a house in Tamworth just before the collapse of the Teardrop Explodes and spent the next few years holed up with his new love, and future wife, Dorian. Virtual recluses, they bolted the doors and permanently closed the curtains. The house was situated opposite a parking lot, and he declared his individuality by painting the dustbin yellow. He saw his parents regularly, and his brother Josh was a frequent visitor, but few others were welcomed. I turned up with a journalist one day for an interview we'd arranged, but he never answered the door. We hung around, politely tapping on the door and calling through the letter-box, but I didn't want to freak him out. I found the nearest payphone and tried calling, but he didn't pick up, so we trudged back to the station. 'Sorry, Mick,' he said, when we spoke a few days later, 'I just couldn't handle it.' There was no point in me getting angry. I hadn't really been surprised. The house was his sanctum and he didn't want to let a stranger inside.

Once Phonogram's great white hope, Julian thought he meant nothing to them without the clout of the Teardrops' name attached, and he'd now been surpassed by Tears for Fears, Soft Cell, Big Country and others. Phonogram hadn't written him off at all and he'd signed up for two solo albums. They weren't entirely sure what to expect but they weren't discounting his making a serious comeback. He already wanted to call his first solo album *World Shut Your Mouth* and had more than an album's worth of tunes. These included one pre-Teardrop Explodes track, 'Bandy's First Jump' (another song about Julie McCulloch), while some dated from the abandoned September 1982 album sessions, including 'The Greatness and Perfection of Love', which Balfey had rejected as 'too sixties'. *World Shut Your Mouth* was recorded in quick time at the Point Studio in Victoria, London – nine of its eleven songs in as many days – and it was wrapped up by January 1984. The sessions reinstated the guitars in preference to weird layered keyboard structures. There were some fine melancholy ballads, while 'Kolly Kibber's Birthday' was a drastic return to early Teardrops fundamentalism, propelled by a rhythm machine and a Casio keyboard, its keys gaffer-taped to the chord of C.

Aside from 'Reward', Mercury always blundered when choosing singles for Julian. Released in the busiest scheduling month of November 1983, 'Sunshine Playroom' was another disastrous choice to mark Julian's return from exile. An orchestrated Jimmy Webb/'MacArthur Park'-style epic about a deep yearning to return to childhood, the single perplexed everybody. It was a brave, bizarre but foolhardy choice that Julian was as much in favour of as anybody else, but he'd shot himself in the foot again. Mercury showed they meant business by hiring David Bailey to direct his first-ever pop video. It cost almost as much as the entire album. They got on fine, but Bailey's art for art's sake rip-offs from *Battleship Potemkin* and gory, violent images meant that no one would show it. Julian's big, belting comeback went only as far as a deflating no. 64, and when the album arrived in mid-February it was torn apart.

The video was made through Paul McNally's new video company, Why B2, which he'd set up after abandoning Why-Fi Records. They specialised in art-house pop promos, using directors such as Derek Jarman and John Maybury. I had now moved from Liverpool Road to share Paul's warehouse space in Metropolitan Wharf in Wapping, six flights up a series of endless stone stairs but with a fantastic view overlooking the Thames that almost made the hike up worthwhile.

I never understood why *World Shut Your Mouth* was so slated in the press. Nothing I'd handled before had got such a mauling; *Kilimanjaro* was a masterpiece by comparison. It was such an about-turn by the entire rock press, but the savagery of the *NME* review really pissed me off. Less than six months before I'd spoken to editor Neil Spencer about Julian writing an article on 1960s garage punk and psychedelia, which duly ran as 'Tales from the Drug Attic'. The piece went down a storm, compulsively written in a babbling, eloquent, informative style that was pure Julian. I felt that the *World Shut Your Mouth* review was such a betrayal by the *NME*. I never complained about bad reviews, but I spoke to Neil, who said, 'We have to respect our writers' opinions.' As I put the phone down, Jack Lemmon's poignant line from *The Apartment* sprang to mind to console me. When Shirley MacLaine's Miss Kubelik, the girl of his dreams, asks why she can't ever fall in love with somebody nice like him, Lemmon's character C. C. Baxter's absurd, understated response is, 'That's the way it crumbles, cookie-wise.'

Nobody screamed at me. I had expected that Dave Bates would, but everybody just seemed resigned to another failure. When I spoke to Julian, he said, 'I know there's nothing you could have done. I have to shrug it off because if I think too hard about it, then it hurts. They finally got to say what they'd wanted to say about me for ages.' I was now working with Mel Bell, then married to my close friend, *NME* journalist Max Bell. She had become my second assistant, and we had joked that the album should have been called *Stop the World I Want to Get Back On*. But now I was screaming, 'I want to get off.' I had a new Brassneck letterhead designed, which some people found tasteless, but it was how I felt: a graphic image of a face with a gun up against one side and a stream of words coming out of the other. They read: 'It's a full-time job getting your own back on the world.' It was a line that jumped off the page from William Boyd's *A Good Man in Africa*, a writer Mel had turned me on to.

Julian went on tour supporting *World Shut Your Mouth* in mid-March, but attendances were poor. I found the shows submissive and professional, with a set that included obscure garage-punk classics by Balloon Farm and the Craig. 'Bouncing Babies' was the token Teardrops song. In Nottingham I went along to a radio interview with Julian. He said he was already recording another album that was going to be darker and edgier. He spoke about getting married in New York in the autumn and honeymooning in Hawaii, and about buying toys at Nottingham fairs. He sounded like he was a little broken by the experience of the past few months.

When the tour reached London's Hammersmith Palais on 25 March, he finally flipped. From high above the stage, where he'd climbed into the rafters, he poured a pot of Gale's honey over himself. Events were triggered by support act the Woodentops' frontman Rolo McGinty stealing his moves, followed by what Julian felt was the crap, sluggish performance his own group had been giving, until the ferocious new song 'Reynard the Fox' brought him to life. He broke the mic stand in half and slashed open his stomach with its sharp edges, reciting Kenneth Williams's last words as Julius Caesar in *Carry on Cleo*: 'Infamy, infamy, they've all got it in for me.' I wasn't allowed backstage, which was probably just as well as Paul Crockford from Outlaw Management was mopping up pools of blood. A week later the second single from the album, 'The Greatness and Perfection of Love', peaked at a miserable no. 52, while the album tumbled down and out of the charts completely.

I didn't see Julian for a while after the Hammersmith Palais episode. I wasn't avoiding him, but of course I was busy with the Bunnymen, who had become a ubiquitous presence in the music press. Julian consoled himself that Mac was letting himself down: the Mac who always wanted to be the great artist had become Jimmy Tarbuck, but it was Mac who was now regularly gracing the same front covers that Julian hadn't been able to command since the end of 1981.

In the aftermath of the Hammersmith weird-out, Mercury's expectations for Julian plummeted. The exception was his new product manager, Cally Calloman, who had joined Phonogram towards the end of 1983. He loved *World Shut Your Mouth*, while everybody else there waited to see if it sank or swam. By the spring of 1983 Cally and Julian were as thick as thieves. In the months ahead Cally would drive to Tamworth every weekend, and if Julian came to the Mercury offices in New Bond Street, he could find a home from home in Cally's bunker. Julian now had a true ally, somebody who was just as enthusiastic about his headful of ideas and somebody able to turn them into a plan of action. He had already decided his second album that year would be called *Fried*. It was how Dorian described his mental state.

Julian was halfway through recording *Fried* before anybody at Mercury but Cally knew anything about it. Donald Ross Skinner, a young guitarist who had turned up on Julian and Dorian's doorstep on New Year's Day, was pivotal. Julian had been impressed by Donald's persistence in wanting to work with him and the fact that his favourite guitarist was Tim Buckley sideman Lee Underwood. Julian's take on *Fried* and its predecessor was that he was making what he called 'back catalogue' albums. He knew they would sell poorly initially, but he didn't care because they'd be rediscovered later. So they were in a direct line to albums he loved by the Seeds or the 13th Floor Elevators. Such an attitude freed him up and his behaviour in the studio marked a return to the kind of Teardrops Rockfield-style madness and drug intake. Julian even insisted upon singing the songs completely nude in the studio.

Fried reintroduced some of the post-punk resilience of old but, more significantly, it anticipated the kind of introspective, strummed, minor-chord ballads that would come to fruition on *Peggy Suicide*. Surprisingly taut, intuitive musicianship keeps *Fried* from drifting too far from its core, even on the disoriented, desolate 'Search Party', 'Laughing Boy' and

'Me Singing'. These songs usually drew comparisons with Skip Spence's *Oar* and Syd Barrett's solo recordings (the implication being that all three, including Julian, were mentally unhinged to one degree or another), but they were just as likely inspired by Tim Buckley's *Happy Sad* and Fred Neil's *Sessions*.

Mercury execs were bewildered by both the album and its sleeve, but it had cost just £19,000 and Cally had pseudonymously put the sleeve together in his own time and presented his bosses with the finished article. The photos had cost just £215, and if ever there was an album where the front-cover photograph has eclipsed the vinyl it houses, then *Fried* is just that. Julian's original idea for the cover had been along the lines of Tim Buckley's bright, sun-blistered *Happy Sad*. How differently would *Fried* have been perceived had it not instead featured a naked Julian crawling across the earth under a turtle shell and looking dolefully at a toy truck (bearing the album's title painted on its side)? That image has haunted Julian ever since.

Fried was released in early November. There was no advance hoo-ha, not even a token single; we did no press to speak of because Julian wasn't around. He and Dorian had secretly married at Lichfield Register Office earlier in the year, but the couple were now in New York undertaking a full, lengthy Greek Orthodox wedding ceremony. Julian hadn't wanted to do anything anyway. He thought he was the problem, not the records he was making, and his crazy persona was now turning people off. Of course, it's impossible to square that with the *Fried* cover image, but Julian is nothing if not consistent in his contradictions. He secretly thought *Fried* would overturn the failure of *World Shut Your Mouth*, and was bitterly disappointed when it didn't. It was no consolation that he was out of the country when *Fried* entered the charts at no. 85 and dropped out one week later. When in February 1985 Mercury chose to release 'Sunspots' as a single, it was an utterly pointless afterthought. Left stranded outside the Top 75, it was a depressing fate for what was arguably Julian's best solo single of the 1980s, his paean to Dorian's green Karmann Ghia.

A few months later Julian sent me a cassette tape of thirteen new tracks, interspersed with backward-taped 'themes'. The inlay card described them as 'St Julian dry runs' and underneath Julian had written 'demobs'. It was only much later that I understood the significance of the deliberate misspelling of 'demos'. It was a brilliant collection of songs that included the hook-laden song 'World Shut Your Mouth' (written soon after the album of the same name). I played it over and over again all weekend, but I couldn't get too carried away in my enthusiasm because I'd thought both albums he'd released in 1984 had been brilliant too, and they'd been pilloried and done bugger-all. I couldn't see how these new songs were going to change the perception of Julian as post-punk's clown prince or alter the stalemate with Mercury. Dave Bates clearly agreed and let Julian go. It was for the best. He needed to be on a new label and he needed a new PR. I'd let him down once too often to have the heart to carry on, and instinctively Julian knew I was never going to embrace his straight-ahead rock 'n' roll *Saint Julian* concept. He signed to Island in late summer 1985, a label that tended to keep its press in-house, so I didn't go pleading to Julian or to Cally, who was now his manager, saying, 'You have to keep me on.' It would have done no good anyway; the word around Island was that I was losing it.

Alan McGee used to say that all people who are drawn to bands are groupies, whatever their role is, whether they're managers or A&R men, publicists or journalists. I guess I became a groupie for a while. It was never about basking in the glory, but when a group or artist you are working with is on the rise, it's so exciting. It's hard not to want to be part of that experience, as long as you don't believe you are some kind of indispensable extra member of the group. You have to hold on to the reason why you're there in the first place. I lost sight of that, particularly with Echo & the Bunnymen and Julian Cope between 1981 and 1984.

I'd thrown myself totally into being a publicist in 1979, and the overnight indication that I was actually good at something went to my head. I was twenty-nine; the average age of the groups was probably twenty-one or twenty-two, so I was old enough to know better than to let the job take over my life. Then, once I struck out on my own, the compulsion to belong grew even harder to resist. I was completely and quite voluntarily sucked into the buzz and intrigue building up around the Bunnymen and the Teardrop Explodes at the end of 1980, and for the next two or three years hanging out with them became almost an obsession.

Nobody but me was to blame for the way I behaved at times. I became this other person who was too easily led astray once the booze, speed, coke and apparent camaraderie kicked in. I was staying out all night, which was not the worst of my peccadillos when it came to screwing up a good relationship. There was no excuse for such loose morality, and looking back I feel embarrassed and ashamed.

The culture of drinking and taking drugs may have come with the job, but I knew it was also a crutch. I couldn't have handled a lot of the social interaction, even going to gigs sometimes, unless I was at least a little high, even though I always knew I could switch off. Problem was, I chose not to. The cheap thrills and allure of the rock 'n' roll lifestyle can engulf you and chew you up unless you are really strong, but the music industry will definitely spit you out once you're too fucked to function. I saw that too often and I may well have been closer to the brink than I care to admit. My long-term relationship ended and I vowed never to get so out of control again. In 1985 circumstances made it easier for me to pull away. Julian moving to Island was the opportunity for me to step back from him, the Bunnymen were less involving that year and nobody could have predicted what happened in 1986, which led to such a barren year. I actually had little other work but I was lucky that several new opportunities came along in 1985. It was down to me not to make the same mistakes again.

8 : IN A HOLE

1984-7

In 1976 Martin Jennings left a senior post at Warner and moved to Australia, where he started a label called Hot Records in the back of a shop in Sydney. It soon became one of the country's leading underground independents, home to the Celibate Rifles, the Apartments,

The Jesus and Mary Chain: William and Jim Reid, October 1987, soon after the release of *Darklands*, and looking dismayed after critics wanted another *Psychocandy* (*photo: Gie Knaeps*).

the Lighthouse Keepers, Ed Kuepper's post-Saints band the Laughing Clowns and the prolific Kuepper himself. In July 1984 Dave Walters, a friend of Jennings from his Warner days, arranged a meeting between me and Martin at the Waterside Inn, near King's Cross in London. Martin wanted me to look after another Hot group, the Triffids, who were due to arrive in London from Western Australia at the end of August. They had two albums in tow: *Treeless Plain* and a mini-LP, *Raining Pleasure*. Rough Trade was set to release them here. I read some of the cuttings Martin gave me while we sat having lunch and liked what I read. 'Let me have a listen,' I said non-committally, but as Martin left he handed me a bag with ten or so copies of each album and thrust £250 in cash into my hand. 'Is this enough to get you started?' he said, and it was fait accompli. I had a feeling I wouldn't regret it, and when I played the records back home, any doubts were immediately dispelled.

The Triffids duly arrived with a wad of cash to tide them over and five fixed-return plane tickets that expired by Christmas. They were all smart, easy-going and unassuming, and none more so than rugged singer and chief songwriter David McComb, who was clearly the star. However impassively, the others definitely deferred to him. I'd fallen in love with the two albums by then. On the surface their influences were similar to those of almost every British band formed between 1978 and 1983 – Television, the Doors, the Velvet Underground and the Stooges – but David's own songs were equally indebted to Dylan, Leonard Cohen and southern country soul. They'd been inspired by a second-hand appreciation of British punk and were avid music fans who waited patiently each week for a month-old copy of the *NME* to arrive at their local Claremont newsagent in Perth.

The Triffids had released their first single in 1981 and now had a stable line-up comprising founder members Alsy MacDonald on drums and David McComb on vocals and guitar, plus David's elder brother Rob, violin and guitar, Martyn Casey, bass, and Jill Birt, keyboards. Once settled in, over the next three months they played every London dive, the first being Dingwalls, where they supported their friends from back home the Go-Betweens using a drum kit borrowed from

Melbourne's the Moodists. They were incredibly tight and were blessed with a formidable frontman, and within a month some were saying they were the best live band in the country. They were fun to go and see as well. There was no angst, no surliness or moodiness beyond what the songs required. When Jill stepped up to sing 'Raining Pleasure', it was like seeing Mo Tucker from the Velvets, with Rob bowing the violin eerily like John Cale. They had no idea just how good they were compared to any British groups and they were a real shot in the arm for me in autumn 1984. My personal life was falling apart, Julian was troubled and faltering, and the Bunnymen were winding down, so the arrival of the Triffids was liberating.

Australian freelancer Lynden Barber wrote the first feature in *Melody Maker*, inevitably headlined 'The Day of the Triffids', which set the scene. All I knew about Perth was that it was home to the WACA cricket ground and the Fremantle Doctor, which Test match commentators always mentioned – a cooling afternoon sea breeze that increased the chance of the ball swinging. The only disappointing thing about the Triffids was that, aside from Rob, none of them cared for cricket. I had no sense of how isolated Perth was geographically. Perth is a relentless, day-and-a-half-long drive from the nearest major city of Adelaide, across the dry, flat Nullarbor Plain, nothing but red desert and a long and unwinding road. The corresponding cliché was how much that contributed to David's bleak, dark songs, which were the Triffids' stock-in-trade.

I didn't miss any of their dozen or so London shows. They projected friendliness both onstage and off, and more often than not they'd invite members of the audience to a party at the weekend. I still treasure a cassette of a covers night the Triffids performed at the Red Parrot in Perth, with everybody clearly having a great night. The Triffids were capable of playing over a hundred cover versions, including the expected Velvets, Television and Stooges songs, but no other group would also play 'There's a Kind of Hush', 'Ring of Fire', 'Ain't No Sunshine', 'Suspicious Minds', 'Gilligan's Island' or the *Bonanza* theme in the style of New Order.

They made the *NME* cover in January, although it was something of a fluke. The first issue of the year traditionally features an act to watch out for. Mat Snow had spoken to the group before the holidays, and the *NME* couldn't resist putting the much-touted Australians on the cover. Their name made it a given: 'The Year of the Triffids'. Back in Australia they added pedal steel guitarist Graham Lee, before returning to the UK in May. He became 'Evil' Graham Lee, as David thought any pedal steel guitarist worth his salt had to have a nickname.

That summer of 1985 they recorded their mostly self-funded third album, *Born Sandy Devotional*, in the tiny basement of Mark Angelo Studios in Farringdon. There was no drum booth, so Alsy had to sit in a junk-filled warehouse next door to the studio and the mic lines were fed around the back. David knew exactly how he wanted the album to sound, but Gil Norton was credited as producer and he brought with him arranger Adam Peters, both of whom had worked on *Ocean Rain*. Australians were often embarrassed about their culture, and making it in England was sought-after validation. One of the many great things about *Born Sandy Devotional* was its sense of longing and nostalgia for home, which was unsurprising since most of the songs were written during that wintertime visit to these shores.

Born Sandy Devotional is the Triffids' sensually atmospheric master-piece, a word I don't use lightly. David's three-minute melodramas, such as the shimmering heat haze of 'Wide Open Road' and the panoramic 'Seabirds', are achingly raw and highlighted by Lee's haunting pedal steel guitar. The pedal steel is always described as haunting, but the term was never more apt than here. The album is often described as quintessen-tially Australian, but the songs are also quintessentially Dave McComb. Nobody was better at embodying melancholy and loss.

Wrangles with Hot Records delayed the album's release until June 1986, when it was greeted with all the critical accolades it thoroughly deserved. The band were back in Europe for its release and now had an Australian manager with them who was tasked with securing a new deal. In November they signed to Island Records, just before heading home for Christmas again. Their Island debut was recorded between

April and August 1987 at half a dozen different studios, with Gil Norton once again producing. Over the course of the year they were sucked into the Island machine, and although I'd helped grease the wheels before they signed, by the time *Calenture* was released in November 1987 I'd been eased out and the press had gone in-house. I was annoyed. I knew I had been instrumental in them making such headway in Britain. My reputation was based on taking groups to the next level; what I had so rarely done was get them off the starting blocks. I'd effectively done that with the Triffids in the summer of 1984 and, unusually for me, I knew I'd done a great job.

Island were typically underhand. Labels tend to do the same thing when they sign bands: divide and conquer. Once signed, they paid David far greater attention and at one point during the first recording sessions tried to oust Alsy from the group. They didn't understand the essence of the group's music or the underlying friendships. Personal bias aside, *Calenture* is seriously flawed; it suffers from too much 1980s click-track production and sheen, too consciously trying to create a hit record that never materialised. Even David considered it over the top, describing it as the Triffids' *Heaven's Gate*.

I had plenty else on my plate in 1987, and we drifted apart. I almost regret now that I was reinstated in April 1989 for their second Island album, *The Black Swan*. Something had changed within the group. The hunger, passion and solidarity of old had been dented and the album had no backbone. Songs such as 'New Year's Greeting' and 'Too Hot to Move' were peerless, but once again it was overproduced. It's an album most bands would kill to have made, but by Triffids standards that wasn't good enough. Living up to its own sense of irony, *The Black Swan* proved to be their swansong. Few expected that the group would disband so soon, but they quietly broke up after a final Australian tour that ended on 15 August. They left behind one LP, *Born Sandy Devotional*, that makes it into my top ten in terms of albums I've been involved with, and it should by rights rank high in any best-album list.

*

The *NME* may have flagged up 1985 as the year of the Triffids, but by its close it had been the year of the Jesus and Mary Chain, who announced themselves in a howl of feedback and buzzsaw guitars on their Creation debut 'Upside Down' in November 1984. It was Creation Records' twentieth release, and it marked the arrival of a label and a group that would both have a major impact on the rest of the decade. I chuckled when I heard that Creation's founder, Alan McGee, who also managed the band, had secured a deal with Geoff Travis's WEA subsidiary label Blanco y Negro. Completing the deal in the corporate boardroom in Broadwick Street was either an act of madness by WEA or a stroke of genius by McGee. Inevitably it ended with stories that ran and ran for weeks about the Mary Chain drunkenly trashing the boardroom, defacing Rod Stewart posters and Simply Red gold discs, and stealing from Rob Dickins's wallet. McGee later said it was all accidental, but he'd been on the phone to the music press almost as soon as they left the building. The stories even made the *Sun*, which had already branded them as the new Sex Pistols after unruly and exaggeratedly riotous Mary Chain gigs at the Ambulance Station and the ICA in London.

I met them a month before their second Blanco single, 'You Trip Me Up', was released in June 1985. Tim Broad, one of the M-Ocean directors (as Paul McNally's video company was now called), had shot the video for their Blanco debut 'Never Understand', and they came to Metropolitan Wharf for a meeting. While Jim and William Reid and bassist Douglas Hart discussed the video on the other side of the warehouse, drummer Bobby Gillespie came over and sat with me and Mel. We were talking about 1960s garage and psych, and Bobby was raving about Julian Cope's 'Tales from the Drug Attic' piece in the *NME*. Years later he told me he was only hanging out with us because he fancied Mel. At one point William sauntered over, sneered at Bobby and said, 'I know what you're doing, you dirty bastard,' and wandered back to the meeting. That aside, they didn't spit on the floor, trash the furniture or steal anything. Paul introduced me, saying, 'Mick looks after Echo & the Bunnymen and

Julian Cope,' not that they gave a shit. I knew better than to say I thought 'Upside Down' was brilliant.

Aside from the Bunnymen, who were a few months into their so-called 1985 gap year, the only WEA act I was looking after was Strawberry Switchblade, although not for much longer. They were signed to Korova and managed by Dave Balfe. He and Bill Drummond published the ex-Glasgow, sweet-singing, punk-girl duo – Jill Bryson and Rose McDowall – and they were also producing them. I'd worked with them on and off since their debut single, 'Trees and Flowers', was released on Will Sergeant's 92 Happy Customers label in July 1983. In November 1984, a few days after their second single, 'Since Yesterday', had become a Top 5 hit, Balfey rang and told me he wanted to shift the press in-house at WEA because I wasn't a pop-oriented enough PR. He was blunt and offered no apology. I was too flabbergasted to point out that I had already secured them the cover of *Smash Hits*. Since this marked the absolute apotheosis of the pop press I figured that was enough of a two-fingered parting gesture. At last I had become a victim of the 'evil' side of Dave Balfe. Strawberry Switchblade failed to make the Top 40 again, their over-embellished, synth-pop-dominated album flopped and the girls split up soon after, bored with doing frivolous interviews about polka dots and make-up for magazines aimed at teenage girls.

I'd always thought it had been WEA's decision to wrest the press from me, so I was taken aback when Moira Bellas called to ask if I'd come in and talk about taking on the Jesus and Mary Chain. 'Never Understand' had been released at the end of February, just weeks before the most infamous of their riots at North London Poly. Clearly WEA didn't want to be in the firing line over any future controversy, and I was brought in as a buffer between the group and the label just in time for a new flare-up, when the release of 'You Trip Me Up' was delayed after staff at WEA's pressing plant refused to handle the single, the B-side of which was called 'Jesus Fuck'. No other pressing plant would touch it either, so the band agreed to ditch the offending track. A carefully worded statement was released saying it was 'Typical of the state of the stale-minded music business' and that 'the group is disgusted by it all'.

I can't recall any strategy meetings with Geoff Travis or Alan McGee. The Jesus and Mary Chain were already a high-profile band. I assumed I was there to contain rather than whip up the press, as McGee had been doing. They needed to broaden their press cachet beyond the shock tactics that were soon going to wear thin. It had always puzzled me why the Mary Chain accepted me so readily, until Bobby said, 'It was because you did the Bunnymen.' Jim and William saw them as kindred spirits of a kind, certainly the early Bunnymen. Not that they ever said as much. The comparisons weren't lost on me. Jim and William were usually sullen and wary, just like the Bunnymen of old, although they made Will Sergeant look like a party animal.

It was obvious they were never going to meet anybody even halfway over the music, but when I met them they made it clear that they already wanted to defuse their confrontational image. I knew that if they made a great album, that would happen anyway. And they did just that. Rob Dickins also saw something similar in them to the Bunnymen, the same conviction to do things only how they wanted. The Velvets and Stooges were just as big an influence on both bands, but Jim and William had a broader canvas. They wanted to transcend those influences as a way of making their own brand of pop music. They didn't just aspire to cult status; they had that already. The Jesus and Mary Chain was a pop group, even if it wasn't pop as anybody else knew it. That's why they wanted to be on a major, rather than remaining on an independent label. Jim regularly rebuffed accusations that they were selling out: 'Before we were part of WEA it was 100 per cent shit. Now at least it's a little bit good.'

The first time I saw the Mary Chain play live was at the Electric Ballroom on 9 September 1985. It was a horrible gig in a horrible venue. Tanked-up beforehand, they ambled onstage an hour late to the sound of William's guitar spluttering and fizzing as he plugged in, and from the start Jim could barely be heard at all above a raw, perfunctory sonic assault. The only song I recognised was 'Just Like Honey', the forthcoming single, but after Bobby's thumping 'Be My Baby' intro and Douglas's opening bass line, which boomed out deafeningly, they stopped playing just as a full-scale riot erupted on a scale that made the North London Poly trouble look like a playground spat. With glasses and bottles whizzing past their ears they wisely walked off rather than remonstrate in any way. I didn't stick around either. The Mary Chain wouldn't play again for the rest of the year, and wouldn't perform in London for over six months. They didn't want a repeat of the Electric Ballroom or the kind of publicity it generated, which had been detracting from the music for too long. When the dreamy, narcotic 'Just Like Honey' became the third Blanco single to pull up outside the Top 40, it was obvious that the focus had to shift towards completing their debut album.

I was given a white label of *Psychocandy* soon after, and it totally substantiated everything they stood for. Fourteen tracks that had the same impact as the first Ramones album, with only one hitting the four-minute mark. Both groups were steeped in rock and pop history, but both albums said, 'OK, that was then, this is now.' The album didn't get the feedback out of their system but it contextualised it. *Psychocandy* was about to shake independent music to its foundations. This wasn't the more readily acceptable sound of the Smiths or New Order or the Cocteau Twins; it was the sound the Reid brothers had imagined in their bedroom on a four-track tape recorder – roaring Shangri-Las and Spector pop smothered in layers of Velvet Underground white noise. It was a rock 'n' roll reboot that soon had the music press in raptures. Released in late November, it was primed to be album of the year – or thereabouts – throughout the music press.

The accolades *Psychocandy* received didn't mean the Reids were suddenly going to cosy up to journalists. They didn't trust or respect them enough. In early interviews they were vitriolic about everything they hated – which was anything journalists brought up to try and bait them with. Venerated as a result of *Psychocandy*, all they wanted to do now was explain what the group was about and what they wanted to achieve, putting their provocative image and notoriety behind them. In truth their interviews were often stilted and almost always done with Jim and William sat opposite the writer in a pub. William really hated doing them. He worried he would get tongue-tied, especially if he was asked about the songs. Jim would speak more freely and then get frustrated, looking at his brother angrily and asking, 'Why don't you say something?' They did very little outside of the music press, and I was never going to ask them to, but it meant their press profile was too predictable.

They were control freaks but never felt at ease dealing with the press, so they usually came away feeling they had been misunderstood or misrepresented. Nothing about the music industry or the media lived up to the 'theatre of dreams' that they had once romantically envisaged. Major-label life shattered William's illusions once he realised it was 'a tacky little affair, a shabby world of shady deals that you try to fit in, and after a while, you just feel disgusted with yourself'.

They had far greater control over their visual image. They dictated the disorientating look and choreographed chaos of their promo videos, while all photo sessions were as detached as possible from the very process of being photographed. They asserted their own house style, which everybody followed, even when they made the cover of *Smash Hits* in July 1986. Glum-faced and half in shadow, the strapline read: 'Loud, spotty and weird!' Spandau Ballet pointedly refused to appear in the same issue. It was a rare moment for celebration.

The only time I saw any kind of bust-up between the brothers was at a photo session where the photographer kept asking them to smile and be more animated, though she didn't go so far as to ask them to throw shapes. Jim was particularly grumpy that day. We took a break, but when the photographer returned with two top hats she was met with a look of furious thunder from Jim. 'What the fuck?' he said, looking at William, who just cracked up. Jim glared at him, saying, 'What's so fucking funny?' and stormed off. They didn't speak for the rest of the afternoon. We carried on a while longer, both brothers looking more dour than usual, before calling a halt. Then, right at the end, the photographer produced the hats again, with an entreating look of 'I don't suppose . . .?' This time both brothers cracked up. In a soft, only slightly menacing snarl Jim said, 'Persistence might pay sometimes, but this isn't one of them.'

In the year after *Psychocandy* the reality of life in the music industry took its toll, once the focus shifted from recording, which they enjoyed, to touring and a growing demand for interviews. The press remained onside, although now that the live shows passed without incident, the Mary Chain were often branded as boring. Their riotous past had certainly not been forgotten by the BBC and the group were victimised by radio and TV producers. In July stand-alone single 'Some Candy Talking' entered the charts at no. 20 and moved up to no. 13, only for smarmy Radio 1 breakfast DJ Mike Read to ban it for its 'obvious' drug references. *Top of the Pops* also refused to book the band, despite any single entering that high usually being guaranteed a slot if the group was available. After they eventually appeared on the show to perform 'April Skies', they were never asked back. All Jim had done was to fail to stick to the camera marks between the run-through and the recording in the evening. 'We never set out to offend people at *Top of the Pops* but we just came across that way. We're not outgoing, we're just awkward in those situations. Our way of dealing with it is to get tanked up and then chaos follows.'

In September they sacked Alan McGee as their manager, claiming he was focusing too much on Creation, as well as managing the Weather Prophets and Primal Scream, the group Bobby had left the Mary Chain to concentrate upon. Sacking Alan was a surprise, even though he and William never really saw eye to eye. Not long after Alan was sacked I was in the Creation office when William stormed in. Alan wasn't there, just his wife Yvonne and partner Dick Green. William walked over to the answer machine and tore it out of the wall, saying, 'That's mine. I paid for that.' I left not long after, only to find the answer machine stuffed in a bin on the street outside.

I could never figure out my relationship with them but I knew I was exempt from their usual hatred of record-company types. I knew they respected Rob Dickins and Geoff Travis, who took over management from McGee for a while. I didn't know Geoff that well, although I'd see him at gigs all the time in the late 1970s, when he looked like Rob Tyner from the MC5. The only time I worked directly for Rough Trade was with the Woodentops, a nicely offbeat group that didn't conform to prevailing stereotypes. The group's leader, Rolo McGinty, had narrowly missed out on becoming the Teardrops' bassist in December 1980 and played on the Wild Swans' 'Revolutionary Spirit'. So it was no surprise that their debut single, 'Plenty', had been the second single released on Dave Balfe's Food Records in July 1984. Morrissey made it 'Single of the Week' in *Melody Maker*. They signed to Rough Trade and supported the Smiths on tour. Morrisey was rather less open-minded when he later described them as 'The Suddenflops'.

The Woodentops always teetered on the edge of a breakthrough and released a series of sprightly semi-acoustic singles during 1985/6, characterised by a frantic, hypnotic, rockabilly attack and singer Rolo McGinty's breathy, refined take on Alan Vega's vocal style with Suicide. The press were supportive but never wholly warmed to them. Geoff would call me into Rough Trade's offices in Collier Street for regular meetings. He was a hard man to impress. I'm hardly the most demonstrative person, but Geoff was rarely enthusiastic or encouraging. His schoolmasterly 'could have done better' assessment coupled with my dissatisfaction with everything I did wasn't a great combination. At least with the Mary Chain he just let me get on with it.

Their second album, *Darklands*, was released in September 1987. If *Psychocandy* was the sound of an angry and disaffected group, then *Darklands* presented them as disenchanted, swathed in a dark existentialism that reflected their post-*Psychocandy* breakdowns. They had stripped away the feedback to reveal songs of a more redemptive resignation. In the studio *Darklands* also confirmed that the Mary Chain was now a Reid brothers-only operation. The studio was always more important to them. Nobody played guitar like William. Few may have wanted to, but most guitarists with far superior technical ability would have envied the freedom and abandon with which he played. *Darklands* didn't wow the critics as unanimously. Too many writers wanted *Psychocandy 2*, but I thought it was the better album. It fell somewhere between the Stones' *Let It Bleed* and Springsteen's *Nebraska*, but I was never brave enough to say that. They hated it when people drew comparisons to others. In one 9/10 *NME* review somebody referenced Duane Eddy's twangy guitar, and William was apoplectic.

Before *Darklands* was released the Mary Chain had back-to-back up-tempo, if not upbeat, hits: 'April Skies' and 'Happy When It Rains'. 'April Skies' went Top 10, and the momentum made *Darklands* a Top 5 album (for all its accolades *Psychocandy* went no higher than no. 31). With a hit act on their hands, WEA tried to take the press in-house in the most effective way possible: by no longer paying me. Most groups crumble when that happens, but the Mary Chain picked up my retainer themselves for the next seven years. I figured I must be doing OK.

Off the back of the Mary Chain I began working with various Creation Records groups during 1986. It was the joint force of personality of Alan McGee and Joe Foster that initially drove the label and launched the Mary Chain. Foster produced them early on and was effectively Creation's house producer, till he was ousted at the end of 1985. They had founded the label with Dick Green in 1983. Creation was something of a closed shop whose rationale was attitude over everything, but by 1986 Alan was trying to do and be everything. He was Creation's ringmaster and found it hard to let go, which meant he was still dealing with the music press a lot, adopting a method of PR that relied heavily upon relentless hyperbole and assertive enthusiasm.

Alan had reasonable cause to be dissatisfied with my inability to muster any interest in a number of Creation releases, including those of his own group Biff Bang Pow! and label stalwarts the Jasmine Minks, but I felt he was also disappointed in me personally. A few years earlier I'd had a reputation that would have better suited the Creation mould, but I'd become a lot more detached, undemonstrative and seemingly unenthusiastic. The last of these was anything but true. Alan and I didn't click as personalities. I deliberately played things down; you'd never find a hint of hyperbole in my press releases. Like *Dragnet*'s Sgt Joe Friday, it was 'Just the facts, ma'am' – a reference that aged me perfectly. Whereas my voice of experience counted when dealing with major labels, Creation's indie attitude was more about chancing its arm, which just wasn't my way of doing things. I never thought that Alan liked most journalists. If they crossed him, they were cunts, and that didn't sit well with me. You have to take the rough with the smooth, and the music press, particularly the *NME* and *Sounds*, had backed Creation to the hilt in its early years.

Alan was such a dominant presence within Creation that some of the groups seemed compelled to conform to his image and bullish behaviour, even the Creation dress code. I was thirty-six and very straight-looking. I had a dodgy haircut, favoured neat casual jackets, never wore shades, before or after dark, and wouldn't have been seen dead in leather trousers. When I'd walk into Creation's tiny offices on Clerkenwell Road I felt like a corporate whore. I knew I was out of place there. Lawrence from Felt caught the same vibe: 'When I joined Creation I thought now I'll be on a label with people who are more like me. There was never any friction with the more rock 'n' roll types. I was never judgemental about how they all behaved but I just didn't want to participate.'

I just didn't fit in at Creation but I knew I was the one being resistant and stand-offish. I had got married in September 1985. It was for the second time, having first tied the knot when I was at university in 1970. The circumstances may have been different, but marriage signified a desire for a degree of normality and stability in my life, and I was seeking that once more. I think the same was true of my new wife, Pauline. She was a gifted graphic designer who had been the great Barney Bubbles's assistant in the late 1970s and then art director at the *NME*, under the name Caramel Crunch. Now mostly designing album and single sleeves, she was responsible for all of Billy Bragg's early artwork and later worked on the design, graphics and layouts for the JAMs and the KLF for several years. Creation thrived on the sort of behaviour and lifestyle we'd both now relinquished. I'd more or less abstained from drinking and definitely avoided taking any kind of drug. The best way I could maintain that was

146

to remove myself from temptation, which left me wondering if I was coming across either as smug or just plain boring.

Pete Astor of the Weather Prophets didn't conform to type either. He was middle class and well educated, and his band had taken its name from Henry Miller's *Tropic of Cancer*. After two initial Creation singles, 'Almost Prayed' and 'Naked as the Day', the latter produced by Lenny Kaye, Pete was desperate to make an album. So was Bobby Gillespie, whose group Primal Scream had released only two singles in twelve months, but the Creation coffers were bare. Alan's resources were often inversely proportional to his ambitions. Rob Dickins had already expressed an interest in signing the Weather Prophets, which developed into the formation of a second-tier label along the lines of Blanco y Negro. Taking the name Elevation, Rob also agreed to sign Primal Scream. I was inked in to do the press once Rob did the deal and agreed that WEA would pay me.

Lenny Kaye was retained to produce the Weather Prophets' album, which was finished by the end of 1986. Everybody was elated by it. Titled *Mayflower*, it was scheduled for May 1987 and Alan began talking it up big time as usual, but *Mayflower* wasn't as radical and exhilarating as *Psychocandy* and the Weather Prophets didn't have any notoriety. It caught WEA napping because it lacked any inbuilt momentum and was slow out of the traps. *Mayflower* charted at an unsatisfactory no. 67. If it had been released by Creation, it would have been an independent no. 1.

It didn't help that *Mayflower* was released the same week as the Mary Chain's first Top 10 smash, 'April Skies'. Did nobody question whether Creation's former flagship band should be going up against Elevation's bright new hope? The Weather Prophets weren't a massively popular press band; they were liked well enough, but Pete tended to take on journalists at their own game. Before *Mayflower*'s release the Weather Prophets appeared on the cover of the *NME*, and during the interview Pete discussed figurative art, described one of his favourite poems, 'The Garden' by Andrew Marvell, in depth and went on to say that his group's music was postmodernist.

Alan and Bobby Gillespie went back a long way, having met at King's Park Secondary School in Glasgow, although Alan was two years older. It was Bobby who had first brought the Jesus and Mary Chain to Alan's attention. At the time he was drumming with them, as well as fronting Primal Scream. The Mary Chain demanded most of Bobby's time in 1985, but Primal Scream signed to Creation and the group's debut single, 'All Fall Down', was released in June 1985, though it was overlooked amid the Mary Chain media onslaught. Bobby left the Mary Chain at the beginning of 1986, and in April of that year Primal Scream belatedly released their second single, 'Crystal Crescent'. It was the B-side, 'Velocity Girl', that showed why Bobby had left the Mary Chain. It was a wondrous eighty-four seconds that epitomised one of indie's signature sounds, marrying a spiralling twelve-string evocation of the Byrds and Love with shades of *Ocean Rain*, or so I thought. I played it daily for the rest of the summer. I always liked Bobby, whose Cope-like enthusiasm for music was such an antidote to Jim and William's moodiness. And I liked the idea of Primal Scream and the way Bobby talked them up, but *Sonic Flower Groove* washed up in a retro 1960s backwater instead of being the celebration that 'Velocity Girl' promised.

Recording Primal Scream was fraught because they were all at sea. One producer thought they were nice guys but impossible to work with, another was largely uninterested. Rob Dickins suggested that his old mate Clive Langer produce a single, 'Imperial', which was recorded at Abbey Road. Coming in way over budget at £100,000, *Sonic Flower Groove* had all the life sucked out of it. Neither the first single from it, 'Gentle Tuesday' – only the group's third in as many years – nor 'Imperial' made the Top 75. Primal Scream were well liked by journalists but they had little enthusiasm for the album. 'Turn On, Tune In, Switch Off' was how the *Sounds* review concluded; a more apt appraisal was that it was too much 'All I Really Want to Do' and not enough *Younger Than Yesterday*. *Sonic Flower Groove* came out in October and crawled to no. 62. Three months later WEA shut Elevation down, and Alan would never again allow others so much control in any future major-label deal.

Felt had a lucky escape when Rob refused to include them in the Elevation deal. Lawrence had already signed to Creation, and after four languid, timeless albums for Cherry Red between 1981 and 1985 Felt were independent stalwarts. Lawrence wanted to be a star, but at the same time was ill-suited to stardom in both his outlook and demeanour. He was the classic reluctant artist, driven by an unattainable musical idealism and an irrational fixation with image, and was dogged by bad timing.

Lawrence was living in an upmarket Birmingham residence and led a reclusive, fastidious existence. His well-known neatness and personal quirks were made central to a November 1986 *NME* feature that set the tone by describing the contents of his kitchen cupboards – all neatly stacked, with the labels precisely arranged facing outwards – and his array of cleaning products. Nobody knew much about OCD in 1986, so he was just an oddball. It was meant to be a cover story but was ousted by a piece about suicide among young people. With its totally blacked-out front cover it was the *NME*'s worst-selling issue that year. Lawrence was distraught. He was always so appreciative, and it was heartbreaking, but I did get him a page in *Smash Hits*, which may have meant just as much to him. He was even more thrilled when he discovered Felt among a sheet of giveaway *Smash Hits* stickers.

I loved his childlike enthusiasm. He was astonished that *Let the Snakes Crinkle Their Heads to Death*, his first offering for Creation, raised so many eyebrows. It was an iconoclastic shift away from Felt's earlier waves of guitars to a collection of cheesy instrumental doodles – most under two minutes long – dominated by the recently recruited teenager Martin Duffy's keyboards. When I asked for a press photo, Lawrence provided an image of four pairs of shoes, arranged as if the group had just stepped out of them. His next offering was *Forever Breathes the Lonely Word*, on which Duffy's Hammond organ emulates the thin, wild, mercury sound of Dylan's *Blonde on Blonde*. It was the best album released by Creation during the 1980s, a classic pop record that was no less true to Lawrence's literate, doomed romantic vision, but it came along before Creation was geared for commercial success. Thereafter, none of the three remaining

Felt albums for Creation bore any relation to the others. Strangest of all was 1988's instrumental cocktail-jazz album *Train Above the City*, for which Lawrence provided only the titles.

Unlike the Weather Prophets or Felt, the House of Love had a similar kind of vibrant life force to the Jesus and Mary Chain in the creative tension between guitarist Terry Bickers and singer and songwriter Guy Chadwick. Guy was also seriously ambitious. He came to Metropolitan Wharf to talk about press before their debut single, 'Shine On', was released in May 1987. By Creation standards it was almost passé epic rock, and we couldn't help but talk about the Bunnymen. Guy said straight away he didn't want the Bunnymen's cult success; he wanted to be as big as U2. Press reaction to 'Shine On' failed to live up to his expectations and he wanted to use a different PR for the next release. That someone was Jeff Barrett, who by then handled most of the Creation press. It wasn't working for me personally at Creation, and Elevation had left a sour taste behind for everybody involved. I wouldn't work on another Creation record again.

One of the few enjoyable things about Alan's deal with WEA was being able to take refuge in Bill Drummond's office. Bill was eighteen months into his A&R consultancy role and had his own office in WEA's Broadwick Street HQ. He was insistent that as an A&R man his office should have a proper piano, an electric guitar plus small amp, an old-fashioned desk, a sturdy chair and tea-making facilities. Once Bill entered and sat down there was little room for anybody else, but in his dreams one day the new Gerry Goffin and Carole King would walk in and play him a song as good as 'It Might as Well Rain Until September'. Bill saw something he liked in McGee, even though their approaches to music-making were completely different. Alan enthused all the time, while Bill was inclined to think everything was shit, including most of the Creation records Alan played him. The liaison brought about a solo album by Bill that was as far removed from Creation's tinny, reverb-heavy 45s as you could get. 'I thought the guy was probably a genius,' said Alan in *Creation Stories*, 'and he was offering to cover the cost himself. There was nothing to lose. We put it out, it got great reviews, sold fuck all, but I was proud of that album.' It was probably the best PR job I did at Creation.

On 21 July 1986, in the sort of self-mythologising prose that soon became his forte, Bill sent a letter to this music-business friends and associates, saying that having reached the age of thirty-three and a third, he was calling time. 'In the past nine years, I gave everything I could, and at times some drops too much, and to those who wanted more, I'm sorry. It wasn't for the giving.' The nine years in question had begun in May 1977 with Bill forming Big in Japan, 'a band that had no right to be'. He said he was leaving behind two gifts: 'The first, Zodiac Mindwarp and the Love Reaction, the only band that can save us from the future, the second is yet to come, and in between was the greatest Album ever made.'

During his two-year stint as corporate man there'd been a resurgence in the Drummond/Balfe axis, which still occasionally operated as a production team, but it was their publishing enterprise, Zoo Music, that proved most fruitful. While Bill had relinquished management altogether, Dave Balfe now had his own label, Food Records, which had links to EMI, and he had moved into management. As well as Strawberry Switchblade, he was soon managing Zodiac Mindwarp and the Love Reaction, another Zoo Music acquisition. To many people's surprise, they also picked up the publishing for the Proclaimers, which would turn out to be a nice little earner thanks to perennial hits such as 'Letter from America' and 'I'm Gonna Be (500 Miles)'. I understood what Bill saw in them. He has very broad, often catholic taste in music.

Balfey was also managing Brilliant, whose debut single, 'Soul Murder', had been the first release on Food in 1985. Brilliant were formed by Youth in 1982, soon after he left punk, heavy-metal and dub hybrid group Killing Joke. Their more conceptual approach aimed to unite NYC-style dance music and hard rock. Brilliant's constantly fluctuating line-up was part of a south London artistic scene centred around Wandsworth, Battersea and Stockwell, and included guitarist 'Jimi' Cauty by the time they signed to WEA. The group was soon honed down to a three-piece of Youth, Jimi and singer June Montana.

Over the next twelve months Bill witnessed £500,000 of WEA's money being squandered by production team Stock, Aitken and Waterman, who were working with Brilliant on a series of singles and an album. SAW had recently fashioned a major hit with 'You Spin Me Round' for another of the original Eric's alumni, Pete Burns, frontman of the group Dead or Alive. Their method of working in their compact studio, already called the Hit Factory, did not allow for the group to play on its own records. Bill and Jimmy (having dropped the Hendrix affectation) watched in disbelief as the producers sampled all the instruments and then pieced the album together. Jimmy was frustrated at doing nothing, but he and Bill were learning a thing or two about the possibilities of sampling. Brilliant were a priority act within WEA but none of their singles struck home, and the exorbitantly costly *Kiss the Lips of Life*, released in September 1986, barely dented the Top 75. The group was already in the throes of breaking up just as Bill called in the removal men to clear his room at WEA.

Written and recorded in ten days, Bill's album *The Man* was credited as having been recorded in the village hall in Newton Stewart, in Galloway, Scotland. Born in South Africa in 1953, Bill and his family moved to Newton Stewart the following year. It was there that he discovered pop music through watching formulaic Elvis films at the local cinema. Bill and I shared a liking for post-army, early-1960s Elvis hits such as 'Are You Lonesome Tonight?' and 'It's Now or Never'. He saw his first-ever live music there too – a local skiffle group. The family remained in Newton Stewart long enough for Bill to see *A Hard Day's Night* before moving to Corby, where so many Scottish families relocated in the 1960s. *The Man* was actually recorded in Dagenham, but 'Newton Stewart was where I was in my head,' explained Bill. It was released on Creation in November 1986 and is characterised by Bill's rich Scottish brogue, as thick as porridge, and by him rolling his 'r's with exaggerated intent. He was accompanied by the Triffids, and between them they created a unique concoction of windswept, middle-of-the-road country, a dash of folk and even a swinging gospel song, 'The King of Joy', spiced with Herb Alpert horns urging you to follow Bill to the ends of the earth.

Funny, enchanting, joyful and sentimental, *The Man* was treated as something of a whimsical curio, but it is full of highly personal revelations. Its major talking point was a song called 'Julian Cope Is Dead', set to a singalong madrigal. Bill theorises that the Teardrop Explodes will be 'bigger than the Beatles' now that he has shot Julian in the head. His touching take on Goffin and King's 'Going Back' includes a revealing rewritten line that reflects on a career in management and A&R now that there's more to do than watch the records slide. Like his resignation letter, it hints too that he's about to try his hand at something new.

Just as the JAMs were about to launch their assault on the music industry in March 1987, Creation Records released 'The King of Joy', a belated single from *The Man*. On the B-side was 'The Manager', the audio track of a short film Bill made with Bill Butt in which he offered to become the manager of the entire 'spiritually bankrupt music business'. Pushing a street cleaner's cart down a Buckinghamshire country lane, with a guitar upside down in the back compartment and a silver disc tied to the front, Bill holds court in an industrial-strength Galloway accent. He was now the manager of 'the complete music thing' and was inviting people to send him a cheque for £100 in return for his personal guidance about 'any problem you have concerning your area of pop'. There was plenty of sound advice: advances should be abolished – 'No great music has ever come from a band that's got a big advance'; no LP should take any more than ten days to record; and, interestingly, there should be 'no remixes'. It was typical Bill Drummond: funny and preposterous but tinged with plenty of common sense.

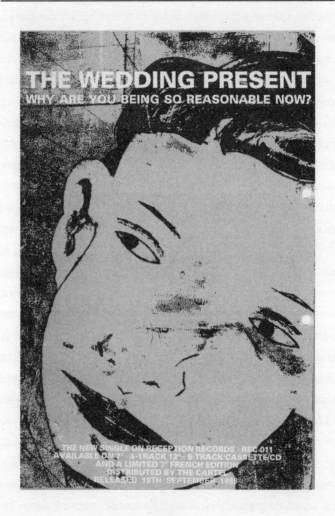

1985-9

In 1986 the impact of *Psychocandy* and the rise of Creation Records had gone a long way towards forging a new attitude on the fringes of independent British pop. The Smiths were no less inspirational, but artistically

The savvy and uncomplicated Wedding Present's final independent release on their own Reception Records in September 1988, before signing to RCA the following year.

Morrissey and Marr were out of reach. The Reid brothers' noise aesthetic and assertiveness, on the other hand, offered a much more attainable template for a crop of new groups and independent labels to follow. Twenty-two of these groups were collected together on the *NME*'s highly impactful *C86* tape, available by mail order in May. Even though much of its content is appalling, it became arguably the most significant compilation of the 1980s. *C86* effectively brought about a resurgence of the old punk and immediate post-punk DIY ethic. *C86* was not a genre in itself, nor a stylistic model, although most of the groups were still essentially guitar-based. None more so than the Wedding Present, whose take on indie pop, with its furious, scratchy guitars, disguised singer David Gedge's student-bedsit mini-dramas.

Both the Wedding Present and That Petrol Emotion released debut independent singles in 1985, but the latter weren't interested in becoming part of *C86* and, in truth, they didn't fit the mould at all. Two of them, John and Damian O'Neill, had been in the Undertones; John, now calling himself Sean, was also a particularly gifted songwriter. The group was completed by guitarist Raymond Gorman and drummer Ciaran McLaughlin, both from local Derry bands, and, in total contrast to his shy and serious-minded bandmates, fronted by ebullient American singer Steve Mack, who could easily be taken as a role model for Damon Albarn.

The Petrols' debut single, 'Keen', was almost released by Creation, but the label's temporary lack of funds saw the band switch to Pink, run by the June Brides (who also declined to be on *C86*). That Petrol Emotion set their stall out right from the start by including a statement on the back sleeve about Northern Irish political prisoners in English jails. As well as offering an alternative information service about Northern Irish politics, which surprised most Undertones fans, Sean and Damian were quick to spurn any Undertones connections that might have been to their advantage. Questions about 'My Perfect Cousin' and 'Teenage Kicks' were given short shrift and the new group never played even a token Undertones song live. Like the Undertones, they did dig deep into their record collections, although That Petrol Emotion's remit was more diverse and Sean's love of the Beatles now wrestled with Pere Ubu, Captain Beefheart, Sly and the Family Stone, and Can. They were also fans of industrial-rock groups such as Einstürzende Neubauten, the Young Gods and Swans, and Swans' drummer Roli Mosimann produced their second and third albums, which made a clear declaration that they wanted to get noise back into pop music. 'A spanner in the works of ugly pop,' I wrote in their press biog.

Yet when their aptly titled debut album *Manic Pop Thrill* appeared in May 1986, it was hard not to hear strong echoes of the Undertones. The new group was no less tuneful but darker and heavier. It was a great debut and, for me, their finest hour. The tunefulness was never entirely banished, but a very different-sounding group soon emerged. *Manic Pop Thrill* had been released by the independent label Demon, but they moved to a major label, Polydor, for 1987's *Babble*, which was much heavier, sometimes bordering on hardcore, but also dancey; they covered Hamilton Bohannon's mid-1970s disco stomp 'Dance Your Ass Off' as half of a double A-side single. At other times their angry agit rock was burdensome, but when they got it right, as with 'Big Decision', they succeeded in marrying a political message – the 'agitate, educate, organise' rap – with hip hop and avant-garde rock in a joyous way. 'Big Decision' saw the band achieve its highest chart position, making no. 43.

Unwisely leaving the supportive Polydor, the Petrols' next single, 'Genius Move', six months later, appeared on the oversubscribed Virgin, the fifth different label in the band's short career. Yet another great track, it was banned by the BBC because of a reference to Gerry Adams on the sleeve. It earnt them the proud accolade of being one of the *Sun*'s ten bands they most loved to hate: 'The anti-British rockers play music as loud as their mouths and sound off about Irish politics.'

A year on, in September 1988, the wantonly diverse *End of the Millennium Psychosis Blues* was their first album for Virgin. Sean, as torn between home life and career as back in the Undertones days, announced his departure during its recording. Drummer Ciaran McLaughlin and guitarist Raymond Gorman stepped up and took over the main songwriting duties and, surprisingly, the Petrols moved towards the more 'pop'-based *Chemicrazy* released two years later. *Chemicrazy* yielded no less than four singles and on the surface was more 'chart-friendly' – had any of the singles charted, that is. Virgin, desperate to claw back some of their investment, spent even more by multi-formatting each single extensively to try and break the Top 40 barrier. It didn't work, and by the time they eventually dropped them in 1991 That Petrol Emotion had earnt the dubious distinction of having the most singles in the Top 75 that failed to make the Top 40 – seven between 1987 and 1991.

Both Polydor and particularly Virgin had marketed the band with very little imaginative flair; on top of that the Petrols were one of the best live bands in the country but never capitalised on it. They should have toured more extensively and sold themselves as an albums band. Their timing was always off too. They went funk when they should have stayed indie, but always played a brand of scuzzed-up alternative pop that was very much ahead of the game. Now you can see them as trailblazers for the Madchester indie-dance scene, pre-dating the connection between rock and club culture.

By the end their enthusiasm for music was tempered by a capacity to complain too much about the state of the industry. It didn't endear them to anyone. Damning the press was definitely out of place because they had considerable music-press sympathy, including plenty of front covers and major features across the board. Between 1986 and 1988 they were always hotly tipped as the next group to break big – that old 'most likely to' albatross. 'We were probably our own worst enemies again,' said Damian philosophically. 'I don't think we tried too hard to be different but, as people, we were by nature incapable of standing still and we were never part of any scene. We were always a band out of time; too late for post-punk, too early for Madchester and Britpop. We could never get past the Undertones either. It just wasn't to be.'

The Wedding Present were in complete contrast. Purposeful and un-wavering in their decision-making, they didn't release singles to have hit records, only ones that were always going to appeal to their fans. They gave them what they wanted, and if they were one-dimensional (certainly compared to That Petrol Emotion), then it worked to maintain and develop a fan base that was steadily stimulated by the amount of live shows they did. It was always easier for northern bands to tour in their extended catchment area; London-based bands like the Petrols often found it harder to build a following.

Taking their name because it was similar to the Birthday Party, the soon-to-be student's favourite band were all university graduates themselves: singer/guitarist David Gedge, bassist Keith Gregory and drummer Shaun Charman (replaced in early 1988 by Simon Smith) had all studied at Leeds University. Guitarist Peter 'Grappa' Solowka, an old school friend of David's, had returned to Leeds after graduating from Liverpool University. As the Wedding Present they played their first gig on 1 March 1985 at the Shires, a pub in the small mining town of Allerton Bywater, in Yorkshire, and within three months released their first single, 'Go Out and Get 'Em Boy'. They pressed up five hundred copies on their own Reception Records, distributed by Red Rhino.

The Wedding Present had developed at their own pace, thriving on the loyalty of a growing band of fans, mostly boys who, David observed, 'were not unlike us'. I paid them little attention, tagging them as the archetypal northern indie band that epitomised the ragged punk have-a-go attitude so beloved by John Peel. They were among the first to be inked in for *C86*, and it's no coincidence that the *C86* tape was parenthesised by its two biggest groups, Primal Scream opening it and the Wedding Present closing it.

The Wedding Present's presence on *C86* won them solid support from the *NME*, and at the end of 1986, soon after I'd agreed to take them on, they were voted ninth best band in the paper's readers' poll, only one place behind the not-so-indie Pet Shop Boys. They also had four songs in John Peel's Festive 50 and had already established a strong bond with the indie world's most influential DJ. The importance of John Peel's show was generational and I'd long since outgrown it. Peel more than anybody helped forge my taste in music, beginning in 1967, when he was a DJ on the pirate station Radio London, mumbling idealistic hippy twaddle between fantastic records on his *Perfumed Garden* show. Years later he'd been instrumental in breaking most of the groups I worked with as a PR, giving them their first plays on the radio and first BBC sessions. The Wedding Present and the Undertones would become two of his all-time favourite bands, and David would echo the Undertones in saying the band's first Peel session was a dream come true.

No longer an avid Peel listener, I hadn't knowingly heard the Wedding Present outside of the *C86* tape till I was approached by Red Rhino, who sent me all the singles so far and a couple of Peel-session cassettes, with a view to my looking after the forthcoming single, 'My Favourite Dress'. It was by far the best and most professional-sounding track of those they sent. I thought long and hard about working with them but decided to say yes after meeting them at a University of London Union gig in late autumn. They were much better live. The sameness and no-frills famil- iarity of every song played live, and the relentless, repetitive, thrashing guitars, had the effect of sucking you in; there was nothing contrived at all. I knew they had strong regional support, particularly in the north and north-west, and the singles thus far had done well in the indie charts. It was the kind of dedicated following that could easily propel them into the pop charts. The press, however, either sat on the fence or hated everything they stood for.

I was even more impressed by their attitude offstage and how self- contained they were. It was just the four of them, no roadies, no entou- rage; they all had their roles and just got on with it. It was a well-oiled machine that didn't require anybody from the outside to be brought in, aside from a sound man. Their touring entourage was minimal and included David's future girlfriend Sally Murrell as roadie and full-time worker for the band; Peter's and Keith's girlfriends dealt with the mer- chandise. They were already wise about that too, and never gave outside contracts for T-shirts, badges, posters, etc. They had complete control of everything, including the design, and while they debated whether they were cashing in on their fans, they realised that if they didn't do it, then bootleggers would. It was a common-sense attitude and approach that I found refreshing.

They never became press darlings because too many journalists found them dull and workmanlike, their singles indistinguishable, and as a frontman the consensus was that David had no charisma and couldn't sing. Most of my closest friends in the press thought I was mad to take them on, but in 1986 there was a new influx of writers who were better disposed towards the Wedding Present. Then, after they released their debut album, plenty of the old-school writers also came around. The shrewd move was calling it *George Best* and using a classic image of the footballer on the front cover. Most music journalists are massive football fans and as a PR I'd always remember the teams they supported; it wasn't a conscious effort on my part, but these things stuck almost as much as remembering every writer's taste in music. I could talk about football and, as a perennially dispirited Charlton Athletic supporter, I could readily lend a sympathetic ear if their team was doing badly.

George Best was an album that was far better than the sum of its parts, but it established David as a songwriter. Till then, the Wedding Present chiefly signified a formulaic, fiercer, fast-paced variant on jangly indie pop. Now people were listening to David's lyrics and it was clear that fans were identifying with them. He was fast becoming the indie everyman with his gift for the vernacular and a love of the mundane. David's songs rarely veered away from commonplace relationships. It was like eavesdropping on one side of a conversation with the girl he has just broken off with or been dumped by, or an exchange with the person she's dumped him for. The Wedding Present were rapidly becoming Smiths fans' second-favourite group or, for those who found Morrissey too precious and his lyrics too fanciful, favourite. David's half-spoken forlorn lyrics about real situations, real people and real feelings struck home. Peel had observed this early on and commented that they made records that were 'direct and uncomplicated', qualities that are regarded as 'vices in some quarters'.

'When *George Best* came out,' said David, 'everyone said what a brilliant marketing idea, but I just thought it was a great name for an LP.' Getting Best to pose with the group for press shots was £500 well spent. 'It's the sort of thing he does all the time,' said David, 'like opening a supermarket. He meets the fans and gets his appearance fee.' Only Peter was a serious football fan and he and David were from nearby Manchester, so the association with George Best provided a certain earthy northern glamour that the band themselves didn't project; it also spared them having to appear on the cover of their own album, something they never did in their entire career. The Wedding Present were a million miles from the George Best myth, so it was a great paradox: old-school, solid, reliable players like Nat Lofthouse or Stanley Matthews, clean-cut and wearing long shorts, their shirts neatly tucked in, would have been more suited to the Wedding Present.

They never asked me what I thought of the records, and I didn't volunteer my opinion either. I never thought *George Best* was as good as most of the reviewers found it. It always worked for me to be honest, sometimes sceptical, even critical, and have journalists prove me wrong. What I thought didn't matter. *George Best* charted at a humble no. 47, but it did dislodge the Smiths' *Strangeways, Here We Come* from the top of the indie charts and eventually sold an impressive sixty thousand copies.

The Wedding Present were oblivious to traditional rock 'n' roll behaviour. There were no 2.43 a.m. moments with David Gedge. They enjoyed what they did but there was never a wild lifestyle. They simply were not indulgent. I always got on well with the group, and when I was around them I tried to be as business-like and professional as they were. I even knew better than to smoke around them. Quite early on I remember David saying, 'You smoke a lot, don't you?' It left me apologising and saying, 'Well, I never used to smoke at all,' to which David retorted, 'So why did you start?' 'I don't know really,' I said. 'Probably because I find it hard being in gatherings of people, especially at gigs.' 'Isn't that an occupational hazard?' he asked. 'Only if I'm not smoking,' I replied, adding that 'I hate loud noise as well,' to which David observed quizzically that I was probably in the wrong job.

During 1988 the group consolidated on the success of *George Best*, releasing a patchy catch-all compilation of their early singles called *Tommy* to tide them over. They had also been in talks with RCA, mindful that Red Rhino was having financial difficulties. They signed to RCA just before Red Rhino folded, where among the releases on hold in their warehouse was a mini-LP that licensed two of their John Peel sessions under the title *Ukrainski Vistupi V Johna Peela*. The ten-inch LP was their implausible take on Ukrainian and Russian folk songs, which Peter Solowka had brought to the table, inspired by his father's record collection. It was a seamless enough diversion into world music, because despite the addition of two additional members playing balalaika and mandolin, they retained their trademark jagged and frenzied sound. Its release was the last thing anybody expected them to announce as their RCA debut at the beginning of 1989. It immediately quashed concerns about whether signing to a major label would swallow them up. They were clearly going to carry on being as cussed as before.

RCA's head of A&R, Korda Marshall, had already signed fellow indie acts the Primitives and Pop Will Eat Itself, and had been courting the Wedding Present for over a year, but the Ukrainian album caused immediate ructions within RCA. The marketing department smelt a hit. They wanted to release 'Davni Chasy' as a single; its tune had been the source for Mary Hopkin's 'Those Were the Days', a no. 1 in 1968 on the Beatles' Apple label. RCA wanted the group to make a video with her (with them dressed as Cossacks, one imagines). The Wedding Present quite correctly said no; it would have smacked of a sell-out. Not only did they refuse to release a single from the album, they also refused to let RCA fill the window of HMV or the Virgin megastore with Russian dolls in the image of John Peel. RCA couldn't believe that a 'novelty' single that they were convinced was a potential no. 1 was rejected by the band because 'We don't want to be no. 1.' Yet this strange album must have exceeded expectations: the mini-LP actually charted at no. 22 – much higher than *George Best*.

The early part of 1989 was taken up by touring and promoting the Ukrainian album, which had been released in April. Most of the songs for the debut RCA album proper, *Bizarro*, had already been regulars in the live set, but two new songs, 'Crushed' and 'Brassneck', were first heard at the Reading Festival and the next day at John Peel's fiftieth birthday party at west London's Subterranea on 29 August. The party was the brain-child of Blast First's Paul Smith, who involved me in organising the press and, more importantly, tasked plugger Scott Piering with making sure John Peel was there. I'd also helped broker for the Undertones to play for the first time since they'd split in 1983. To everybody's amazement, they agreed – including Feargal Sharkey – until the O'Neill brothers' father died and they had to pull out. The Fall and the Wedding Present were both on the bill, and the House of Love deputised for the Undertones. It turned out to be something of a PR coup for me because the celebratory *NME* cover featured Peel flanked by David Gedge and Guy Chadwick, with Ian McCulloch standing incongruously behind them.

'Kennedy' was the first proper single released on RCA, in October 1989, and the group's first Top 40 hit. It sliced through the vibrant sound of Madchester with an abrasive edge that would have cleared the floor at a rave as quickly as the cops bursting in. *Bizarro* followed just weeks later. That, too, reached a respectable no. 22, in one of the busiest months for record sales. The group's aim was not to produce something that rep-licated *George Best*'s glum urban vignettes, but to make the transition to the more hardcore sound and dissonant power of underground US groups like Sonic Youth and Big Black. *Bizarro* put their old sound to bed and was more brash and extreme, especially David and Peter's patented unison guitar sound, which they took to an almost unbearable conclu-sion on the nine-minute 'Take Me', half of which was given over to an unremitting three-chord strum.

David became more solemn too. It was in keeping with them aban-doning the three-minute pop simplicity that the majority of people within RCA had been expecting. *Bizarro* veered towards a series of songs the group declared 'all sounded exactly the same', almost Quo-like in their simplicity. Korda Marshall aside, RCA insiders must have scratched their heads, as the Wedding Present's music was too harsh ever to cross over and their attitudes were too radical for them ever to fit on a major label. They were even more disarmed when they met the group, who were as well behaved – though sometimes dismissively rude – as they were stubborn in their ideals.

The recurring theme in the press had long been that the Wedding Present were just too ordinary. Detractors found them boring and, depending where you sat, either applauded this or were dismayed by their lack of image, but that very normality is what made them stand out. They were unhip. 'So what?' I'd say defensively. The Jesus and Mary Chain were hip and fashionable, but Jim and William Reid led a pretty ordinary life away from touring. And when it came to making records, both groups had a strong work ethic. By the end of 1989 the purportedly predictable Wedding Present had outsmarted everybody, and they weren't finished yet.

After the collapse of Elevation, Alan McGee and Creation had to take stock. It was down to the House of Love to revive their fortunes and their reputation. No longer hitched to the corporate machine, Creation gathered momentum during 1988 with the release of a series of dynamic House of Love singles, such as 'Christine' and 'Destroy the Heart'. Their thrilling debut album was released in May 1988 and saw them touted as potential inheritors of the Smiths' mantle, but by the end of the year they had jumped ship to sign to a major label. A second Primal Scream album arrived in 1989, but they now drew inspiration from the Stooges and the MC5 rather than Love and the Byrds, yet still couldn't make it happen convincingly. The Scream came close to breaking up before finally finding the right formula, the right drug in ecstasy and the right man in Andy Weatherall, who turned an overlooked album track into the game-changing 'Loaded'.

It came too late at the end of 1989 to prevent Creation suffering another cash-flow setback, which had serious repercussions for Lawrence and his secret masterplan that in ten years Felt would make ten LPs and ten singles and then disband. Felt's swansong, *Me and a Monkey on the Moon*, came out just under the wire on the Cherry Red imprint él in 1989. Produced by Adrian Borland, whom Lawrence had wanted to produce Felt's debut, *Me and a Monkey on the Moon* stands alongside *Forever Breathes the Lonely Word* as the best of Felt's post-Cherry Red albums. It abandons arch poetry for Lawrence's most direct and honest lyrics, often sung in harmony with Strawberry Switchblade's Rose McDowall and highlighted by steel guitar and analogue synths in a cycle of songs about growing up in the 1970s, a theme he would explore in a very different way with his next group. The album was also a fine farewell for keyboardist Martin Duffy before he committed to joining Primal Scream.

'I hated that we were called indie,' said Lawrence. 'I thought we completely defied any category. I never told people about the plan to release ten singles and ten albums in ten years but it was there from the start and the band knew about it. I wanted to do something that had never been done before but I never made a big announcement in case we failed. We set out to produce this great body of work that people could look back on and it would all make sense.

'It was a great way for us to split up but nobody was that bothered, and Felt ended on a quiet note of achievement rather than a blaze of glory.' The guileless Lawrence had been hoist with his own petard. 'I wanted there to be something mysterious about Felt. Maybe I succeeded too well and became such a mystery figure that no one [ever] discovered us.'

Felt played their final gig at Burberries nightclub in Birmingham on 19 December. It was another tenet of Lawrence's plan never to play his home town till that final show. It wasn't the triumphant farewell tour he'd envisaged in 1980: the agent could only arrange six shows in total, dotted all around the country.

Released in March 1988, 'Sidewalking' was a stand-alone single by the Jesus and Mary Chain that deserved better than a lowly chart position of no. 30. Lyrically it was Jim and William's own revamp of Bo Diddley's 'Who Do You Love?', and it pissed them off when reviewers suggested it was an homage to vintage early-1970s T. Rex. They were seething that a non-LP single that broke new ground didn't register with the public. It came just a month after their 'B-sides and alternatives' compilation *Barbed Wire Kisses* went to a surprising no. 8. The album was dominated by their early sound of unfettered feedback, manic, squalling guitars and surf-pop melodies. These weren't B-rated songs, and plenty preferred the collection to *Darklands* since by its very nature it was rawer and closer to *Psychocandy.*

Despite the public indifference, 'Sidewalking' prefaced Jim and William's approach to their third album, *Automatic*, released in October 1989. They had added a distinct dance pulse. 'Sidewalking' had sampled drums from a Roxanne Shante song and sought to do something more sequenced in terms of drums and bass, which Jim usually played in the studio. But a reliance on drum machines effectively gave critics a rod to break their backs; the usual comment was it would have been better with *actual* drums and bass.

Chart-wise *Automatic* only reached no. 11. They released a couple more singles off the album, including a semi-video hit in the States with 'Head On'. So it was there that they turned their attention, undertaking a series of gruelling tours during 1990 that began with three months in Europe, before an epic US jaunt. When it all came to an end, Jim and William weren't talking. It was the last tour with Douglas Hart. Spiritually, Douglas was as much a part of the band as Jim and William. It was a difficult but pragmatic decision because Douglas was contributing so little to the on-stage sound, but William wished they had stopped touring altogether – it had stopped being fun. It's a cliché: the Ramones said it, the Undertones said it, the Bunnymen said it, but they all carried on for longer than they should have.

By 1990 the Mary Chain were no longer the worst-behaved group in the country. Manchester's influence had been spreading wildly since 1988. The Stone Roses' 'Fools Gold' and the Happy Mondays' *Madchester*

EP signalled the future. The Madchester scene revelled in bad behaviour, but what had always isolated the Mary Chain and caused them to be discriminated against was having the opposite effect in the changing culture of the late 1980s. By the 1990s groups could almost get away with murder. I was happy to have missed out on the baggy revolution. Andrew Lauder, who had founded Silvertone in 1988, sent me an early tape of the Stone Roses' debut for the label, with a view to my taking them on. All I could hear in my head was Primal Scream's scorned *Sonic Flower Groove*. I gave the Stone Roses only a cursory listen before telling Andrew, 'Sorry, but I'm too busy right now.'

Sometime in November 1988 I had a call from Paul Smith, asking if we could meet up. I didn't know who he was but had at least heard of his label, Blast First. Like Creation, Blast First had started up in the mid-1980s. Where McGee sought out and cultivated the music press and was in the papers more than some of his groups, Paul built a wall around his label, fostering an us-against-them attitude that extended to almost everybody. Blast First's groups reflected the label's belligerent attitude, to the point where a label overview was released in 1989 called *Nothing Short of Total War*. When I asked around about Blast First, nobody in my circle knew much beyond the fact that the label's roster included Sonic Youth. That much I knew. I'd not actually listened to them in any meaningful way. They were often described as New York's equivalent to the Jesus and Mary Chain, but aside from an obvious propensity to make what many regarded as a tuneless racket, comparisons ended there.

Sonic Youth had begun their career by abandoning any pretence of following traditional rock 'n' roll conventions. Founding members Lee Ranaldo and Thurston Moore spoke about reinventing the guitar and detuning their instruments, taking their cues from the long-running experimental and improv scene in New York. The Jesus and Mary Chain were trying to reinvent pop music through an approach that was essentially informed by only a rudimentary ability to play their guitars. I doubt they knew how to tune them, let alone how to detune them. Sonic

Youth had come together in downtown New York during 1980/1, and had released three albums and toured Europe in 1984, before the Mary Chain's 'Upside Down' was released.

Sonic Youth were Blast First's main calling card, but in 1988 the label released three albums by US groups – the Butthole Surfers' *Hairway to Steven*, Dinosaur Jr's *Bug* and Sonic Youth's *Daydream Nation* – which collectively shook up independent music in Britain by reinstating loud, distorted guitar music to drown out the predominant *C86* jangle. At the forefront was *Daydream Nation*, which was widening people's awareness of Sonic Youth by adding more melody to their trademark guitar noise. It showed that the group could adhere to more traditional song structures if they chose to, unleashing classics such as 'Silver Rocket' and 'Hey Joni', as well the college-radio-friendly 'Teenage Riot'.

No longer regarded as a sidelined art-rock curio, Sonic Youth's rampaging post-hardcore approach was now offering an antidote to the stultifying values of *C86* that the press had been blindly flogging for the last three years. In that time Paul Smith had been slogging away determinedly to get recognition for his provocative bands. He had formed Blast First in 1985 purely in order to release Sonic Youth's albums in the UK, beginning with *Bad Moon Rising*. The deal came about through Lydia Lunch, one of the more familiar voices of the New York underground. Paul had facilitated the release of her mini-album *In Limbo* on Cabaret Voltaire's Doublevision label, which he ran with the group; Thurston Moore had played bass on it, and she told him that Paul was an OK guy to deal with. Thurston then sent him a cassette of what was essentially a two-thirds complete *Bad Moon Rising*. Paul described hearing it as a moment of epiphany that inspired him to try and get the record a European release. The only way he found that possible was by starting his own label, Blast First, and setting up a manufacturing and distribution deal with Rough Trade.

It took a series of lengthy phone calls to Lee Ranaldo in New York to agree a deal, and then, after two missed mortgage payments, Paul managed to raise the advance for the UK and European rights to *Bad*

Moon Rising. By the end of the year he had already fallen out with Rough Trade over the cover of Sonic Youth's twelve-inch 'Halloween'/'Flower': a grubby photocopy of a voluptuous topless girl. Starting as he meant to go on, he wouldn't back down. Paul was soon offered a new home by Daniel Miller at Mute, who ran a much more laissez-faire operation far better suited to Paul's quixotic way of doing business. He gave Paul a free hand and sufficient funds to run with.

Blast First was a revelation to me, as was Paul Smith. So in what was a state of embarrassing ignorance I was being vetted with a view to try and take Sonic Youth to the next level. The first few times I met Paul had usually involved lengthy drinking sessions that I found hard to keep up with. I was out of practice. Despite having been warned that he could be a prickly customer, we immediately bonded over our denial of being in the music business, or in my case more a healthy disregard for it. I can't remember how it came up, but we talked about how our respective mums found it hard to tell the neighbours what we did for a living. Paul had to settle for his saying he drove groups around in a van rather than that he ran a small independent record label. My mum could never understand what a publicist did, but when I was a journalist I'd written a couple of chapters for the *St Michael Book of Rock*, which was sold exclusively through Marks & Spencer's. She'd kept it on the sideboard for everybody to see.

Paul was absolutely driven and focused on what he was doing. Before long I realised that he had a hustler's instinct and an attitude not dissimilar to Bill Drummond's: that nothing is unachievable. Paul's attitude was pinpointed by something Lydia Lunch said in a *Guardian* interview a few years ago: 'If you're doing it for the money, you're not doing art. You're doing commerce.' I'd been unaware of Paul's particular crusade, but it made total sense to me immediately. I'd bumbled into something special once again.

Once I heard *Daydream Nation*, and then its immediate predecessors, *Evol* and *Sister*, it was like, 'Fuck, what have I been missing?' But first Sonic Youth had to approve me, and I couldn't believe it when Paul asked if I'd travel to New York to meet them. Nobody had suggested that in ten years. Admittedly I didn't know that Mute was bankrolling Blast First, but here was a small independent label stumping up to send me to New York. Paul booked me into the Washington Square Hotel in Greenwich Village and gave me directions to his apartment between Mulberry and Mott in Little Italy. It was all too good to be true.

I did my homework, mostly just listening to the records; I couldn't find too much written about Sonic Youth. Looking at the front-cover shot of their first album (released on avant-garde experimentalist Glenn Branca's Neutron label), I could see obvious parallels with Talking Heads: they came out of New York, they had a female bass player – Kim Gordon had even studied visual art in LA – and with an image that said they were a pretty straight bunch. They probably wore watches. But I wasn't going to play the Talking Heads card or even the Ramones card, and it was some time before I learnt that Lee and Thurston had witnessed the original Bowery scene first-hand and that the Youth had played CBGBs. They'd play the occasional Ramones cover, asking, 'Do you want to hear one Sonic Youth song or three Ramones songs?'

Meeting them was a job interview, a job I wanted. I'm not good at selling myself at the best of times, and they didn't ask me anything – in fact, they barely uttered a word – so I was floundering and we tumbled around each other, enduring long silences, while Paul said nothing either. I found them intimidating. Kim was glaring; Thurston pretended to doze off. I couldn't find any way to break the ice and was desperate not to bring up working with the Ramones and Talking Heads, but they weren't going to make it easy. I knew the Bunnymen card wouldn't work either, or the Mary Chain's. I felt they were playing mind games and couldn't have cared less that I'd travelled from London just to meet them.

So thank God I'm an old hippy at heart, in musical taste at any rate. I finally struck a chord with a shared passion (particularly with Lee) for the Grateful Dead, which some of the meandering, textural flights on *Daydream Nation* reminded me of – that and Jefferson Airplane. I kept it to myself, but Airplane guitarist Jorma Kaukonen and the ferocious

'Spayre Change' from *After Bathing at Baxter's* were clear touchstones for me, and Thurston reminded me of the Airplane's wholesome, all-American college-student lookalike Paul Kantner. We had finally struck up some sort of dialogue, before Paul wrapped things up. I left convinced that they didn't want me to be foisted upon them.

As it turned out, there was little opportunity in 1989 to break any further ground with Sonic Youth. *The Whitey Album*, by their alter egos Ciccone Youth, was their only release that year. It represented a more playfully experimental sideline, their first outing having been their deviant take on Madonna's 'Into the Groove' in 1986, which sampled the original, giving the impression of a Thurston–Madonna duet. *The Whitey Album*'s mix of lo-fi fragmentation, repetitious loops and guileful cover tunes included a rather too knowing minute of John Cagean 'Silence' and Kim Gordon's deliciously droll karaoke-backing-track version of 'Addicted to Love'. The album was either taken at face value as a bit of an in-joke by existing fans or seen as further evidence that Sonic Youth's career so far had been 'propelled by a tide of pseudo-intellectual sycophancy and a stupid respect for pretension'.

They played a week-long UK tour with Mudhoney in March, and onstage they were everything I expected and more, tearing into their guitars but with a sound that swelled and subsided in waves and a deep and rumbling bass that loosened the bowels. Some Sonic Youth virgins whom I'd invited along to the Kilburn National found them relentless, to the point where they were driven to the exit doors. Offstage they continued to play hard to get and were a little too smart-arsed, but having seen them tear up the stage in Kilburn, it was definitely worth riding the challenge.

It was clear that Paul was their manager, entangled in every aspect of their business. His apartment in Little Italy was effectively Blast First's New York office, and he was spending more of his time there attempting to shift Sonic Youth to a major label. It was something they wanted too, after a series of disappointing experiences with US independent labels. Then, sometime in June, in between various major-label encounters, Paul was told his services were no longer required. The group owed so

171

much to his drive and determination, and Sonic Youth definitely broke out internationally after having first made an impact in the UK. Typical British blokes, Paul and I never really spoke about it. Why spoil valuable drinking time? The situation was then compounded when both Dinosaur Jr and the Butthole Surfers also flew the coop soon after. When Sonic Youth signed to Geffen, I was shocked to get the call. I'd done nothing for them in the brief time since I'd been brought in and didn't have any relationship with them. I felt a loyalty to Paul and was uncomfortable saying yes, but I did so with nothing but his blessing and encouragement.

There was a steady flow of releases on Blast First throughout the year, some of which were deliberate attempts to shake up people's perceptions of the label. One such was a Sun Ra compilation, *Out There a Minute*, the first ever to appear on a rock label. It made total sense for Sun Ra to be on Blast First. His music was part of the label's DNA, especially these particular recordings from the end of the Arkestra's 1960s New York period. A tour in 1989 had to be postponed, but Paul brought the Arkestra to the UK a couple of times the year after. By then he was decelerating and diversifying Blast First, which became weirder and less guitar-friendly and more of an umbrella for a series of events and projects that were stimulating and always tremendous fun to be involved with.

10 : THEY DON'T WANT TO UPSET
THE APPLE CART

1986-9

On New Year's Day 1987 KLF Communications was born, and on that day Jimmy Cauty and Bill Drummond formed a group called the Justified Ancients of Mu Mu.

They may have backdated their beginnings for the sake of historical symmetry, because the first the world knew of the JAMs wasn't until March 1987, when their first single, 'All You Need Is Love', was unleashed on an unsuspecting world. It embraced a familiar basic DIY ethic that was nothing new to Bill. Zoo Records was born out of this ideology, but the JAMs were not inspired by punk; this was crudely recorded white hip hop for the techno age, utilising a bunch of records, two decks and a £400 sampler. Its amateurish bravado was a smokescreen, since it had been created by two cunning collaborators in their mid-thirties who sought the anonymity of aliases, masquerading as a couple of Scottish rappers from Clydeside, King Boy D and Rockman Rock.

'All You Need Is Love' was originally a one-sided twelve-inch released

The ubiquitous pyramid blaster logo signified the JAMs more than any other image in 1987 and has endured in Bill Drummond and Jimmy Cauty's work to this day.

on their own The Sound of Mu label (via KLF Communications, which would release everything by them over the next five and a half years). It was a fabrication of audaciously illegal samples, the core of which mashed together Samantha Fox's 'Touch Me (I Want Your Body)' and the MC5, while brazenly copying the intro to the Beatles original of the same title. There was even a synth steal from the Osmonds' 'Crazy Horses'. Over the top of the rumpus a demented Scot was claiming the JAMs were the hottest MCs on the River Clyde and demanding to know what the fuck was going on. The results were jarring, irreverent, hilarious and simultaneously very dumb and very clever. They cleaned it up enough to release it officially a month later through Rough Trade.

Bill turned up one day in February 1987, played me 'All You Need Is Love' and explained that he'd made it with Jimmy Cauty, whose name meant nothing to me at all. In the past I've said I thought it was complete tosh – at least, that's how I'm often quoted – but that's not true. I just didn't get it and I didn't think they could get away with it. I thought jour-nalists would realise straight away that it was Bill's next project after the *The Man*. We listened to it again and I was still left feeling a little ambiv-alent, but I knew not to doubt Bill's instincts or his passion and intensity, all of which amounted to: 'This is what I'm into now, Mick, and I've no idea where it's leading. This may be all there ever is.'

'I don't want you to do anything right now,' Bill said. 'We'll send copies round to the music-press types ourselves, with our own hand-scrawled notes. I know it will give the game away if you do it.' Bill left me a box of the one-sided twelve-inch singles and said, 'Do what you want with them.' I gave him a few names and addresses in return.

The JAMs owed a lot to *Sounds* journalist James Brown for getting the ball rolling. He genuinely believed they were two blokes from Clydeside when he made 'All You Need is Love' 'Single of the Week' on 14 March and ranted that with no guitars or synthesizers, it was making a direct assault on the way records were put together. They later gave him some of the twelve-inch singles which he passed on to likeminded journalists, whereas I adopted a more speculative 'Not sure what you'll make of this, but . . ' ploy. Once the *NME* followed suit with another 'Single of the Week', the JAMs were up and running. In May James wrote a cover story for *Sounds*, interviewing Rockman and King Boy. Anybody who'd met him would have just about been able to recognise Bill wielding a guitar like an axe on the front cover.

It was an instant success in terms of music-press buzz, and 'All You Need Is Love' established a modus operandi the JAMs followed for the rest of 1987. It exceeded their expectations in the way it was received, and they just ran with it. In interviews they – or rather Rockman and King Boy – would say that 'We did the single and that was all we intended, but it somehow turned into an album.'

I first met Jimmy sometime in April, and I didn't see a great deal of him all year. What contact I had was usually with Bill, and from the start he grabbed greater attention in the press because they knew who he was – a lot of journalists knew him personally – and the JAMs became good copy almost overnight. Jimmy was an unknown quantity, but I soon discovered that theirs was a unique partnership that didn't conform to any known constructs. This wasn't 'I write the songs and he writes the music,' and the lines between them as to who did what were always blurred. The way I worked with them was entirely reactive; I just did my best to keep up.

Jimmy was born near Birkenhead, on Merseyside, but his family moved to Kettering, in the Midlands, and later to Totnes. He's the relaxed counterpoint to Bill's coiled-spring intensity. Both are reserved characters, although people find it hard to believe that of Bill, who is given to sudden raucous outbursts. While Bill lived in the Buckinghamshire countryside, Jimmy lived in a five-storey squat in Stockwell that became the JAMs HQ. Having moved to London earlier in the 1980s, he played guitar in a series of groups prior to joining Brilliant, none of which are remembered by anyone other than his fellow participants and JAMs/ KLF obsessives.

Unlike Bill, he didn't attend art school and was entirely self-taught. He had made a tidy fortune at seventeen, when he was given £500 plus a 12 per cent royalty for his painting depicting Gandalf from *Lord of the Rings*, which adorned the best-selling Athena poster of the 1970s. It graced the walls of almost every teenage bedroom and student bedsit of the day. He did other posters for Athena and even the cover of a 1977 album by a Steeleye Span spin-off duo, *The King of Elfland's Daughter*. His graphic style at the time was intricate and spindly, drawing from the pre-Raphaelites but in a direct line from 1960s fantasy artists and *Oz* magazine. In the mid-1970s Jimmy had seen the theatrical version of *Illuminatus!*, which had transferred from Liverpool to the Roundhouse. I'm not sure either he or Bill had managed to get all the way through the books when they took the name the Justified Ancients of Mu Mu from the trilogy.

They appropriated what they needed but never openly traded on Robert Anton Wilson and Robert Shea's mythology. Bill never said anything to me about the origins of their name, nor did I make the connection at first. Right from the start we agreed there'd be no JAMs biog or any photos, just very basic press releases or statements where necessary. Others may have made the connection, but James Brown's *Sounds* cover story was the first time I recall any mention of the name's *Illuminatus!* origins. Their usual dismissive line was that 'We nicked a lot of stuff from *Illuminatus!*, in the same way we sampled records.' The idea of the JAMs as Discordians whose aim was to bring down the music industry was never on the agenda. 'We're not taking on the record industry,' said Jimmy,' and we're not out to prove anything. There's no point to any of it. We just do what we do.'

The Justified Ancients of Mu Mu were the time-travelling anarchists – the Lords of Misrule – in the counter-culture conspiracy novels by Wilson and Shea, an organisation or disorganisation as old as the Illuminati. Anybody familiar with the books would have understood the significance of the JAMs pyramid blaster logo – a beatbox superimposed over a pyramid where there should be a third eye – or the number 23 synchronicity principle: 23 was the catalogue number for the first JAMS single. They'd just say that 23 was their lucky number.

Their antics were manna from heaven for an expectant music press, and it didn't matter if an individual journalist thought their music was pointless, revolutionary or just plain fun; they knew a good story and were well aware of who King Boy D and Rockman Rock really were. I always thought it was a shame they were photographed for press features, but at least we stuck to not sending out any official publicity photos. Instead, they engineered a campaign of using graffiti to daub posters or paint slogans on buildings that was a kind of anti-art hijacking of commercial advertising. They were adopting promotional tactics that were as brazen as their sampling.

The first image they provided was of two meter maids standing in front of a government Aids warning poster covered with graffiti that just said, 'The JAMs', the letter 'A' being their pyramid blaster logo; the second had 'Shag Shag Shag' (a chant from the single) splashed over a photo of police chief James Anderton's face on a *Today* newspaper billboard. The latter image was later used on the cover of the edited 'All You Need Is Love', itself an attack on the media coverage of the Aids crisis. On its release they covered the entire front window of Tower Records in Piccadilly Circus with promo posters saying, 'Out Now, Justified Ancients of Mu Mu single'. It took the whole of the next day to remove them.

They didn't stop there, saving their most ambitious act to herald the release of the JAMs' debut album, *1987 – What the Fuck's Going On?* Having already painted the name of the LP on the top of a twenty-storey block of flats in Stockwell, they did the same on the side of the National Theatre building on the South Bank, scaling the walls in the pouring rain using ropes and planks of wood and painting '1987 The JAMs' in twenty-five-foot-high letters. It was the night of Thatcher's third election victory. Walking into work the next day the National Theatre's director Sir Peter Hall saw it and demanded it be cleaned up; it was gone in twenty-four hours. Such exploits backfired only in so far as the pair became renowned for so-called pranks and scams, terms which annoyed and frustrated them and have dogged them ever since.

The album continued their assault on copyright law, with the Monkees, Dave Brubeck, Scott Walker, AC/DC and Hamilton Bohannon among their latest victims. They laughably juxtaposed the introductory chords of Stevie Wonder's 'Superstition' with Julie Andrews singing 'The Lonely

Goatherd', but its cornerstone track was 'The Queen and I', a synth riff that sounds like Donald Duck squawking along to the chorus of Abba's 'Dancing Queen' before crashing into the Sex Pistols' 'God Save the Queen'. The album was well enough received, but while applauding their audacity in sampling such major acts, the method in their madness was already becoming repetitious, with reviewers increasingly observing that the magic moments on the record came from other people's work, not the contributions of the JAMs.

'We just thought no one was going to take any notice of it,' was their usual line of defence over the sampling, but they knew they were asking for trouble and that it would come at some point. It took five months before they were eventually sued, and fortuitously, in terms of them making a stand and generating publicity, it was by Abba. First reported on 12 September, it was announced that Abba's lawyers, acting through the music-industry watchdog the MCPS, were demanding the JAMs cease all manufacturing and distribution of their album *1987*, take all possible steps to recover the copies and then destroy them all under the supervision of the MCPS, destroying all the masters too.

Advised by their lawyers, Bill and Jimmy knew they couldn't afford the likely twenty grand they'd need to fight the case, so they decided they'd have some fun with it. Bill worked out an elaborate defence on artistic grounds and had the idea of confronting Abba face to face, artist to artist. Abba's publishers rejected the idea, so it was time for the grand gesture. With James Brown, now writing for the *NME*, and photographer Lawrence Watson in the back seat, they drove to Abba's Polar Studios, in Stockholm, in Jimmy's 1968 Ford Galaxie American police car, arriving at three in the morning. They'd mocked up a gold disc for sales in excess of zero to hand over to the group, but of course there was nobody there, so instead they handed the disc to a blonde Swedish prostitute, claiming they thought Agnetha had fallen on hard times. They had all the remaining copies of the album (or most of them) in the boot of the car. Some they tossed over the side on the return ferry, the rest they piled up in a Swedish farmer's field before starting a bonfire.

The trip to Sweden was a crucial piece of JAMs iconography. The inevitably thwarted jaunt sealed their fate as pranksters. By taking along the *NME*, where it was written up and occasionally embellished by James Brown as being such a great romp, it was always going to come across as a scam. Bill and Jimmy are their own worst enemies. They take what they do very seriously but don't behave in that way. That's the contradiction that lies behind much of their work.

I instinctively knew I'd serve them better by maintaining as invisible a presence as possible. In fact, the less I knew, the better in terms of maintaining my own sense of disbelief when speaking to the press. Had I gone to interviews it would have sent out the wrong signals, and could even have been inhibiting. For a group that was creating controversy and spreading misinformation, any PR presence would have looked too much like it was all being staged purely for the media. Cynics might argue that it was, but that was never the JAMs' prime motivation. The downside for Bill and Jimmy was that you can't whip up a storm of publicity and then complain about being misrepresented. Every act has consequences.

The clandestine nature of the JAMs' actions and a measure of inscrutability on my part was always going to be more effective than my ringing round, saying, 'Guess what the JAMs have been up to this week? And here's the photo to go with it.' To try and put a lid on the Abba story once and for all, in late September the JAMs issued an edited version of the *1987* LP with all the samples removed and leaving nothing but silence in between their own parts. What was left was rendered nonsensical and was sold as a twelve-inch, along with instructions on how to recreate the original album. As an idea it was too calculated, and people were already thinking the JAMs had taken the joke far enough.

Their two final cut-and-paste releases that year moved towards dance music and away from hip hop. 'Whitney Joins the JAMs' expertly looped riffs from the theme to *Mission: Impossible* and *Shaft* around the chorus to 'I Wanna Dance with Somebody'. It's the JAMs' best recording. Their final single, 'Downtown', disappointed many because it lacked any illegal samples. They hired the London Community Gospel Choir and even had permission from Tony Hatch to sample Petula Clark's classic. I knew they were getting more and more uncomfortable with the amount of news coverage appearing in the music press and hated idea that they were a cult music-press band. After twelve months it was time to kill off the JAMs, and in late January they released *Who Killed the JAMS?* It closed with the chimes of Big Ben on New Year's Eve 1987. The album was the same collage of familiar riffs and fragments from pop history, corralled by insistent electronic beats and with Bill lairding it up, but the dominant voices were now those of a conventional female chorus. The sampling is more surreptitious – Hendrix, Wagner, the Shangri-Las, the Doors; the plagiarism is more blatant – Sly Stone's 'Dance to the Music', Betty Wright's 'Clean Up Woman'. Enough was enough. Its release was followed in March 1988 by the first single in their new guise as the KLF, the rap-free 'Burn the Beat'.

The JAMs' final act soon after was to take out a full-page advert in *The Face*, offering the last five copies of *1987 – What the Fuck's Going On?* for sale at £1,000 each. The copy read: 'Invest in the Past Now, for the Future'. They claimed they sold three copies, which covered the ad's cost. The language they used, the typography and its audaciousness laid down a marker for the future.

Released in late May 1988, the unexpected Timelords single was a happy accident. It grew out of an idea to use the *Doctor Who* theme, but they couldn't make it work as a dance beat and the only thing that fitted was the pummelling Glitter Band drumming, specifically Gary Glitter's 'Rock 'n' Roll (Part Two)'. The intention was not to make the ultimate crass pop record but that's what materialised, so they threw in the kitchen sink, adding Dalek samples, a lift from Sweet's 'Blockbuster' and Harry Enfield's ubiquitous Loadsamoney catchphrases, delivered in the voice of a Dalek. There were no half-measures in the making of 'Doctorin' the Tardis', and that was its saving grace.

It could have completely backfired on them, and it was only after I took it into the *NME* offices and played it to editor Danny Kelly that I knew they would get away with it. He absolutely loved it for exactly what it was: the greatest – or worst – lowest-common-denominator single of all time. 'This is genius,' Danny proclaimed unequivocally, grabbing anybody he could find to come and listen to it. He would have dragged people in off the street to hear it if the *NME* offices hadn't been on the nineteenth floor of King's Reach Tower. The paper ran a massive news piece the following week, along the lines of 'It's the worst record you've ever heard and it will be no. 1.' A few weeks later the Timelords appeared on the cover of *NME*, by which time Bill and Jimmy had brought Gary Glitter on board the Tardis and remixed the single with him so that he could front the performance on *Top of the Pops*, as ludicrously camp and over the top as back in his glory days.

The Timelords were an extension of the music press's love affair with the JAMs. They didn't just champion the record but bought into the entire ludicrous idea that the car, Ford Timelord, was the star who instructed the rechristened Lord Rock and Timeboy in the making of the record itself. The logical extension of this was that only the car would do interviews. It was absurd, yet all the four of the weeklies, as well as the pop press, turned up to a car park in central London to interview a wired-up talking car that spoke like Del Boy. The press were happy to conspire in something that was undermining their own part in the process. The Timelords were acceptable; this wasn't Joe Dolce or Timmy Mallet.

Everything about the Timelords was monstrously tacky. The video was the antithesis of big-budget epics, with their Ford Galaxie cop car driving round mythical Wiltshire chasing crudely constructed Daleks – the BBC wouldn't allow them to create anything that looked like a 'real' Dalek. With even less shame Bill and Jimmy, in contrasting black and white top hat and tails, vulgarly posed with silver miniskirted models who were dubbed the Delightful Escorts. 'Doctorin' the Tardis' was a freak international hit record and a no. 1 in the UK, so it gave them a substantial amount of money to play with and more than enough to resist following it up. They did toy with the idea of marrying Alan Freeman's 'Hi there, pop pickers' chart countdown theme with Rolf Harris's 'Sun Arise', long a favourite of Bill's. If they ever recorded it, Harris's fall from grace guarantees it's now safely locked away for ever alongside 'Doctorin' the Tardis'.

On the surface the rest of 1988 was quiet. In making remixes for 'Doctorin' the Tardis' they came up with the idea of minimal dance twelve-inch releases, which they described as 'Pure Trance'. Beginning in late summer they planned to release a series of five 'Pure Trance' singles. They were titled and sleeved, but only two were definitively recorded and released. The first was 'What Time Is Love?', to be released in October. That was when I went to Trancentral, their spiritual home, for the first time. Trancentral was the basement of Jimmy's shambolic squat in Stockwell, where their rudimentary studio was set up. We sat in the kitchen, which was heated only by the open door of a gas oven, the crumbling ceiling supported by a plank of wood between two metal poles.

They wanted to go through their plans for the next few months, the first of which was to turn their trash pop hit even further to their advantage by writing and publishing *The Manual*, a money-back-guaranteed, step-by-step series of instructions on how to have a no. 1 hit. It was as good a set of guidelines about the mechanics and machinations of the music industry as any ever written, demystifying the process with basic, no-nonsense advice and funny, irreverent polemic: 'If you are already a musician, stop playing your instrument. Even better, sell the junk . . . if you are in a group, split up now.'

They played me 'What Time Is Love?' at blistering volume. 'You won't get it, Mick,' shouted Bill over the pulsing noise. 'It makes no sense at all unless you're out of your brain and it's late at night.' I loved the track, even while just sipping tea in Jimmy's kitchen. What I heard was relentless, minimalistic, instrumental dance music with no middle eight that I thought owed something to avant-garde composer Terry Riley. They wanted to send 'What Time Is Love?' only to specialist shops or direct to clubs. 'We don't want any promotion,' continued Bill. 'We don't want this reviewed. We're already thought of as too much of a music-paper-type band, and that means nothing in the club/DJ world this is meant for.' As with the first JAMs single, they wanted me to do nothing, which was always fine by me. By the end of the year the first 'Pure Trance' single had made no impact whatsoever, but by then they were making a movie.

In their own make-believe mythology, the film was about a journey they were contracted to make by some higher order, to a place called 'The White Room'. They were further impelled to portray that journey artistically. It was originally going to be represented as a joint art exhibition, before they decided on making a road movie instead. It would begin at Trancentral, before heading to Spain in November, where they frittered away a quarter of a million pounds filming in the spaghetti western terrain of the Sierra Nevada region, utilising the crew that had just finished the latest Indiana Jones film. Bill Butt took on the role of Steven Spielberg. Once Bill and Jimmy start something, it takes over, and *The White Room* was no exception. This was two men fulfilling their whims, making a film with no storyline. Unforeseen persistent bad weather and other setbacks didn't help, and they knew it wasn't working, but they just carried on in the blind belief that 'It's a road movie; we have a car and we know where the road is.' I left the meeting thinking it was going to be a typical road-movie folly, a genre that was rarely anything other than tedious. It would be just another atmospheric, existential parable like *Two-Lane Blacktop*, built around two rock stars, neither of whom could act.

I didn't see them again until early in February 1989, when they were locked away in a Soho edit suite looking through the footage. Jimmy was the only one there when I turned up; he was looking weary from viewing hundreds of hours of footage of him and Bill driving through Sergio Leone's Spain. He was typically honest in his assessment. 'It's completely boring,' he said of the footage on which they had squandered the money earnt from 'Doctorin' the Tardis'. When Bill arrived, they returned to a conversation that was as endless as the footage, revolving around the question of 'How can we turn this into something we can use?'

Bill Butt persuaded them to see it through, and during February they found enough money to shoot the interior scenes in London, but in order to do more they needed something commercial to fund it. So *The White Room* soundtrack shifted shamelessly towards a more marketable Europop sound, signalled by a new KLF single, 'Kylie Said to Jason', which was released in July. For two and a half years Bill and Jimmy had

done little wrong. Even the Timelords single had worked within the context of the JAMs as provocateurs. 'Kylie Said to Jason' didn't have that
cachet; described by one reviewer as sit-com house, it was lyrically shal-
low, run-of-the-mill synth pop, with a hushed, carefully enunciated vocal
by Bill, doing his best to emulate Neil Tennant's delivery. There was nothing radical about it; it was no more than another synth-pop-duo single.
The buzz within Rough Trade, the pluggers and Bill and Jimmy themselves was that it was a surefire Top 10 hit that would rescue them from
bankruptcy, but after entering the charts at no. 105 it went no higher.
Instead of going straight onto the Radio 1 playlist, producers rejected it
for mocking their most beloved superstars. TV producers also blanked
the shimmering video, which utilised handsomely shot scenes from the
film. The duo even did a glossy, conventional photo session, trying their
best to look like pop stars. Bill was dressed sombrely, staring into the distance, straight-backed and awkward-looking, while Jimmy was wearing
what appeared to be a flowing striped nightshirt, with a long strand of
hippy beads round his neck.

It was the first time Bill and Jimmy had seriously fucked up. With no
hesitation, they scrapped the more or less finished soundtrack to *The
White Room* and pulled the release. They didn't ditch the film, though,
and by the end of summer had an edited version that ran for fifty-two
minutes, which they thought might work as a backdrop to the KLF performing a live soundtrack. Instead, it was premiered at the Arri Kino in
Hamburg in February 1991, where a flock of sheep was let loose in the
foyer. It was never shown anywhere else, nor was it ever completed.

If there was a silver lining to the failure of the ill-judged 'Kylie' single, it was that it kept their club cred intact. While they'd been filming
and fretting over the footage, 'What Time Is Love?' had become an
unexpected underground club hit in Europe. They released a remixed
'What Time Is Love?' in May, with the original on the reverse side, while
the second 'Pure Trance' single, '3 a.m. Eternal', appeared just as 'Kylie
Said to Jason' was sinking. The knock-on effect saw the KLF being feted
in the UK by the rave and acid-house scene, which had been building

over the summer, and 'What Time Is Love?' became an anthem for what the tabloids were now calling the 'new summer of love'.

The KLF finally made their debut live appearance at Land of Oz (at Heaven nightclub in London) at the end of July, performing a fifteen-minute version of 'What Time Is Love?', during which they splattered the audience with polystyrene pellets fired from a giant wind machine. It was the only one of their live performances that summer that I saw. I never went to any summer raves: off my head or not, I couldn't handle crowds and avoided festivals like the plague. I couldn't picture Bill at a rave either, out of it on ecstasy, jumping up and down with one arm raised. He'd told Julian he didn't need to take acid, and I wondered if he followed the same advice with regard to ecstasy. I missed out on that whole scene because of my own fears and paranoia, but wished I'd been there at the Helter Skelter event in Chipping Norton, where the KLF showered the crowd with a thousand Scottish pound notes, on each of which was written 'Children We Love You', and I couldn't help but envy the rush Jimmy described of seeing five thousand people at the Sunrise rave dancing to 'What Time Is Love?', a tune he'd come up with in his bedroom in fifteen minutes.

They also dreamt up 'ambient house', the antidote to the rave experience, a soporific exploration of pastoral bliss. With its Pink Floyd parody front-cover artwork, they delved into their own pop history to complete *Chill Out*, which was recorded live at Trancentral. The album was executed using two DAT machines, a cassette machine, samplers and computers. It took them two days to put it together as a continuous piece with no edits. Having lined up all the different elements, Bill described the process as like 'spinning plates', hoping they could get to the end without any of the plates crashing to the floor. If not, they'd start again from the beginning.

Among others, samples were drawn from Glen Campbell's 'Wichita Lineman', Fleetwood Mac's 'Albatross' and Acker Bilk's 'Stranger on the Shore', as well as Graham Lee's steel guitar from *The Man*, all interspersed with the sound of bleating sheep, chirping crickets and other natural sounds. I loved *Chill Out*, but it was nothing new beyond their giving ambient music a different name. I had my own favourite atmospheric albums that used natural soundscapes. Acoustic folk and country albums by John Fahey and Mickey Newbury, and electronic and experimental music by Beaver and Krause, notably *In a Wild Sanctuary*, achieved the same early-morning come-down mood that *Chill Out* did.

I'd been working with Bill for ten years, and for most of those ten years he'd never been 'the difficult artist', though I was often 'the difficult publicist'. I knew Bill well enough to question why he did certain things and where, how and whether I fitted in. At the end of 1989 I considered that they might be better off without me. I feared that in my hands *Chill Out* would be dismissed as some kind of loopy twist on ambient music. It was a tough call. Bill thought I hated *Chill Out*, but the new rave culture and the magazines, writers or DJs who mattered in that world were just not on my radar, nor my contacts list. So I suggested they hire Jeff Barrett, telling them that he would totally get it. 'Jeff takes the right drugs,' I assured them. And I wondered if I was making a huge mistake and that they'd stick with Jeff in the future.

By January 1986 Echo & the Bunnymen had released one single in the year and a half since *Ocean Rain*. The group were creatively spent, bored and had no decent new songs written, but nobody anticipated what would happen next: Pete de Freitas went AWOL. 'Pete flipped his wig and went off to America with a bunch of mates,' was Will's take on it. 'They were sponging off him and getting shit-faced and taking loads of drugs and supposedly making an album that Pete was bankrolling. Pete was amazing. Before he went he had this boyish spark, a kind of innocence. When he got back he was a completely different person.' I knew exactly what Will meant. It was as though he'd been taken over like the people in *Invasion of the Body Snatchers*, replaced by alien doubles that came out of a giant aubergine-like pod. He wasn't the same Pete. In fact, neither he nor the group were ever the same.

It was *Sounds* that broke the story in February, reporting that Pete had gone missing and was travelling across the US with members of a religious sect, the Children of God. The truth was even stranger. His disappearance had been prompted by years of pent-up frustration with the Bunnymen, combined with a drinking habit that sent him over the edge. At least there were no mysterious religious cults involved. Pete had disappeared to New Orleans, taking with him a group he'd formed called the Sex Gods, for whom he played guitar, not drums. He planned on filming and recording the new group, which was made up of his housemate and former Deaf School drummer Tim Whittaker, Bunnymen roadie Andy Eastwood and Steve 'Jonno' Johnson, sometime bassist with Julian Cope and Wah!. A local Bunnymen fan who went by the Kerouac-style name of Louisiana Paul had arranged free studio time in New Orleans.

What they were getting up to was eventually pieced together through the increasingly strange, deranged and worrying phone calls made by Pete over the next three weeks. With an alcohol and drug intake that Julian likened to 13th Floor Elevators' Roky Erickson – Pete was reputedly so high he stayed awake for eighteen manic days – there were wild schemes that pre-empted the JAMs' exploits. Apparently, Pete wanted to hire a helicopter to fly to New York and spray a message on the World Trade Center. All his calls had everybody seriously concerned. I received two, both at around three in the morning. One was complete gibberish about needing to build a gigantic platform in order to contact the aliens who had the answer. I never found out to what. The other was Pete pleading with me to wire him some money. Bill and Mick Hancock flew to New Orleans to try and bring him back. It takes a lot to shake Bill, but he said he couldn't get through to him, and he barely recognised the Pete who eventually returned home, via a stopover in Jamaica with a girl he'd met in New Orleans. When I met him a month or so later, he really was different: he had a vacant stare and spoke only tangentially. He was still hoping to salvage something from the recordings made by the group, but whether they ever taped anything, and what became of any tapes, he couldn't say.

A US Bunnymen tour was due to start in March and there was a new album to record, but Mac, Will and Les refused to take Pete back. Nor was he in a fit state to tour. However, after drafting in Blair Cunningham, formerly of Haircut 100, the dates went ahead. With Pete still shut out, the band spent three months at Amazon Studios in Liverpool, using various drummers to try and record their fifth album. In mid-summer Rob Dickins was due to come up and hear the album. They asked me as well, more for moral support. I arrived before Rob, to find Mac and Mick Hancock totally wired. They were pacing the floor, while Will and Les sat around busying themselves doing nothing. It was an uncomfortable couple of hours of listening back to half-finished songs that went nowhere. I returned on the train with Rob, who'd been completely underwhelmed, and tried to gloss over what I thought. A few days later he'd rejected the album on the grounds that 'even Mick Houghton thought it was shit'.

Realising they needed him, Pete was allowed back, but on their terms; he became a hired hand and was no longer a full member of the group. At Rob's suggestion they once again brought in the painstaking Laurie Latham to produce the album, and then spent a gruelling six months in studios in Cologne, Brussels, London and Liverpool trying to complete it. The torturous year and a half since Pete had absconded meant that everybody wanted to wash their hands of the new album even before its release. As Mac recalled, 'We were in Brazil when it was remixed by someone in America, and we listened to the mixes down the phone. I just never wanted to hear it again.' Nor did Will: 'We ended up at loggerheads. Mac would go one way and we'd all go the other and there were arguments over royalties, with Mac wanting an additional, separate split because he wrote the lyrics.'

The first single was 'The Game', released in June, a month prior to the album. After a three-year wait it reached a disappointing no. 28. Mac described it as a 'Dear John' letter to the others. He wanted to call the album *The Game*, but the rest were against it, so it was simply called *Echo & the Bunnymen* and came in a plain, stark, grey sleeve with a black-and-white photo of the group; Pete is facing in the opposite direction to the rest. 'We couldn't be bothered to come up with a title,' said Will, 'or agree on anything. It was grey by name and grey by nature.'

The Bunnymen played no UK shows ahead of the album. They'd had no presence on home turf for two years. They needed to do something, and while it may not have been up there with any of Bill's great notions, it was my idea that they should launch the album on the week of its release on 6 July 1987 by playing a lunchtime set live on the roof of the HMV music store in London's Oxford Street. They played three of their own songs and a version of 'Twist and Shout'. While clearly intended to evoke images of the Beatles' rooftop gig at the Apple building in nearby Savile Row, it was too tame and little more than an in-store appearance – or indeed, on-store. I should have persuaded Bill and Jimmy to scale the walls of the HMV building and write on it 'Do It Clean' or, better still, 'What the fuck is going on?'

Three years after *Ocean Rain* the grey album still went Top 5, but the reviews smacked of indifference and the group's irrelevance. The once-supportive music papers, which were now frothing wildly about the JAMs, were the harshest critics. While the band was increasingly losing interest, the record company wanted to claw something back on their renewed investment. Having plateaued out in the UK, WEA wanted the Bunnymen to concentrate on the US and was pressuring them to tour there more extensively. In one regard it worked: they ended up having their two biggest US hits, 'Lips Like Sugar' and 'People Are Strange', and *Echo & the Bunnymen* became their best-selling album stateside. Secretly, though, they all knew that stepping up the touring in North America was too little and definitely too late, and the idea that they had finally broken in the US was an illusion. 'We never did what U2 and Simple Minds did,' said Mac, 'and spent months out there touring. Perhaps we should have.' Les could only pour scorn: 'On our first US tour in 1981 some of us felt homesick before we reached London airport. We saw it as like doing National Service.'

After touring stadiums in the US in a series of double-headers with New Order during August and September 1987, the Bunnymen finally returned to play major concert venues in the UK at the end of the year. These included an undersold Wembley Arena. The stage set was an embarrassment. A Roman temple with pillars either side of a stage draped in black netting showed none of the theatrical flair they were known for. Playing at Wembley was something they had always said they'd never do; it was everything the Bunnymen weren't about. I'd gone by then. WEA had taken the press in-house, and I was relieved. My heart wasn't in it any more.

I rang Mac after the tour, and he told me he was going to leave the Bunnymen in the spring, after yet more dates in the US and then Japan, where the show in Fukuoka on 26 April 1988 proved to be their last. Prior to going on stage for that final concert, Les had the courage and decency to tell Mac that his father, who'd been ill for some time, had suffered another heart attack and was in hospital; nobody else wanted to tell him until after the show. With no available flights until much later, they played the gig anyway. Mac got on a plane that night, and some twenty minutes before touchdown, his dad died.

When the announcement that Echo & the Bunnymen had split up was finally made in October, a month short of their tenth anniversary, it went all but unnoticed.

Having signed to Island Records in summer 1985, Julian Cope's rock-star resurrection wasn't a long time coming, but within two years it was a long time gone again. I had mixed feelings when his first single for the label, 'World Shut Your Mouth', saw him back in the Top 20. I had no reason not to feel pleased for him, but it's hard to take when you are no longer part of something. And here was Julian all over the press again and back on TV – on *Wogan*, of all things, and *Top of the Pops*, atop of what he called his 'cosmic asshole' mic stand. The maddeningly slick, radio-friendly 'World Shut Your Mouth' was everywhere, but that was as good as it got. The *Saint Julian* album followed in March 1987, with Julian adorning a glossy cover that was the very antithesis of *Fried*'s, his arms outstretched in a confident Christ-like pose. The record was too garish for my taste – and this was not sour grapes. It hung around the charts for nearly three months, and for the rest of that year Island had him touring relentlessly. I couldn't help but wonder if history would repeat itself, since his reaction to high-profile success had been so severe in 1981.

Sometime in January 1989 I saw him on Jonathan Ross's Channel 4 show *The Last Resort*, plugging a really odd choice of single, 'Five O'Clock World'. I found it hard to believe he had chosen to cover the Vogues' lightweight 1960s US pop hit. He looked unhealthy and desperately thin, and although I hadn't spoken to him for a couple of years, I wanted to call him up like a concerned mother and say, 'Are you sure you're eating enough?' He was nothing but skin and bones. After an excruciatingly patronising interview with Ross, for which he was completely bonged out, he performed another cover. The Animals' 'We Gotta Get Out of This Place' must surely have been a statement of intent. His second Island album, *My Nation Underground*, which had taken six months to complete, had completely stiffed on release a few months earlier.

I heard that he had sacked Cally, the co-architect of his initial triumphant return at Island. He was clearly disenchanted by success again, and self-destructing. In advance he had talked about the new album as a cross between Funkadelic and Can, but it had turned to be something so insipid he wanted to call it *The Great White Hoax*. Now referred to as 'the Scottish album', Julian has long since disowned it as 'underachieving cack'. This may be in part due to the circumstances surrounding a last-ditch attempt by Island to salvage the album by releasing a belated third single. 'China Doll' was an exquisite ballad that was *My Nation Underground*'s only true jewel. By the time it was released in late June, Julian could not have cared less, after an unexpected tragedy shook all of us who knew and loved Pete de Freitas.

Julian had become particularly close to Pete over the years and had asked him to star in the video for 'China Doll'. It was a tackily romantic treatment in which a rugged, leather-clad Pete tumbled around in bed with a French mademoiselle and come morning climbed onto his bike and rode away. It was perfect casting. Then, on 14 June, Pete's cherished Ducati 900, which had featured in the video, was hit somewhere on the A5 in Staffordshire by a car driven by a seventy-five-year-old woman, causing his death.

Julian's devastation at Pete's passing triggered a two-year series of visions he once described as 'physical eruptions inside his head'. They opened his mind to the possibilities that would ultimately inspire and shape his work during the 1990s. Pete's death shook him out of any complacency about how he should make music in the future. He'd had it with meddling record-company men and unsympathetic producers and was determined to get back to basics. This was a drude awakening.

Only a year after the Bunnymen split Ian McCulloch released his debut solo album, *Candleland*, in October 1989. *Candleland* had been recorded in London, in a small studio in Pimlico, Mac working closely with producer Ray Shulman, who had recently worked with the Sundays and the Sugarcubes. Shulman played bass and keyboards, but the guitars were all down to Mac. Cure drummer Boris Williams was one of the few outside contributors. I saw a lot of Mac when he was recording the album and I could tell that his confidence was shot, but at the same time he wanted *Candleland* to be a personal feat he could be proud of having made, so usually it was just him, Shulman and the engineer working closely together. It is a subtle, at times downbeat affair that looks back on his childhood and recent losses. His father haunts an unusually reflective, introspective album. He could still command the cover of the *NME*, but this wasn't the moment for Mac the Mouth to return. *Candleland* reached a respectable no. 18 but didn't sell well thereafter. It deserved better but was completely out of sync with the Madchester scene that was about to erupt.

To Mac's dismay, Echo & the Bunnymen announced they were carrying on without him. Contractually, if there was a majority of original members, they had the rights to the Bunnymen title, so he had no say in the matter. Will made no secret of how delighted he was that Mac was so cheesed off, especially since the group had been retained by WEA. Rob Dickins wasn't happy that Mac had left the group at a point when he thought they were poised to break big in the US, and he had encouraged Will to replace him.

Mac's take on it was that they had become Echo & the Bogusmen.

11 : LOTS OF LITTLE OSMONDS

1990-5

My life was a bit of a mess at the start of the 1990s. My second marriage was over, and not through any indiscretions on my part this time. We had reached a point where we no longer fulfilled each other's needs and desires, and for the first time in my life I didn't go straight into another long-term relationship. I found myself nomadically renting flats, sharing houses and, in between, living in the upper level of my new office space. I'd moved into a separate unit between the Riverside and Roadside warehouse spaces in Metropolitan Wharf. It was a tip. I had a futon bed, a small Sony TV, a kettle, a microwave and even running water and an old butler's sink. I wasn't looking for a home or a steady girlfriend and just

The House of Love: Chris Groothuizen, Guy Chadwick, recently recruited guitarist Simon Walker and Pete Evans seated in a cable car overlooking Barcelona during an *NME* trip in May 1990 (*photo: Kevin Cummins*).

threw myself into work. I had clung on to the Jesus and Mary Chain and the Wedding Present, but everything else I'd been doing was in a state of flux. I wasn't to know that during the 1990s I would become busier than I'd ever been.

At the beginning of the decade Pam Young came to work with me. We'd known each other for ten years through her working with Zoo, and I knew she was incredibly organised but great to work with. I definitely needed both those qualities. When she left after eighteen months, Louise Nevill joined. She had no experience whatsoever. She loved all the groups and had spent time hanging out with the Pogues, which was as good a grounding for PR work as any. I'd met her at one of Jimmy Cauty's infamous parties, and revelry definitely remained an integral part of the job for the next three years.

I felt like I was starting out all over again, just as outlets for music were proliferating in the press as never before. The *NME* and *Melody Maker* were no less pivotal, despite falling sales, even after *Record Mirror* and *Sounds* closed down in April 1991. The change was due to the rise of so many specialist music monthlies – *Q* since starting up in 1986, and now *Vox*, *Select* and *Mojo* – lifestyle magazines – *Loaded*, *GQ* and *FHM* – and expanding tabloid and broadsheet press coverage. Even the 1980s metal mags came into play, and within a few years *Kerrang!* was outselling the *NME*. I held none of the aces and successfully dodged Britpop and grunge, just as I had the baggy scene and shoegazing. In fact, little of what I was doing in the 1990s made a great deal of sense if you placed all my artists side by side.

None more so than two bands I took on early in 1990 who had emerged from the indie wasteland: Birdland and Cud. Both groups polarised opinions and nobody gave either of them a prayer, but I couldn't have cared less what it did for my credibility. It was a terrible time in British music, and a host of scrappy, mostly independent groups had sprung up from grass-roots level to a point where they couldn't be ignored. The so-called Stourbridge bands Pop Will Eat Itself, the Wonder Stuff and Ned's Atomic Dustbin, south London's ironic, drum-machine-driven social agitators

194

Carter USM and others such as the Mega City Four, Senseless Things and the New FADS were all being feted by the music press. Cud certainly ran with the same motley pack. They also very much fitted in with that enduring British art-school tradition of acts who made great, hook-laden singles loaded with ideas, but whose albums were patchy and didn't sell. I liked that Cud were down to earth and didn't take themselves too seriously, yet the group had two Top 30 hits for A&M in 1992, 'Rich and Strange' and 'Purple Love Balloon'. They'd changed from underachieving amateurs to solid professionals who had got farther than they or anybody else expected. When Cud made the cover of the *NME* in July 1992, I was besieged with calls wondering if I was blackmailing its editor, Danny Kelly.

Birdland were truly loved or totally loathed. There was no middle ground, although much of the derision towards them was down to their appearance: four Brian Jones lookalikes with bottle-blond fringed haircuts, all dressed in matching silk shirts. Detractors cruelly dismissed them as the Bros of the indie charts. They had four independent no. 1 singles in a row and could headline Brixton Academy. Such was the momentum that after I came on board in January 1990, 'Sleep with Me' gave them their only Top 40 hit, and there were *Melody Maker* and *NME* front covers either side of it. I take no credit whatsoever. I just ran with it, and for a few months they were a mini-phenomenon. Then, within a year, their self-titled debut album was dismissed as indistinguishable and tuneless, making a one-week-only chart appearance at no. 44. They crashed and burnt, which was the perfect end. I wish more groups would do so, rather than sticking around for too long.

Buoyed by the success of their eponymous debut album, the House of Love signed to Phonogram's Fontana label for an advance of £400,000. Alan McGee continued managing them, which brought him and the group head to head with Dave Bates, and a clash of unstoppable forces and an immovable object would soon ensue. That first album had set the tone. Guy Chadwick's moody, self-reflective songs were offset by Terry Bickers's atmospheric, textured and alternating soaring guitar leads and hooks;

the two of them played off each other's personalities and musical aspirations. The group began recording their Fontana debut in spring 1989 and soon clashed with Bates over 'Safe', a leftover Creation single that they had recorded with Daniel Miller. Their choice of single was overridden and the newly recorded 'Never' was released in mid-April to an unexpected press panning, before reaching that worst of chart positions, no. 41.

The House of Love continued to record in different studios and with different producers for the next six months. Their excessive alcohol and drug intake in the studio and their habit of changing producers from one month to the next, ditching sessions and then switching studios, were common knowledge. A paranoia-inducing mixture of hedonism and despondency was getting the better of them as Bates rejected tape after tape. Costs were mounting too: six weeks spent at Abbey Road didn't come cheap, and with nothing to show for it except more misery. The album was eventually finished after six months. In the end four producers were credited on the album sleeve. According to Julian, Bates had been dismissing the recordings after unknowingly listening to them through a faulty speaker system in his office. At some point the tech guys hired to service all the equipment at Phonogram pointed out that his system badly needed calibrating.

Julian's story may not have been true, but such was the jinx surrounding the House of Love's recordings, who is to say it wasn't? The cost of the album eventually came in at a reputed £500,000, upped by outlays on videos, B-sides, artwork and other marketing, which brought the cost of the entire project in for half as much again. Allegedly, the group's taxi bills amounted to £10,000. Whatever way you look at it, it was a shameful amount of money.

Having finished the album, the group planned a seventy-date, back-to-basics UK tour, beginning in November and ending in March, ahead of the album release. There would be two singles along the way, commencing with 'I Don't Know Why I Love You' in November; it too stalled at no. 41. I could imagine the shitstorm and recriminations between Bates and his marketing staff and the pluggers at Fontana, and the ongoing inquests presided over by Bates, McGee and publicist Jeff Barrett, who hadn't put a foot wrong in marshalling the press so far.

Then the roof came down during four dates in Wales between 29 November and 2 December. By now everybody was getting deeper and deeper into drugs and further out of control, and the already mentally unstable Terry Bickers was becoming estranged from the others. Over the next week the press got wind that he had been sacked. It was announced that he'd left only temporarily, as a result of suffering 'mental and physical exhaustion', but another guitarist was brought in immediately – Simon Fernsby, stage name Simon Walker. He was taught the songs while travelling in the van to the next scheduled gig in Portsmouth on 4 December.

The heavy touring schedule continued in the New Year, but they were now permanently without Terry. Jeff Barrett was ousted before Christmas, and I was brought in at the beginning of 1990. I hadn't seen that one coming. Since the collapse of Elevation I'd had nothing to do with Creation. It was Bates who called me, and I'd not seen or spoken to him since Julian had left Mercury five years back. He filled me in up to a point but glossed over the gory details. My role was to exercise as much damage limitation as I could. It would all rest on what journalists made of the album and whether the next scheduled single – a re-recorded version of 'Shine On' – was a hit.

I had no qualms about taking the band on. I felt as if there'd been a mid-season transfer, whereby I had bowed out from looking after *Chill Out* and was now taking on the House of Love. All Jeff said was a stony-faced 'Good luck, mate.' It was only when I saw them on tour a few weeks later that I could see what was really going on. The group had a heavy-looking, scary road crew who seemed to dominate the band when on tour. Their behaviour was quite unbelievable, and clearly nothing had changed since Terry left. When I walked into the dressing room after a mid-January gig at Thames Valley College in Slough, they were all off their heads amid flaring strobes and ear-splitting music. I was greeted by the odious sight of one of the party crapping into a pint glass. From the little I knew of them back in 1987 they'd struck me as an unassuming bunch. The only thing that had been off the scale then was Guy's ambition.

'Shine On' was released at the end of January, and given the intrigue over Terry's departure it made an *NME* cover pretty much a foregone conclusion – their last, as it turned out. It charted at no. 22, rose to 20, and they played on *Top of the Pops* for the first and last time. Even the artwork on the band's second album smacks of confusion or deliberate obfuscation. Like its predecessor, it is self-titled and is usually referred to either as 'Fontana' (as it says on the spine) or the 'butterfly album', a reference to its cover image. The sparse credits on the back are written in tiny type, as if nobody wanted to put their name to it.

The album was by no means a disaster, but it was always going to be viewed as a case of promise unfulfilled. Everyone feared a mauling, but the reviews were decent enough for an album that inevitably lacked cohesion due to its piecemeal recording and it never quite bristles with the excitement of their Creation debut. The press had cooled towards them, but the knives never came out. When the mammoth tour picked up in January, they finally gathered some impetus, and to great relief all round the album charted on 10 March 1990 and reached a face-saving no. 8. (Primal Scream's 'Loaded' had charted the week before and was Creation's first Top 20 single.) The group sold out the Royal Albert Hall, receiving a hugely enthusiastic response from the audience, but it was something of a hollow victory. They'd got away with it by the skin of their teeth, and the album was ultimately enough of a success to spare Dave Bates's blushes. Figures can paper over cracks, but it sold over four hundred thousand copies worldwide, a quarter of those in France alone. The root of the problem was not the dirty linen discarded on the floor but the group's revivalist guitar rock 'n' roll, which didn't fit in with the club-conscious pop scene that was still gathering momentum. To their credit, the House of Love never tried to jump on the baggy bandwagon.

Fontana continued to throw money at them. At the beginning of April, as they trekked off to Europe 'Beatles and the Stones' became the fourth single taken from the album. In came in a ridiculous twelve different chart-eligible formats and was backed up by an £80,000 video recorded in Los Angeles. It earnt them a no. 36 chart placing. To add insult to injury, Creation's latest flavour of the month, Ride, charted four places higher with their *Play* EP and virtually no marketing spend whatsoever.

In the eyes of the press, the House of Love never recovered from Terry Bickers leaving and the manner in which he did, casting Guy as somebody with megalomaniac tendencies. They had all made up their minds that without the Guy/Terry dynamic, the House of Love would never be as good again. Simon Walker was no slouch and the live shows sparked, but the creative dynamic was diminished as Guy took complete control. The group's plight wasn't helped by an over-fussy Bates and an increasingly disinterested Alan McGee. It took two and a half years before the next album appeared. The group wanted *Babe Rainbow* to be recorded quickly, but Bates kept rejecting the songs Guy was coming up with. Maybe his speaker system was still faulty.

Aware they'd not been heard from for over a year, on 31 August 1991 they returned, playing three different London gigs in one night, a different set at each venue. It was an isolated stunt that worked, but a few months later their only release that year, the moody and warmly greeted 'Girl with the Loneliest Eyes', was another flop. By then McGee no longer wanted to manage them. He and Guy were hardly speaking. Like the Mary Chain before him, Guy reckoned Alan was too preoccupied with other Creation business, so he sacked him over the phone.

Babe Rainbow had restored considerable faith in the group, but its positive reviews counted for little. Two weeks in the charts and a peak of no. 34 confirmed they'd left it far too late. Guy desperately wanted another *NME* cover, and I told him the best we could expect was a feature spread. There was nothing to justify a cover, however much Danny Kelly was a fan of the group. So Guy asked if we could go in and see him. I was uncomfortable to say the least and knew Danny wouldn't make any rash promises for old times' sake. Guy ended up virtually begging him to change his mind. He said he'd do anything for the cover photo – strip naked, wear a dress . . . you name it. Did he even offer to wear a Nazi uniform? I may have either blanked that out or made it up over time. Danny paused before coming up with a proposition. He'd go for it if Guy would pose back to back with Terry Bickers, both holding duelling pistols. Deflated, Guy just shook his head. He was crestfallen. Danny shrugged and made further apologetic noises, and we left.

With Guy playing all the guitars himself, the group's final Fontana album was recorded and mixed in under three weeks. *Audience with the Mind* was tantamount to a solo album, appearing only a year after *Babe Rainbow*. Sales were negligible. It was an introverted and understandably emotional listening experience that warranted a re-evaluation that never came. The band split up before the year was out, leaving Guy wondering if they might have fared better had they stayed on Creation, now that McGee had sold half the company to Sony. They weren't the first artists to have been tainted by money, drink, drugs and record-company indulgence, and they certainly won't be the last. For me, it always felt like chasing rainbows.

Meanwhile, the thrifty and incorruptible Wedding Present had been disappointed that their RCA debut proper, *Bizarro*, hadn't gone far enough in achieving the fuller sound they wanted. They decided to re-record 'Brassneck', but this time with Steve Albini producing a four-track EP with them in London. The group had seen Albini's monstrously loud group Big Black in Leeds in 1987, since when he'd built up a strong reputation as an engineer/producer, responsible for helping create music that ran along similar basic, exacting lines to his own, which had paid dividends in the recording of the Pixies' *Surfer Rosa*. It was an inspired move to use him, and the Wedding Present were the first British group to do so.

A new album followed, recorded at Pachyderm, a snowbound residential studio in rural Minnesota, and completed in twelve days. By Albini's standards it had been expensive, coming in at $25,000 – more or less the House of Love's taxi bill in 1989. David Gedge likened Albini's approach to doing a Peel session: just play it live and record it. The brutal Albini technique meant bass and drums loud, guitars even louder, overdubbing the vocals later if need be. *Seamonsters* was released in May 1991. Rather than the passive, romanticised break-up scenarios that featured on past records, its themes were lust, greed and jealousy; it was no longer 'OK, see you later,' but 'You better watch out next time you do.'

These were bleak, single-word-titled songs driven by visceral, dissonant guitar play. Gone was the fierce jangle of old, *Seamonsters* replacing their usual frenetic energy with textures and layers of guitar noise. It charted at no. 13 and hung around the charts for a month. This didn't impress most of those at RCA, who thought the Wedding Present were an awkward bunch, but their fans didn't desert them over their more uncompromising sound. In January 1989 they had been voted the *NME*'s band of the year, and three years later they were still in third place. It's all too often overlooked that the unfashionable and uncontroversial Wedding Present were hugely popular with the slavish indie crowd.

Peter Solowka left after *Seamonsters*; with David he had been as responsible as anybody for the Wedding Present's signature buzzsaw sound, and there was some concern over his departure. It helped the transition that Peter left to follow the Ukrainian direction (and, indeed, formed the Ukrainians), so it was never seen as a coup to bring in another guitarist. That guitarist was Paul Dorrington, a one-time member of experimental Sheffield guitar band AC Temple, who had released two albums on Blast First. As it was, the group confounded all expectations anyway by coming up with the inspired *Hit Parade* concept. The idea was to release a single a month throughout 1992, each one available only on seven-inch and strictly limited to fifteen thousand copies. The A-side would be an original new song, the B-side a cover version, and it worked a treat; each of the singles sold out within a week, and they had twelve consecutive hits that year. The fifth one, 'Come Play with Me', was their only Top 10 hit, a further seven made the Top 20 and the lowest entry was no. 26. The *Melody Maker* hated the group, bar one brave writer, and moaned like fuck every month, but it was a small and almost smug victory when we made the paper's cover for the first time at the beginning of 1993.

The single-a-month game plan was a brilliant idea and proved really subversive in exposing the vicissitudes of the pop-chart formula. It also flagged up a decline in the record industry, when a mere fifteen thousand singles was sufficient to achieve such consistent success. It gave the Wedding Present a *Guinness Book of World Records* citation for equalling Elvis Presley's feat of a dozen chart hits within a single calendar year. Both recorded for the same RCA label, although Elvis sold considerably more than fifteen thousand copies of each of his 1957 hits. It was such a simple idea that few if any other groups could have made work. It relied upon the strengths of the Wedding Present: a fervent fan base and a rigorous work ethic. It was demanding even without the extra commitment of coming up with twelve sleeve designs and making twelve videos. It was a tough ask because David wanted to record each single afresh, although they had to settle for recording them in four batches of three, each batch with a different producer, including famed Rolling Stones producer Jimmy Miller.

Some of the singles were pretty ropey, but even that added to the seditious nature of the plan, as each song took its place in the chart rundown. They also made four less than scintillating appearances on *Top of the Pops* that hit out at its ritualistic nature. Of the dozen A-sides, some would not have worked outside the confines of the concept, but the B-side covers were far more bold and unpredictable: a brilliant Sonic Youth-like assault on Julee Cruise's 'Falling' (the *Twin Peaks* theme); a grungey take on Neil Young's 'Don't Cry No Tears'; a soaring remake of the Monkees' 'Pleasant Valley Sunday'; and despite the Mancunian dialect, a surprisingly respectful 'Theme from *Shaft*'.

Despite the Wedding Present's extraordinary record-breaking feat, they were dropped by RCA the following year. The times and the company personnel had changed. They re-emerged on Island Records in 1994, a label whose values were completely at odds with the Wedding Present's singular disdain for being cool or stylish. Island released just one album, the vastly underrated *Watusi*, on which the group adopted a fascinating lo-fi pop approach. Needless to say, Island took the press in-house and managed to bury the album completely, but it was impossible to see where the Wedding Present belonged in a year that was torn between the enduring grunge sound they no longer favoured and self-absorbed Britpop.

By the end of the 1980s Lawrence had fashioned his own flawed legend after executing Felt's ten years, ten albums, ten singles plan. His reputation was built around his oft-catalogued eccentricities and insecurities and the sense that he was acting in a way that you're not supposed to act until you have actually achieved stardom. Even before the dust had settled on Felt's disassembly, Lawrence had bought a plane ticket to New York. He'd been living in Brighton but found it boring, even though he was sharing a flat with Alan McGee, so he decided to live in what he thought was the most dangerous place in the world, 'but I ended up living in a really nice apartment on Sullivan Street in Greenwich Village. I'd buy the *NME* every week and straight away realised I was in the right place at the wrong time. I was reading about the Stone Roses and all these happening bands, and even Primal Scream were on *Top of the Pops*. It was all happening back in Britain. I started thinking about growing up in the 1970s and how awful the '80s had been.'

So Lawrence bought a round-bodied acoustic guitar from a pawn shop, started writing songs and plotted his return. The group he created was Denim, and it was the last thing you expected him to do. The band laid down a partial blueprint for Britpop. Lawrence always had very fixed ideas, and one of these was that Denim was a studio band that never played live. He wanted to sign to a dance label because rock music was finished and it was only DJs who could get records into the charts. He'd seen that with Primal Scream, through whom he knew Andy Weatherall, co-founder of the label he signed to, Boy's Own Records. The label operated through London Records, and for the first time in his career Lawrence was affiliated to a major label.

Another first was that *Back in Denim* was recorded and mixed by a 'name' producer, but Lawrence scrapped John Leckie's mix and his typical attention to detail further delayed the project. *Back in Denim* eventually went out to the music press in the run-up to Christmas 1992. It jump-starts with the pounding Glitter beat of the title track and maintains a powerful mix of glam and pop hooks, encased in a musical framework of Mickey Most productions and Lee Perry. It very consciously denounced the popular classic-rock canon of the Beatles, Byrds, Beach Boys and Big Star. Lyrically, it's the antithesis of Felt's poeticism. Here Lawrence reminisces about his West Midlands childhood in a deadpan voice that casts him as a Brummie Bowie. In the centrepiece song, 'The Osmonds', he remembers men in flares looking like Jesus, chopper bikes, bovver boys, stringy beards, Jeremy Thorpe resigning, George Best retiring and the Birmingham pub bombings in an epic list that shifts surreptitiously between darkness and light. It's a truly great song, but people saw Denim as a jokey band and Lawrence was always regarded as too screwball to be taken seriously.

Back in Denim was a shrewd and clever precursor to Britpop in its method and manifesto, and Lawrence was honourably mentioned in *Select*'s April 1993 'Yanks Go Home!' issue, which arguably marked the beginnings of Britpop. It featured Suede's Brett Anderson in front of a Union Jack on the cover, with mentions for the Auteurs, Pulp, Saint Etienne and Denim. 'It was like Felt all over again,' lamented Lawrence. 'We were just one step ahead of everybody else. We influenced other people to copy what we'd done. I always thought that if people could enter my world, they would really like Denim, but it felt like the Great Wall of China was in front of us.'

Denim were also hampered by muddled decision-making within London Records, who did a deal with independent distributors Pinnacle so that the band could remain independent. What Lawrence wanted was that unstoppable major-label machine behind him. As it was, it was only the press that grasped what Denim were about. *The Face* ran a feature before the record was out, and we had incredible reviews, all leads. *Melody Maker* declared Denim was the most exciting thing to happen since . . . well . . . probably Suede. Then it all went wrong.

The mountain of accolades took London by surprise, so they put the album on hold for three months, during which time the momentum was lost. When Lawrence refused to play live, London said there was nowhere to go with the band. A year later they were dropped. The project hadn't come cheap and, largely through London's ineptness, had fizzled out. Denim signed to Chrysalis subsidiary Echo, but the second album, *Denim on Ice*, took another four years. Lawrence had stockpiled so many songs that it was a double album, but his vision was diluted and he slipped into parody and cheesy humour. Lawrence had been at the forefront of Britpop but ended up being left out in the cold. He was even persuaded by Echo to take Denim on the road, opening for Pulp, a group he'd been on a par with five years earlier. He insisted on using the same top session musicians as on the record and had to cover the income they were losing by being out on the road. It was a financial disaster. The tour was a complete waste of time and money, the band playing in massive venues before anybody had even arrived.

Denim were dropped again but surprisingly picked up by EMI within a year. The group's only release was the stopgap album *Novelty Rock*. The songs were true to its title – short, sharp and silly – but his concept didn't catch on. Lawrence knew that Denim would only survive on EMI if he could come up with a hit record, so he wrote 'Summer Smash' to order. 'It was like something out of a terrible film about the record industry. I took it in two weeks after I'd written it, and the guy was sat there behind the big desk – he should really have had a big cigar – and he goes, "That's a hit record."'

We'll never know. It was 'Single of the Week' on Mark and Lard's daytime Radio 1 show, with the full weight of EMI ready to get behind it – all very encouraging. Then on the Sunday, the day before it was due to be released, Princess Diana died in a car crash. EMI pulled the single on the Monday. 'So they destroyed all the records that week in case it offended the monarchy and dropped me soon after,' sighed the ill-fated Lawrence. 'After "Summer Smash" I felt cursed. So I shut the door, and put the guitar in the cupboard. I had a complete lack of motivation to do anything for two years. It was a mental breakdown.' His life fell apart and he ended up homeless, before getting a council flat by the Barbican in 2008. Cherry Red, the label he started out on, came to his rescue. He was given his own label imprint, West Midlands Records, which released the first album by novelty rockers Go-Kart Mozart in 1999, *Instant Wigwam and Igloo Mixture.* In 2018 Go-Kart Mozart released their fourth album in twenty years.

I often wonder how Lawrence is doing. But you can't call him up or email him. The only way to get in touch is to write to him on a brightly coloured postcard, not a letter because he won't open it, and hope he'll call you back. He is as proud of Denim as he was of Felt, although neither band was validated by hit singles or albums. 'I cannot sell out because there is nothing to sell out. I'd rather do nothing if I can't do it my way. Even having no money shouldn't stop you if you have that resolve.'

The last time I bumped into Lawrence was in the food hall of Marks & Spencer's Moorgate branch, near the Barbican. It was a Saturday and the store doesn't open on Sundays, so you can pick up generously marked-down sandwiches and other bargains. Lawrence was stocking up for the week, but so was I. It's too easy to mock him. Anybody who has worked with him has a hatful of stories they can trot out, and I'm as guilty as anybody. There's a touch of Forrest Gump about him and the happenstance of his career, and he has every right to pose the question, 'What's normal anyways?' When Lawrence says, 'I'll never let my dreams disintegrate,' he means it, and against the odds he still has those dreams intact.

As far as anybody in Britain knew, the Jesus and Mary Chain had gone into hiding from late 1989 to early 1992. They had actually been trekking despairingly across North America during 1989–90, arguing all the way, but there'd been no tours or records at all in 1991. Jim and William had been setting up their own studio. It was a smart move for them to buy the studio at 9a Amelia Street, in south London's Elephant and Castle, which they renamed the Drug Store. It was the perfect set-up, enabling them to work as and when they wanted to without running up studio bills.

Their absence worked to their advantage since in the meantime there had been an upsurge of so-called shoegazing bands – Ride, Moose, Slowdive and Chapterhouse among them – who had all been inspired by *Psychocandy*. When the Mary Chain returned in February 1992, the song that heralded the new album was anything but dream pop. 'Reverence' was powered by an electrifying, corrosive groove, while spewing forth their most nihilistic and controversial lyrics since 'Jesus Fuck'. After the muted response to *Automatic*, Jim and William were uncharacteristically thrilled when 'Reverence' rocketed into the Top 10 and was greeted with the kind of unified rapturous reception they'd not experienced since *Psychocandy*.

It reaffirmed what the Mary Chain were about, and *Honey's Dead* was a consoling mix of grinding, piercing guitars and snarling, lascivious, seductive, low-life lyrics, including the X-rated 'Teenage Lust', side by side with a couple of William's most tortured ballads, the gut-wrenching lament 'Almost Gold' and 'Sundown', where William writes that the planet's more fucked up than he'll ever be. *Honey's Dead* was released on 23 March, just ahead of the UK leg of their ambitious 'Rollercoaster' tour.

Taking its name from their 1990 EP, the Mary Chain's eleven-date tour saw them curating and headlining a bill with My Bloody Valentine, Dinosaur Jr and Blur. 'Rollercoaster' visited mostly UK arenas, ending with three Brixton Academy shows. It was seen as a steal of Lollapalooza, but Jim and William saw it as a return to the package tours of the punk era, when the Clash, Buzzcocks, the Stranglers and the Jam played on the same bill. The line-up was intended to cover all aspects of independent music, hence the presence of Blur, who always came last in the competition to see who could be the loudest. The order of play rotated each night, aside from the Mary Chain closing, and nobody relished following My Bloody Valentine, whose finale was 'You Made Me Realise', their harsh, discordant, endless loop of guitar and feedback at unbearable volume. I saw the Mary Chain more on that tour than on any other and they had a great band, including additional guitarist Ben Lurie, who stuck with them till the bitter end in 1998, while they went through a new rhythm section every year. Jim and William never wanted the Mary Chain to be a 'tight' band, and changing things around was a way of keeping their edge.

Lollapalooza followed, but playing to bored Red Hot Chili Peppers and Soundgarden fans in bright, mid-summer sunlight for six weeks took its toll. Back there for the US leg of 'Rollercoaster' with Spiritualized and Curve, they began the next album at the beginning of 1993, with both Jim and William suffering the usual post-tour burn-out and detox. In the studio they had always been abstemious and disciplined. The new album, however, was recorded almost entirely under the influence of booze and drugs. Eighteen months later *Stoned & Dethroned* marked another departure from their usual recording method: rather than Jim and William playing everything themselves, they recorded as part of a band.

Their frustrations during recording were exacerbated by William's relationship with Mazzy Star singer Hope Sandoval, who was there much of the time, which Jim found hard to deal with. William and Hope's relationship was as volatile as that between him and his brother. Hope does contribute significantly to *Stoned & Dethroned*, on which she sings a duet with Jim called 'Sometimes Always', though the original intention had been to feature Lee Hazlewood rather than Jim in a Lee and Nancy Sinatra-style duet. The track was the album's first single, but it only reached a worrying no. 22, which suggested that Mary Chain fans still wanted feedback squall. The other guest singer was Shane MacGowan. Jim and William were big Pogues fans. Shane loved the Mary Chain, but recording his vocal for the song 'God Help Me' was stressful. After multiple takes were pieced together his contribution turned out to be wonderfully moving. I asked William if he'd written the song for Shane, since the lyric was so right for him. 'It could have been,' he said, 'but "God Help Me" was how I felt at the time.'

Lyrically, *Stoned & Dethroned* was as fucked up as any of their albums. They are pouring their hearts out on songs such as 'Dirty Water', as well as 'God Help Me'. Emotional despair was always a thread running through Mary Chain albums, as much their trademark as their guitar barrage. It really bugged me that critics branded *Stoned & Dethroned* as country-tinged after hearing 'Sometimes Always', which didn't reflect what might be the blackest album they ever made. The climate was changing. We didn't get an *NME* front cover, which was a significant sign of the times. As the title hinted, they'd been dethroned (as well as being stoned when they made it). Released in August, it reached no. 13. Oasis's *Definitely Maybe* came out the same week and became the fastest-selling debut album in the UK. The parallels between the two groups are obvious – Creation, sibling rivalry and bad reputations – but what had always worked against the Reid brothers seemed to work only in the Gallaghers' favour. They learnt quickly how to manipulate the press, whereas Jim and William would never stoop to the barefaced media pandering that was such a feature of Britpop.

I ceased working with them at the beginning of 1995. I hadn't been there when they signed to Creation and I wasn't around for the disintegration three years later. They loved making records and hated the rest of it, which included what I was hired to do. Jim and William were too insular to enjoy the success they had and too principled and uneasy to kiss music-industry backsides. I never wanted to intrude on their privacy but I wish I could have got closer to them over the ten years. Behind the facade they were smart and droll and projected an air of disdainful menace that I never found threatening. A lot of their bad reputation was a hangover from the early days, though it was reinforced later on when they continued touring, especially in America, and couldn't stand the sight of each other. They could be their own worst enemies at times and were much misunderstood. Their music really mattered; it still matters. To have been around when *Psychocandy*, *Darklands* and *Honey's Dead* were released was really something.

12 : K CERA CERA

THE MUTHA' OF ALL AWARDS SAYS

LET THE PEOPLE

CHOOSE

Hannah Collins	☐
Vong Phaophanit	☐
Sean Scully	☐
Rachel Whiteread	☐

WHO IS THE WORST OF THEM ALL

On the 23rd of November 1993 the K. Foundation will award £40,000 [cash] to one of the shortlisted artists who in the opinion of the jury has produced the worst body of work in the preceding 12 months. **The K. Foundation invite you "the people" to be the jury.** Put your mark in the box next to the artist's name of your choice. Then post this ballot paper to the K. Foundation. PO Box 91, HP22 4RS the UK to arrive no later than Friday the 13th of November 1993 Multiple entries will be accepted. Visit the special exhibition of the four shortlisted artist's work opening at the Tate Gallery. London on the 3rd of November 1993 and fully flex your artistic critical faculties or just stay at home and use your innate prejudices. Either way don't waste this chance to promote public discussion in contemporary British art

Remember democracy is a gift not a birthright.

Will I be pretty ? Will I be rich. ? THE 1993 K FOUNDATION AWARD

1990–5

The original 'Pure Trance' version of 'What Time Is Love?' had taken the KLF underground and into danceland, and was covered and sampled so often that, facing bankruptcy once again, Bill and Jimmy decided to

The first mysterious K Foundation ad appeared in July 1983. Finally, on 12 September the public were invited to choose the perpetrator of the worst body of art from the same shortlist as that year's Turner Prize.

exploit 'the riff that refused to die' themselves. They added a rap by MC
Bello, sirens, bleeps and plenty of pop thrill, and 'What Time Is Love?
(Live at Trancentral)', featuring Children of the Revolution, was released
in July 1990, reaching a high of no. 5 during its three-month chart life.
Its initial progress was boosted by their first attention-grabbing *Top of
the Pops* appearance, which set the bar for the kind of unmissable, outlandish, theatrical presentations that had people switching on their tele-
visions at 7.30 p.m. on a Thursday purely to watch the KLF.

The rest of 1990 passed quietly, but in the fifteen-month period between
January 1991 and March 1992 the KLF had four consecutive Top 5 hits: '3
a.m. Eternal', 'Last Train to Trancentral', 'Justified and Ancient' and 'America:
What Time Is Love?'. Two of them reached no. 2, while '3 a.m. Eternal' gave
Bill and Jimmy their second no. 1 single. The JAMs also re-entered the fray
with a pulsing litany of northern towns, 'It's Grim Up North', which also
made the Top 10. In March 1991 the soundtrack to *The White Room* was
tactfully released. It peaked at no. 3 and sold over a million copies worldwide by the end of the year, although sales eventually trebled that figure.
The KLF were now coining it to such an extent that even Bill and Jimmy
couldn't spend all the money they were making, however much they tried.

The White Room was a rare let-down that saw them playing it surprisingly safe. It was too diverse and too polished, and was such an anticlimax because for two years the KLF were the most exciting and original
pop phenomenon the world over. In January 1992 it was revealed that
they were the best-selling pop outfit in Britain, which was all the more
remarkable because KLF Communications was such a small-scale operation: they were self-managed, they made the records, produced them
and came up with the video concepts, a combination of feats that meant
they were self-sufficient in every aspect of the pop process, including
loading boxes of records into the back of a van.

There was nobody to contain them and nothing to stop them rethink-
ing and re-examining increasingly elaborate goals. Money was never an
obstacle to anything they wanted to do, nor an incentive. They never
thought, 'What shall we do?' but 'What would the JAMs do now?' or 'What

should the KLF do next?' and soon 'What the fuck is the K Foundation all about?' In the world of the KLF everything was possible.

At the beginning of their remarkable run of success, KLF Communications was still operating on a shoestring, not unlike a stock theatre company. They'd pull in friends and associates – not least Jimmy's wife Cressida, Bill's partner Sallie Fellowes, Jimmy's brother Simon and film-maker Bill Butt – to make their low-budget videos and eye-catching *Top of the Pops* appearances look so spectacular. Cressida helped with the design and choreography, while the others lent a hand building the sets and models, making the costumes and eventually prancing around in them. They brought in some so-called professionals, myself included, and crucially Scott Piering's TV/radio promotions outfit Appearing. They were amassing a repertory team of DJs, engineers, producers, musicians, rappers and singers – Maxine Harvey, Ricardo da Force, MC Bello, Wanda Dee, Duy Khiem, Tony Thorpe, Nick Coler and Mark Stent – each of whom played their part at different times. They all had the ability to think and act instinctively and in tune with Bill and Jimmy.

Bill and Jimmy were both in their thirties when they started up the JAMS and had long since parked their egos. They weren't irresponsible kids fucking up; they were irresponsible adults who only occasionally fucked up. They were motivated by setting new challenges but had the skills to back them up. I don't think they analysed why they did anything; the driving force was basically, 'OK, let's go do it . . . or die trying.' They left it for others to offer retrospective criticism or look for cryptic meanings.

The bigger they got, the more anonymous they became. They didn't see themselves as pop stars and at the height of their commercial success went largely unrecognised. They were often photographed in the music press, but on TV or in videos they were hooded figures, their faces concealed beneath a cowl with a single protruding horn, or else hunched over guitars, wearing oilskins, their backs to camera. Instead, they gave prominence to the singers and rappers who fronted their records. On their final *Top of the Pops* appearance they were inside two suffocating life-sized ice-cream cones designed for them at great expense by *Spitting Image* puppet-makers Fluck and Law.

The music press still offered a safety net. We were still getting cover stories in the music weeklies and specialist magazines; Bill and Jimmy even reviewed the singles in the *NME* and paid some lip service to the pop press. There wasn't a broadsheet piece about them till 1991, by which time they'd had two Top 5 hits and a Top 3 album. The serious press was dismissive and condescending, displaying that in the way they do it best: by ignoring them. For the tabloids, of course, they were simply bonkers. So we stopped doing interviews altogether. It was only radio play and TV that really mattered. Taking their own advice from *The Manual*, the essentials were to be on the Radio 1 play list and to make a splash on *Top of the Pops*. I never kidded myself that what I was doing was anything other than window dressing.

Nothing in 1991 topped the KLF's celebration of the summer solstice. They flew a group of fifty people to an unknown destination – actually the Isle of Jura, off Scotland's west coast – to document and be part of an unspecified event. The centrepiece was the dramatic burning of a sixty-foot wicker man in a pagan ceremony they called 'The Rites of Mu'. The invitees were journalists and industry folk – one representative from each territory – who were required to don yellow robes, chant 'Mooooo' and take part in a procession ahead of the ritual burning. It ended with a post-ritual rave, and the next day they returned to the mainland via a stopover in Liverpool, where the KLF's acolytes took to the stage to sing 'Justified and Ancient' at the Festival of Comedy.

I refused to go along. I was behaving like 'the difficult publicist' again. I didn't agree with their choice of taking *ID* magazine, and said there was no point in my being there. 'The Rites of Mu' was something Bill and Jimmy admitted had no real purpose other than to do it. 'Not everything is a publicity stunt,' said Bill at one point, which only made me madder. My beef was being kept in the dark about what they had in store. I wasn't prepared to turn up at Glasgow airport with my passport, heading for God knows where. I'm just not one for orchestrated, enforced participation, so I missed out on something quite amazing. I consoled myself that staying home was better than freaking out on a barren island.

The year ended on a high that made up for it. 'Justified and Ancient (All Bound for Mu Mu Land)' was a song that had opened the JAMs' *1987* album (under the title 'Hey Hey We Are Not the Monkees') and closed *The White Room*, but it had been given a complete facelift. It's the apotheosis of the KLF's recording career. Everything that was great about them is encapsulated in that one single and its accompanying video, not least for incongruously featuring Tammy Wynette as the Queen of the Lost Continent of Mu. It was Jimmy who suggested asking her to sing the lead vocal; it was the ultimate example of their ability to identify the component that turned good into great. Through Clive Davis at Arista, their old-school US record-label man, approaching Wynette had been surprisingly straightforward. Bill flew to Nashville to record her vocal in a downtown studio. Tammy insisted he stay at her expansive First Lady Acres estate, and even cooked him grits for breakfast. By the evening he was on a flight back. Speaking ahead of her show at the London Palladium on 24 November, just before the single was released, she said, 'I don't think it's a love song. It's called "Justified and Anxious".'

She'd learnt the title by the time she spoke to Terry Staunton, while she was in London to shoot the video. She also told him that she 'knew about ice cream vans but I'd never heard of a 99. Bill explained it to me and now it makes perfect sense'. Filmed at Pinewood's massive 007 stage, Wynette sits on a throne in the gargantuan video, atop a pyramid with steps leading down to the water. There, our two hooded figures sail away in a mini-submarine, as Wynette and her mermaid-like backing singers and dancers gleefully wave goodbye. It was shot back to back with the video for 'America: What Time Is Love?', which made use of the same mini-submarine but added a Viking longship that had been used in Terry Jones's 1989 film *Erik the Viking*. The KLF gave it to the Dark Age Society afterwards. The two extravagant video shoots set them back £250,000. I went down to the 'Justified and Ancient' shoot and was introduced to Tammy Wynette. She was utterly charming and signed my copy of the twelve-inch. 'Mu Mu Land looks a lot more interesting than Tennessee,' she said, 'but I wouldn't want to live there.'

Although it was the bookies' favourite, 'Justified and Ancient' was denied the Christmas no. 1 spot by the death of Freddie Mercury and the re-release of Queen's 'Bohemian Rhapsody'. Asked to appear on the Christmas *Top of the Pops*, Bill and Jimmy wanted to perform '3 a.m. Eternal' as a thrash-metal version with Ipswich hardcore merchants Extreme Noise Terror (they'd already begun recording a speed-metal album to be called *The Black Room*). The producers thought it unsuitable and turned them down.

In January it was announced that the KLF had been nominated for three BRIT Awards: 'Best British Group' (which they won, shared with Simply Red), 'Best Producer' and 'Best Album'. They were also invited to open the 11th annual BRIT Awards show, to be held on 12 February at London's Hammersmith Odeon, but in the time in between something snapped. Both Bill and Jimmy were showing signs of an increasingly fragile mental state, a result of the extreme exhaustion that hit them at the beginning of the new year. However relentless their capacity for work, nobody could continue operating at that level without eventually spiralling out of control. I could see Bill was cracking up; with Jimmy it was harder to tell.

You don't invite the KLF to perform live at a stuffy industry event unless you are expecting them to make headlines the next day. The year before Jonathan King, who was now organising the event for the third time, had withdrawn the KLF's invitation after hearing of plans to fill the stage with a horde of spear-carrying Zulus and white angels, while Bill and Jimmy rode in astride a pair of elephants. What they proposed in 1992 was far more doable, although King must have suspected they had something up their sleeves beyond the shock value of an unrecognisable, ear-splitting version of '3 a.m. Eternal' with Extreme Noise Terror.

We met up every day in the run-up to the event, and at the beginning of the week they told me what they were thinking of doing. Put simply, it was to carve up a dead sheep live onstage and throw buckets of blood over the front rows of the auditorium, where the industry bigwigs would be seated. This would be in front of a likely ten million TV viewers in the UK and seventy-five million worldwide. If I initially thought, 'You're joking,' I soon realised they meant every word. They had flipped. They'd had enough. They wanted to quit and disappear, and they wanted it to be permanent. There was no coming back from what they were planning, it was such an act of artistic suicide and extreme bad taste. It would have alienated the industry and the public.

They told me they were having sleepless nights over it, and once I knew, so was I. Rightly or wrongly, I thought, 'I can't let you go through with this,' so on the Tuesday before the event I leaked the story to the *Daily Star* and the *Sun*. That would be enough to alert the organisers and the BBC, who would nix the idea. In the early hours of the next morning I met up with Jimmy and Bill, who had driven up to Northampton in a van and returned with the carcass of a sheep, bought from a local slaughterhouse; there were several buckets of blood on the side. Bill opened the back doors to the van and there it was, a dead sheep with blood congealing around its mouth. I'm a city-dwelling wimp, and I felt queasy. I'd never seen a dead animal, and it looked huge. It was the morning of the rehearsal at Hammersmith Odeon, where I'd also arranged to meet Danny Kelly and Kevin Cummins from the *NME* to make final arrangements about the cover story they'd agreed to do. I said nothing about the *Sun* and the *Star* and hadn't checked whether anything had run, but Bill and Jimmy were hauled backstage, where BBC lawyers took them to one side and told them the 'rumoured stunt' would have serious legal implications. I'd left by then, having sorted arrangements for the *NME* – Bill and Jimmy would meet them at Jimmy's place later in the afternoon – so I went back to the office. Aside from anything else the BRIT Awards that year was a black-tie affair, so I had to change and then get back to Hammersmith and take my seat – thankfully a good halfway back.

'THE KLF VERSUS ENT,' hollered Bill. 'This is Freedom Television.' And the games commenced. Dressed in a kilt and full-length leather coat, he was spewing out indecipherable new lyrics berating the BPI to something that sounded more like Motörhead's 'Ace of Spades' than '3 a.m. Eternal'. It was fucking loud too. At the end, now chomping on a cigar and for no apparent reason walking on crutches, Bill produced a machine gun and fired a burst of blanks at the startled audience. The rest of the group fell about in an act of standard guitar-abusing rock 'n' roll petulance, while Bill and Jimmy hurled the contents of two buckets into the crowd. To a few pantomime jeers it was clear they contained nothing but a kind of confetti.

They'd clearly had a Plan B. Even Bill and Jimmy didn't carry a machine gun and a box of blank cartridges around with them. It was a real weapon too, not a plastic toy, as was reported. At the run-through Bill had pretended to gun people down with the crutch, but I'd thought nothing of it. Nor did I know that at the end of their performance, an American voice (Scott Piering's) would boom out over the PA system, announcing, 'Ladies and gentlemen, the KLF have now left the music business.' I'm not sure that even registered with me – I was too relieved they hadn't chucked blood over the audience – but it did dawn on me that the KLF's performance hadn't caused much of a furore at all. People were only taken aback by the deafening racket. The only visible protest had been when eminent Hungarian conductor Sir Georg Solti, who had been sat in the front row, fled the auditorium, pursued by people with clipboards, within seconds of Extreme Noise Terror striking the first chords of '3 a.m. Eternal'.

Whether the KLF had left the music business or not, they had left the building, and they hurtled off in their van, with only a dead sheep for company. I sat through the rest of the show not knowing whether they were accepting their BRIT Award or not, so the second-best moment of a dreary show was seeing a motorcycle courier in full leathers and helmet dashing onstage to pick up their gong, while a bemused Mick Hucknall looked on. Backstage they had tried to deny the fake courier access, but he managed to break away, get up onstage and grab their gong, only to be relieved of it by security when he came offstage. I didn't stick around too long after the show, but there was no buzz about the KLF's antics.

I rang Pam at the office a few hours later, who said Danny Kelly had called in a strop to say that Bill and Jimmy hadn't shown up. A tuxed-up Danny wasn't happy sitting around all afternoon with the boys from ENT. I was due to meet Bill and Jimmy the next morning, so I assured Danny I'd sort the interview out, hoping they hadn't scarpered for good. When I turned up at the post-awards party at the Royal Lancaster Hotel, everybody was talking about two masked men who had dumped a dead sheep by the entrance before driving off, hotly pursued by the police. Tied to the carcass was a note saying, 'I died for you. *Bon appetit!*' The next day strict vegetarian Jimmy was concerned by their depositing the dead sheep outside the hotel. He was worried they had gone too far. It made me feel better about scuppering their original plans. I never owned up to it, although they must have known. It was never even discussed.

The post-BRITs reactions were predictable. The dead-sheep incident eclipsed Bill's gunfire burst, and the KLF were blasted as sick. 'Teenage fans screamed in horror as masked men heaved the animal into the hotel entrance,' railed the *Star*, who quoted an RSPCA spokesman who was 'appalled at young fans seeing their idols pull such stunts'. The broadsheets and red-tops ignored the ceremony itself, beyond saying who had won what.

When the *NME* piece ran, Danny Kelly said he'd been appalled when Bill cited the guy from the Hungerford massacre – Bill couldn't recall his name (Michael Ryan). 'We looked into our souls and entered into the same arena that Charles Manson must have entered,' he said by way of explaining that he'd reached a point where he was capable of doing something more horrific than anything he could have contemplated previously. The day before the BRITs I'd been sitting in a pub with Bill and Jimmy, where a sleep-deprived, wild-eyed Bill was talking about taking an axe and cutting off his hand onstage. We were all laughing nervously, but he was so maniacal it wouldn't have taken much to trigger him to do it.

At the time we all thought the announcement that the 'KLF have now left the music business' was a joke. I'm not sure Bill and Jimmy knew they meant it till the futility of 'getting back to business as usual' during

March confirmed they'd lost the plot. They'd gone back into the studio with Extreme Noise Terror to record *The Black Room*, its title now taking on a truer meaning in keeping with their precarious mental state. Within a few days the sessions were abandoned.

I heard two or three tracks sometime later, but the only one that stuck with me was one called '38', on which Bill despairingly screamed 'I'm thirty-eight and I'm losing control' again and again and again. It reminded me of Peter Finch in *Network* hollering, 'I'm mad as hell and I'm not going to take it any more', to passers-by outside his window. In the film his character, Howard Beale, threatens to commit suicide on live television.

The final KLF single, 'America: What Time Is Love?', duly appeared two weeks after the BRITs. It was more overblown than anything they'd ever done. It had been five years since they first pressed up five hundred copies of 'All You Need Is Love'. They once said they'd originally planned their first album to be a cover of the entire *Deep Purple in Rock*, till they got into sampling instead, so for their parting single they recruited former Purple frontman Glenn Hughes to scream over a jumble of screeching rock guitars, Wagner, 'Song of the Volga Boatmen', Motörhead and hardcore techno. They only very discreetly sampled the original 'What Time Is Love?' riff.

Despite scrapping *The Black Room* sessions, Bill and Jimmy had to return to the studio to remix some of their hits from 1991 for the umpteenth time, for a compilation they owed to one of their licensees. They revisited 'Make It Rain' from *The White Room*. Searching for ideas, they booked a bunch of session singers, who they instructed to sound like 1960s Parisian vocal group the Swingle Singers in order to jazz it up. Bill rang me, saying, 'It's not working. It's rubbish.' Jimmy said, 'I just don't want any more of this. I think we're done with music.' It was all meaningless. It had become too easy to be them and rattle off the hits, knowing that whatever they did was going to be lapped up by adoring fans and drooling critics. Only now it wasn't so easy; they couldn't do it any more. In March Bill had even applied for a job as a warden at a nature reserve near Arundel, in Sussex. He had always been a keen bird-watcher. He got the job too. I asked him, 'Do they actually know who you *are*?' And Bill said, 'Yes, I told them I'm a musician, wanting to take some time off.'

At the beginning of April I went with Bill to Brighton to see the 'Rollercoaster' tour. He wasn't too interested in watching the groups, but backstage he seemed happy enough talking to Jim and William Reid, Damon from Blur, Douglas Hart and Bobby Gillespie, and every so often I heard a loud, deeply Scottish cackle coming from Bill's direction. He got completely pissed. It was the first time I'd ever seen him drunk. We came back on a late train and he fell asleep.

A few weeks later Bill called to say it was over and that he and Jimmy were going to disappear for a while. They were taking out an ad on the back page of the *NME* to make the announcement the following week, and he wanted to let me know. It was a tongue-tied conversation both ways. Bill apologised in advance for all the calls he knew I was going to get, adding that they weren't going to be around. The rumour was that he and Jimmy fled to Mexico, but I'm not sure they ever left the country. I'd known the end was coming but I was still shocked. I didn't ask about any future plans.

The ad ran in the issue dated 16 May 1992. After a typically ostentatious preamble, the statement read: 'For the foreseeable future, there will be no further record releases from the Justified Ancients Of Mu Mu, The KLF, or any other past, present, or future name attached to our activities. And as of now all our past releases are deleted . . .' It was dismissed by many as a publicity stunt, another grand gesture to set up a triumphant return at a later date, and it was flawed, of course. In reality, they had licensing deals with Arista in the US and Toshiba in Japan, and other deals in European territories, and the decision to delete everything wasn't theirs to make. It wasn't an entirely token act; they were, after all, cutting off any future royalties by making no further recordings.

Bill and Jimmy had turned the traditional Faustian pact on its head. They were trying to buy back their souls so they could leave behind not just the music industry, but that monster of their own creation, the KLF. They had grown tired of their own success and infamy. Whatever they did they'd have to top the next time. The public and the media were waiting, open-mouthed, to see what that might be, and Bill and Jimmy were concerned they were slipping into self-parody. There was a danger that success at the level they had achieved was now inhibiting them. The industry which they had always operated outside of was now swallowing them up. They became victims of their own success, and rather than get away with murder any longer, they committed career suicide instead.

As the dust settled, the final KLF Communications Information Sheet, appropriately enough no. 23, was the final word from King Boy and Rockman:

> Have the real Justified Ancients Of Mu Mu slipped unseen from our here and now into some other reality to create havoc and intrigue, leaving Jimmy Cauty and Bill Drummond to ponder on the footnote in rock legend that is their legacy? [. . .] Do they gather dust with Ashton Gardner and Dyke, the Vapours, and the Utah Saints, or does their influence live on in unseen ways, permeating future cultures?

The K Foundation

Nothing further was heard from Bill Drummond and Jimmy Cauty until 23 February 1993, when they announced they were investing much of the money that KLF Communications had made and which was still rolling in from around the world in setting up the K Foundation, of which they were both trustees. The K Foundation was a body dedicated to 'the advancement of kreation'. One of its first acts was to record a piece of music entitled 'K Cera Cera (War Is Over If You Want It)' with the Red Army Choir. This was to become the interstellar anthem of the K Foundation. The recording, however, would only be made available once world peace had been firmly established. They hoped it would be played at various major sporting events, mass rallies and music festivals.

It was sent to Michael Eavis to play at Glastonbury, but he thought it was one of the worst things he'd heard in his life.

After nearly eight months everybody's favourite pranksters were back. The press assumed they'd formed another band. I said that wasn't the case, but I had no idea what it was all about. Nor had they. The K Foundation was an idea with very little flesh on the bone, except that its aim was to 'go further'. It was an open mandate.

Then, beginning in July 1993, the first of a number of mysterious full-page ads appeared on the back page of the *NME*, headed 'Divide & Kreate' and with a six-inch K Foundation logo in the centre. Like all the ads that followed, it was printed in white type on a black background. The ad made little sense, while the next two were mere statements of fact about the Red Army Choir recording. The next ad on 18 July left nobody the wiser. 'Time Is Running In,' it stated. 'Switch to K Time Now'. If the point was to get people talking, it was working. 'What's with all these ads?' I'd be asked. 'No fucking idea,' I'd say in one way or another to KLF-starved fans who were still hoping it was all a smokescreen for a new record.

Then, on 1 August, another ad in the *Independent* commanded us to 'Abandon All Art Now' and 'Await Further Instructions'. Next came 'Major Rethink in Progress'. This was a holding measure while Bill and Jimmy did just that, piecing together the idea of a K Foundation Award. Then at last, on 29 August, they revealed their intentions: 'It has been brought to our attention that you did not Abandon All Art. Serious Direct Action is therefore necessary. The K Foundation will award £40,000 to the artist who has produced the worst body of work in the last 12 months.' This was to be handed over on 23 November. Their nominees were the artists selected for the Turner Prize, which was also being announced on that day. Finally, on 12 September the K Foundation invited the public to nominate the worst artist from the Turner Prize shortlist. 'Let The People Choose' was followed by a ballot paper on which you made your mark against one of Rachel Whiteread, Vong Phaophanit, Sean Scully or Hannah Collins, before returning it to the K Foundation. The Foundation's prize of £40,000 was double that of the Turner Prize.

By a quirk of fate, Rachel Whiteread won the awards for both best and worst artist. She had been the clear winner of the K Foundation's prize too – or loser – with a substantial percentage of the three thousand-plus votes cast. Of all the nominees she was by far the best known because of the controversy over her concrete casting of a house in a derelict part of London's East End. She was informed by the K Foundation that she had won their award on the morning of the Turner Prize ceremony, and at that point agreed to accept.

The night of 23 November 1993 was one of the absolute best and weirdest nights of my life. It unfolded thus:

6.30 p.m. Twenty-five invited witnesses are welcomed by the K Foundation's master of ceremonies David Ball at the Gloucester Hotel in west London.

7.30 p.m. The guests are to be transported to a secret location near London to witness and document the 'Amending of Art History'. Poor visibility and freezing conditions mean that the party cannot be taken by helicopter as planned. Instead, waiting for them at the pick-up point, are seven stretch-limo Cadillacs with luxury leather interiors and chilled champagne provided. Even the drivers don't know where they are heading, but they are instructed by Ball, who leads the fleet in a gold Cadillac.

The entourage is made up of a mixture of people, including music journalists from the *NME* and *The Face*, Pete Wylie and Tony Wilson; others are from the art world, with writers from the *Modern Review* and *Frieze* magazine and sculptor Andy Elton among the invitees. Elton had written a series of angry letters to the K Foundation, which he dismissed as a piece of shit. Five arts editors and writers from the broadsheets complete the party, along with me and my assistant Louise. All the witnesses are given orange construction helmets and vests to wear.

I decide I have to be professional, for a while at any rate, and travel in the car with the broadsheet editors. They are po-faced and dubious and know very little about the KLF. I tell them they will soon be receiving further instructions. I envy Louise swigging champagne in the fun car with Wylie and the music journos. For now I have to keep focused as the inquisition will soon be stepped up.

8.00 p.m. We stop at Heston motorway services. All twenty-five witnesses are presented with a white envelope. There is £1,650 in crisp, unused £50 notes in each one and a page of instructions announcing plans for an exhibition, *Money: A Major Body of Cash*, which the K Foundation plans to stage the following year. One of the £50 notes is effectively a sample to be taken and spent as proof the money is not counterfeit.

The arts editors almost turn on me after being handed their envelopes. 'It's not a bribe,' I assure them. 'Read the instructions, it's all made clear.' 'Humourless buggers,' I think. It is further explained that every witness is being given £1,600, which collectively makes up the £40,000 K Foundation award.

The Turner Prize is sponsored by Channel 4, whose £20,000 prize money is coincidentally equalled by the amount the K Foundation has spent on advertising time. In effect, the K Foundation is paying for both awards. Unbeknownst to the witnesses, the K Foundation has booked space during the three ad breaks in Channel 4's hour-long coverage of the Turner Prize ceremony. The first, in trademark white out of black type, notifies viewers that 'the motorcade to the Amending Of Art History is on its way'.

9.00 p.m. The motorcade arrives at a clearing in a wood near Woking, where we all get out, now standing in a cold, frosty field. The sight before us, lit by four arc lights in each corner, is amazing. Two orange Saracen armoured cars driven by Bill and Jimmy are circling the perimeter, blaring out Abba's 'Money, Money, Money' and the Red Army Choir's 'K Cera Cera (War Is Over If You

Want It)', interspersed with the Greenwich Mean Time pips.

Once our eyes adjust to the dazzling light, everyone is drawn to the sight of a huge easel in the middle of the clearing, to which £1 million in bundles of fresh fifties is nailed. Two hefty bouncers in black suits and dicky bows are stood either side, both as stern-looking and uncommunicative as the Household Guards outside Buckingham Palace.

Hot soup and rolls are served, while everybody is handed a catalogue that explains that this is the first in a series of K Foundation art installations, all involving sums of cash. The reserve price of the works has been set at half the face value of the cash involved, including the one in front of us all, *Nailed to the Wall*, up for sale at £500,000, postal applications only. The exhibits will decrease in value, down to a fiver as the reserve price for the £10 exhibit. The point which was ultimately lost was that the face value would eventually be diminished by inflation, while the artistic value should increase.

9.15 p.m. MC Ball barks instructions through a megaphone, telling us that we have to take our £1,600 and nail it to another pallet. This will later be delivered – as a guilt-edged piece of artwork – to the K Foundation's prize-winner, Rachel Whiteread. Chaos ensues while Ball tries to herd everyone into performing their task before ushering them back to the cars. It is already clear that there are four spaces where no wads of money have been nailed down, while other wads look decidedly skimpy. Despite requests for the four people to come forward, nobody moves. I go up to David Ball and ask what we he wants to do. 'Nothing,' he says. 'Unless you want to frisk everyone.' There is a tight schedule to keep to, so the motorcade moves on. Later it is revealed that the prize money is £8,400 light.

At this point I'm beginning to think I'm living out a modern-day Ealing comedy. Any moment now Alec Guinness will run

225

out in front of the motorcade in a bright white suit. Where is Jack Warner, the sensible beat copper from *The Ladykillers*, to appeal to everybody's sense of honesty and get them to cough up the missing loot?

The arts writers are still not very amused. They are appalled that four people have stolen the money. The lady from the *Telegraph* then realises she's actually nailed down £1,650 – 'I forgot we were supposed to keep one back.' I decide it's time to uncork the champagne and look forward to arriving at the Tate, where I can ditch my sceptical and tiresome charges and join the rest of the now boozy and coked-up members of the entourage.

At 9.45 p.m. Rachel Whiteread is announced in the third TV ad break as the winner of the K Foundation award. She has yet to learn she has won the Turner Prize too.

10.45 p.m. We arrive at the Tate, and David Ball takes the prize in its gilded frame from the back of his Cadillac and hands it to a man in a balaclava, the K Foundation's trusty aid Gimpo, who chains it to the Tate's railings. As the art world elite start filing out of the ceremony for the prize-giving, they are unsuspectingly greeted by a throng of merrily drunken people in plastic vests variously chanting either 'Take the money' or 'Burn the money'.

Whiteread is now refusing to accept the K Foundation award. Amid the confusion somebody rushes inside to tell her that if she doesn't come out to accept her rightful prize within five minutes, the cash will be burnt. Gimpo is standing with matches and petrol at the ready. 'He's totally wired,' I remember overhearing one of the broadsheet witnesses say. 'You can see it in his eyes, he's really going to do it.' Eventually, a flustered Rachel Whiteread appears, mutters that she is 'honoured', grabs the frame full of cash – missing £8,400 – and fights her way back inside. It is later explained that the full amount will be topped up the next day; she in turn says she will give the money to needy artists and to Shelter. It is not only the

K Foundation that has ruined her big night; she has already learnt that Bow council has voted to demolish her *House*.

Midnight: At an after-show event at Filthy McNasty's bar, Bill and Jimmy, who witnessed the events at the Tate from a vehicle parked nearby, are still in hiding in the adjacent smaller bar, while those witnesses who have come to Filthy's are buying drinks with brand-new £50 notes, some of which have clearly been tightly rolled up to suit a different purpose. The barman eventually refuses to take any more large-denomination notes. He's totally out of change.

There was major coverage in the press the next day, but it was all about the high jinks outside the Tate. The cavalcade of Cadillacs, the amendment of art history and the £1 million art installation that was meant to be the centrepiece of the night's activities were scarcely mentioned. The conceptual-art aspect had been dwarfed by the 'spoof' award.

Once it became a news story, the art critics were let off the hook. They didn't have to bother commenting. It was simpler to dismiss Bill and Jimmy as pop stars with too much money and even less sense who were merely dabbling in the art world. It was Bill and Jimmy's recurring nightmare; they'd gone to great lengths and great expense, only for the main event to be written off as another silly scam. They were no better than McCartney, Sting or Bowie and their inept efforts as painters. The K Foundation were dubbed as self-styled art terrorists. One of my companions in the limo couldn't even get Bill's name right – he named him as Phil Drummond. And a day later it was yesterday's news. There had been no attempt to explain or even mention *Money: A Major Body of Cash* and their intention to stage a series of exhibitions. Bill and Jimmy had effectively squandered what eventually amounted to over £250,000 in vain.

The *Guardian* did say, 'As a PR exercise it was a Picasso,' but even that was just another way of saying 'publicity stunt', which still begged the question as to what they were publicising. It was too obvious a statement about art and money that had been made before. Rachel Whiteread's agent Karsten Schubert certainly thought so, commenting in the *Guardian* that

'The thinking behind it was confused and contradictory. The whole affair was a non-event. They achieved nothing and they were left looking like real prats.' He called Bill and Jimmy cowards for not being there, with Bill telling him it was because they were publicity shy.

Whiteread felt she'd been morally blackmailed. She came out of it with great dignity, having been placed in an impossible situation. What always surprised me in the light of what took place nine months later was how appalled everybody was at the idea of Bill and Jimmy – or their man Gimpo – threatening to burn £40,000. Would they have gone that far? Absolutely.

When Bill and Jimmy returned the £1 million from *Nailed to the Wall* to the Bank of England, officials pointed out that because all the notes had a hole through the middle, they were unusable. It is a criminal offence to tear notes, put holes in them or deface them, but not, apparently, to burn them. The K Foundation was fined a further £60,000 to cover replacing the spoilt £1 million, which was later burnt by the Bank of England.

A few months later I went with Bill to a reading by Iain Sinclair that Paul Smith had organised, and afterwards we went to a pub, where Bill ended up standing right next to Rachel Whiteread at the bar. She had no idea it was him; he didn't know it was her either. After Bill left I was introduced to her by Paul as somebody who worked with the K Foundation. I told her what I did, and she said disgustedly, 'And you can sleep at night?' She paused before adding, 'Fucking KLF.' So I thought I should tell her she'd just missed Bill, and her face darkened. 'If I'd known that, I'd have set my boyfriend on him.' She glanced down at her glass ruefully and said, 'You're lucky this is empty.' I offered to buy her another. She smiled but declined.

The following year the *Guardian* rang me to ask what the K Foundation had planned for the 1994 Turner Prize. I've said some dumb things when put on the spot over the years, but this time I came up with a real peach: 'Nothing,' I said. 'Enlightenment never strikes twice.'

23 August 1994

In 1994 Bill and Jimmy spent the early months trying to make arrangements to exhibit *Money: A Major Body of Cash*, but all attempts failed. Even those who were interested eventually said it was impossible due to issues of security and insurance. Sometime in June Bill and Jimmy's frustrations reached the point where they ended up thinking, 'Fuck it, let's just burn the lot.' The idea grew from unthinkable to real. That in turn raised the questions of where and how they would do it. They made further attempts to organise some kind of public torching, under the auspices of a gallery or through a recognised agent, but this hit the same brick wall of health, safety and sanity considerations. It appeared that the art world, still seething at Bill and Jimmy for upstaging the Turner Prize, thought, 'We're not going to let a couple of pop stars buy their way into our world.'

Once they'd decided the only way forward was to burn the money themselves in a neutral location, they brought me in to discuss how best to involve the press, or whether they should at all. We had several meetings during August: some where it was only me; others where Louise or Paul Smith joined us. To begin with the general air was one of levity and bravado as to how best to go about torching the money. There were certainly no ethical concerns. Why they were doing it or whether they should was never discussed. I never confronted them, nor did I once think they wouldn't go through with it. We were discussing it as if we were wondering how best to promote a new album.

By mid-August it got serious, and from frivolous ideas about hiring the Royal Albert Hall or hooded men with protruding horns storming Trafalgar Square with flamethrowers, they settled on there being just one witness. Various names were kicked around. Damien Hirst was first on the list. My suggestion of asking Rachel Whiteread was met with blank stares. They decided that Jim Reid was the chosen one. I only knew Jim as a former *Record Mirror* journalist who hated all the groups I worked with. Worse still, he liked the Jam and most of the groups I hated. He and Bill were friends, and he was now writing for the *Observer*. There was never any question of me being there. I was frustrated they were burning the money so inconspicuously; it denied me the opportunity of being in the thick of it, as I had been with the Amending of Art History. It wasn't long, though, before I came to appreciate that I had been spared the nightmare of reliving it.

I knew that burning the money in secret was the only way, otherwise it would have been another grand gesture, another scam, and we wouldn't still be discussing it today. 'People think we're jokers,' Bill said at one point. 'You know me, Mick, I'm very dour. I approach everything I do very seriously and I'm usually the last person to see a funny side to it.' They told Jim to be ready to travel with them on 22 August and to tell no one. He knew they had the money with them but thought they planned to bury it. Only when they lit the first £50 note did he realise what they actually had in mind. The only other attendee was Gimpo. It was only at the last minute that they thought to take along a camera.

So on 23 August 1994 Jimmy Cauty and Bill Drummond set fire to £1,000,000 of their own money and burnt the lot. It was witnessed by Jim Reid and Gimpo. It took place in a derelict boathouse on the Isle of Jura, Scotland, and the burning was filmed. Jim wrote about the experience in the *Observer* on 5 September. The next day Louise and I sat in the office, expecting a deluge of calls. I had absolutely no idea what I was going to say but I prepared various trivial examples of how far a million pounds would stretch: the wing of a jet plane, a yard of motorway, a limb of a footballer. It didn't matter because nobody rang. Nobody believed it was true. It was too shocking and improbable to contemplate, even for a pair of known pranksters. It had to be a hoax. Nobody in their right minds would burn a million pounds.

Only when a local Scottish islands paper reported clumps of burnt notes being washed up on shore did people start to think it just might be true. Finally the calls started coming in, usually asking, 'Did they really do it?' 'I wasn't there,' I'd say, 'but I believe they did.' And I did believe it too. I'd met them at Euston station on their return. They were carrying two large suitcases that contained the ashes, and we'd arranged for Kevin Westenberg to photograph them. It was in their eyes. They looked devastated by something; they looked different. My usual comment was that they looked like GIs returning from Vietnam.

The reactions to the money-burning came in three stages. The first was disbelief. The second was abject indignation. It didn't matter whether people believed it or not, the prevalent view was that it was indefensible. So the second wave of calls was more often abusive, both from journalists and members of the public. I got tired of people saying, 'They could have given some of it to me,' or 'They could have paid off my mortgage.' The outrage was less about the public good the money could have contributed towards than 'What about me?'

The third stage was, 'Why did they burn the money?' – something Bill and Jimmy have been asking themselves ever since. What's significant, twenty-five years later, is that it's gone down in history that the K Foundation Burnt a Million Pounds, and very few people now question it.

I was never that shocked myself, and I think my response was tempered because I'd been in the music industry for twenty-five years. It was the same for Bill and Jimmy too, and in music-business terms £1 million is nothing. Bill and Jimmy certainly had previous in wasting money on lost causes. Brilliant blew £500,000 of WEA's money on an album that sold diddly-squat. The KLF squandered £250,000, and probably a lot more, shooting *The White Room*, a film that's since been permanently shelved. The two videos for 'Justified and Ancient' and 'America: What Time Is Love?' set them back another £250,000, and two years later the total spend on the Amending of Art History was over £250,000. So there's over a million gone, and for what?

The music industry is a money pit – it certainly was in the 1980s and '90s – and only a few years before Bill and Jimmy's heinous act the House of Love blew £800,000 in less than a year on their debut album for Phonogram. What was commonplace in the 1990s was a group like That Petrol Emotion going unrecouped by over £1 million when they were let go by Virgin. Julian Cope would have been bankrolled by Island for close to that figure when he was dropped. The music industry is essentially a bank for artists, where you can overdraw as much as you like and then the debt is written off. Or perhaps it's more like a casino? The industry gambles more and more on recordings, videos and promotion, throwing good money after bad, particularly in the pursuit of hit singles, knowing that, hit or miss, the artist will rarely earn that money back. That was our background, operating in a music industry run on the basis of 'Spend, spend, spend', then cut your losses.

The £1 million was Bill and Jimmy's money, after all, and twenty-five years later it no longer matters whether they burnt it or not because the idea is out there and it has effectively eclipsed everything they did before. I always thought that was one of their main objectives. Deleting their back catalogue hadn't been enough; they wanted to delete their history, to erase those five years between 1987 and 1992 altogether. Of course, there was no one overriding reason why they burnt a million. No one thing drives anybody to such extremes. It certainly wasn't to make the ultimate art statement, although that must have crossed their minds. They burnt £1 million because they had £1 million, and because in the end, stymied and thwarted by the art establishment, torching it was the only option left.

The most prevalent attitude is still that of the local cabbie in Liverpool who drove me to one of the events at the Bombed Out Church, during the launch of the JAMs book *2023: A Trilogy* in 2017. 'They are cunts, aren't they?' he said angrily, and went on to explain why and how much good they could have done. I wasn't about to try and trivialise £1 million, but I was tempted to tell him that on top of burning it, the money was also taxed as 'drawings', so they did actually contribute £400,000 to health, welfare, education and the defence of the realm.

23 August 1995

On the first anniversary of the burning Bill and Jimmy returned to the Isle of Jura for the premiere of the sixty-three-minute hand-held film that Gimpo had made. *Watch the K Foundation Burn a Million Quid* starts with the first match being struck and ends with the last embers fading. After the screening they discussed why they had done it with the local villagers. They then toured the film, taking it to unlikely and potentially confrontational settings, including Cheltenham Ladies' College, a Mind drop-in centre, an anarchist club in Bradford and a Friends Meeting House. After a full month of screenings during November Bill and Jimmy ceased taking active part in the discussions, although they did continue to attend.

Furthermore, they announced a twenty-three-year moratorium banning them from discussing the reasons why they burnt £1 million on the Isle of Jura. This was announced by the K Foundation in the *Guardian* on 8 December, one of two simultaneous full-page ads that day.

23 December 1995

The second ad, which appeared in the *Independent*, was altogether more mysterious.

In a square white box in the middle of a totally black page the text simply read: 'SIX THOUSAND TWO HUNDRED AND THIRTY SEVEN CANS OF TENNENT'S SUPER'. It was eventually divulged that to celebrate the moratorium, the K Foundation would be distributing said number of cans of Tennent's Super to London's street drinkers on Christmas Eve.

I was to hold the press release until 23 December. It explained that the 6,237 cans were being stacked to form a perfect cube. They saw the 'red, white and blue cans of Tennent's Super as the ultimate 90's icon symbolising the arse-end of our culture'. The cube was to be loaded onto a flatbed truck emblazoned with a Union Jack and driven to the south side of Westminster Bridge, by the Lambeth Palace gates. There they would begin their 'super kitchen round' throughout the known haunts of London's street drinkers since, with the supermarkets and off-licences closed, 'those most in need of alcohol will have their supply cut off'.

We met up to discuss it. Unlike the money-burning, I thought that ethically this was indefensible. Also, their argument was: 'If you were on the street over the holiday, you would rather have a can of Tennent's than a bowl of soup.' Whatever my viewpoint I knew they hadn't thought this idea through. 'The streets will be empty,' I said. 'And there'll be nobody to report it.' The rest of my reasoning went something like this: organisations like Crisis at Christmas will have rounded up all the homeless and found some sort of shelter for them long before midnight on Christmas Eve; and aside from a skeleton staff, the papers and news broadcasters will have all shut up shop, so unless you are committing a terrorist act or bumping off one of the royals, forget it. Any other day of the year, and with enough notice, you'd have a posse of indignant news hounds following you around. At best we might get one of the news agencies to send somebody down, but it would still be days before anything would run. That's how we left it. They took everything I said on board and went ahead as planned.

I wasn't entirely correct that nobody would write about the final act of the K Foundation. A few months later they were sent a cutting from a Christmas Day edition of an Indonesian national newspaper out of Jakarta. The headline story was about two British pop stars who had planned on giving London's homeless a bit of Christmas cheer, but the cans of lager they were distributing had fallen off their lorry in front of the Houses of Parliament. The streets were deserted and the only people to get drunk were Members of Parliament. Bill and Jimmy assured me this was true and they loved it, even more because of the ridiculous spin that the Indonesian hack had put on the story.

1990-8

Pam Young had always been really close to Julian, who'd been living in London since 1987, moving from Tamworth first to Elephant and Castle and then to Tulse Hill. Pam said Julian wanted to come and visit, and I

Krautrocksampler, the second of four books published by Julian Cope during the 1990s. He was already in danger of being taken just as seriously, if not more so, as a writer than a musician.

was thrilled at the prospect of seeing him again. Sometime in January 1990 he cycled over, stuck his head round the door, grinned, bounded in and gave me a huge hug. We sat around, drank gallons of tea, ate beans on toast and nattered like there was no tomorrow, picking up where we'd left off four years ago.

Eventually he produced a white-label copy of an album called *Skellington* in a mocked-up, colour-photocopied sleeve. It was an album he'd talked about in 1985, but it was never recorded. I looked at the titles and there were plenty of songs I knew, including 'Robert Mitchum', which Mac always claimed was his, and, at last, the notorious 'Out of My Mind on Dope and Speed'. In 1985 Cally had told Julian that if he was looking for a new deal, then the *Skellington* songs weren't fit for purpose. So Julian put them to one side to concentrate on the demos for the *Saint Julian* concept, which led him to Island.

Five years later Julian was now at loggerheads with them, and with top dog Clive Banks in particular. Julian had recorded *Skellington* on the sly at London's Townhouse 3 studio in a day and a half during April 1989, but when Banks eventually heard the sketchy, spontaneous, frivolous recordings, he threw up his hands in despair. He said that there was no way Island could release *Skellington*, nor would he allow Julian to release it himself. Banks thought it would ruin Julian's career for ever and he'd be even more of a laughing stock than he was already. Julian had hatched a plan to release it subversively, without Island Records' knowledge or consent. 'Count me in,' I said, and he left me his sole white-label to loan to a sympathetic journalist, and that was that. He trusted me to do the right thing. Conspiring against Island Records was an added bonus.

The sympathetic journalist I approached to review *Skellington* was *Melody Maker* freelancer Bob Stanley. I'd met Bob a few times and knew he was mad about music and mad about Julian. He wasn't the obvious choice because *Melody Maker* was always the most likely to ridicule Julian as some kind of rock nutter; in 1988 he'd been voted their Nobody of the Year. Approaching Bob turned out to be a good call, and his half-page review in February described the album as marvellous, classic Cope gobbledegook. The deal was that *Melody Maker* would follow the review with a feature, Julian's first interview of the 1990s, in which he effectively set out his stall for the next few years in remarkably accurate detail. Julian always planned years ahead and would have entire albums and concepts, even titles and artwork thought out. He'd more or less finished his autobiography and talked excitedly about a new album that in his head was already good to go. *Peggy Suicide* was going to be more rock 'n' roll, very live, at least sixteen songs and over sixty minutes long. He even explained the concept of Sqwubbsy, a monstrous puppet that he'd recently found in a theatrical shop. 'There's nothing worse than a serious artist,' he expounded, 'so you've got to trivialise your trip all the time, but utterly mean it.'

Yet before *Skellington* surfaced, Julian had given his old label Mercury permission to release what could be salvaged from the unfinished third Teardrop Explodes album. Julian suggested Mercury adopt the rejected title for the Teardrop Explodes' debut, *Everybody Wants to Shag the Teardrop Explodes*. His usual line about the abandoned recordings was that they weren't as terrible as he remembered them. They very much fitted in with Julian's new mindset: 'You don't have to put out only your incredible stuff, put out your shit as well.'

The supposedly shit third Teardrops album was much lauded for once and since the *Melody Maker* review of *Skellington* there was a healthy buzz building up around it. For Julian rock 'n' roll was always about capturing the moment. He said this time and time again. It was how all the great rock 'n' roll records of the 1950s and punk and psych records of the 1960s had been made, and that's exactly how he'd recorded *Skellington* – everything was done in one or two takes. It became his default setting from that point onwards. As more and more reviews appeared, *Skellington* struck a chord with the Cope faithful. Although Island threatened to take action over what was effectively a bootleg, they never followed through. It couldn't have escaped their notice that Mr Nobody was becoming a somebody again.

I'd arranged for Julian to write an exclusive report about the poll tax riots in central London for the *NME* on 4 April, which described how a peaceful protest turned into a 'maelstrom of madness' in which the government 'turned the poll tax issue into a fight', he wrote, 'protesters versus the police'. The march marked an unlikely debut appearance by the grotesque seven-foot Sqwubbsy and his companion Big Baby, once they were allowed upstairs on the 2b bus from Tulse Hill to join the protesters. Julian also played his first gig for two years at the Fridge in Brixton, an 'Anti-Poll Tax' benefit headlined by the Wedding Present and Cud. Joined by Donald Ross Skinner on guitar and drummer Rooster Cosby, surprise guest Julian strolled onstage and announced to wild applause, 'Good evening. This group is called Skellington. I'm Julian Cope and I'm not paying my poll tax.'

The Julian of old was not known for displaying any great interest in politics, but now he was inspired to write openly political songs and he never missed an opportunity to express his hatred of Thatcher. In a Q&A piece some years later he was asked what his final three wishes would be. He was going to put an end to Christianity back in 363 AD, bump off Ma and Pa Hitler before they had sex, while the third one involved somebody he knew who had a crush on Margaret Thatcher. 'So he and I would manifest in her front room just before her first election victory. I'd allow him one shag then I'd shoot her dead.'

Julian's answer to Island's threats over *Skellington* was to release another eponymous alter ego album within two months, this time as Droolian; the subterfuge was that it was only being released in Texas to support a campaign to get Roky Erickson out of jail. More fragmented and sonically challenging than *Skellington*, it hinted at the shape of Julian's extracurricular albums to come with its astral ramblings, spoken pieces and off-the-wall incidental music. The cover star was the Cope family dog, Schmelvin.

The promised *Peggy Suicide* was completed in November 1990. It was longer than he'd predicted, its eighteen songs sprawled across more than seventy minutes, and was the real game-changer. The recordings had been made on the QT once again, but this time paid for by Dave Bates out of a Phonogram demo slush fund. He'd agreed to release the album on Mercury but would get his money back if Island had the sense to put it out. In the week before Christmas Julian gave me a personally inscribed white-label copy – to 'Micky the Hoot'.

The last thing I expected, though, was that Island Records would hire me when *Peggy Suicide* was released in March 1991. It laid the ground-work for a complete makeover that would take Julian into the most cre-ative phase of his career, which lasted through the 1990s. *Peggy Suicide* showed the first signs that Julian was beginning to shed the past and reha-bilitate himself. Or, in Cope-speak: 'True fuckheads always win through.' Finally distancing himself from both his beleaguered post-punk persona and earlier pretty-boy pop-star image, the misfit had found his rightful place in the world. Exploring issues of sex, religion, ecology and social collapse, above all *Peggy Suicide* reflected Cope's compassion for the socio-ecological plight of the planet, defining the themes that have pre-vailed in his music ever since.

The album was loose and spontaneous and powered by a guitar-driven garage sound that was rarely better than on 'Hanging Out and Hung Up on the Line' and 'Double Vegetation'. The epic 'Safesurfer' was a scourging song that used Aids as a metaphor and took its title from a German brand of condoms. Julian was brilliantly aided by regular guitarist, sideman and co-producer Donald Ross Skinner and drummer Rooster Cosby. Julian even got to play electric guitar himself, but it was Liverpool's best-kept secret, guitar-hero Mike Mooney, who jacked the songs up to another level.

Peggy Suicide even generated a couple of minor hit singles, in the form of the Caribbean calypso 'Beautiful Love' – a song Julian held back from *My Nation Underground* – and the tough yet funky 'East Easy Rider'. Neither single was a substantial hit, but it no longer bothered Julian because he knew it was the bigger picture that mattered, and the pic-ture was getting bigger all the time. *Peggy Suicide* was moulded into a cohesive whole by Julian's explanatory sleeve notes – a fixture on all his albums since – in which he was unafraid of inviting accusations of self-indulgent preaching or cheap New Age philosophising. To paraphrase one of Julian's favourite sayings, this was no-bullshit-Sherlock time.

Julian, Dorian and their two young daughters, Albany and Avalon, moved from south London to the Wiltshire market town of Calne, just six miles from Avebury, whose Neolithic monuments have never ceased to inspire him. A few years later he would move from the small house in Calne to more spacious converted stables in Yatesbury, usually referred to as 'The Unstables'. His new environment brought him even closer to the Mother Earth of his visions and he was soon to take to the archaeological trail around megalithic Britain. Julian talked freely about writing *The Modern Antiquarian*, explaining it was a guide to Britain's Neolithic remains. Having exhaustively promoted *Peggy Suicide* worldwide, his touring schedules were now arranged as a means of visiting the more remote structures in every corner of Britain.

The first of Julian's solo 'Highlands and Islands' tours opened in Findhorn on 3 July 1992, the six dates taking in the Isles of Skye and Orkney, as well as mainland Aberdeen. These effectively provided the blueprint for his solo performances to this day. He cut an extraordinary sight in Aberdeen, his bleached, flowing locks now perched on top of his head in a haystack-like bun, and dressed in black leggings and Daffy Duck boxer shorts, worn externally, of course. To the delight of everybody, including a rowdy section of dissenting oil-riggers, he cavorted across the stage like Nureyev in *The Nutcracker*. It was almost stand-up, like a New Age Bill Bailey or Eddie Izzard with a catalogue of hit records behind them. Julian thrived on the jeers and heckles as much as the adulation. 'These stone circles blow my mind,' he raved. 'They make me hard and moist at the same time.' There were plenty of songs too, which dispelled any comparison with the original recordings. A barnstorming 'Reynard the Fox' was delivered a cappella, while the Teardrops' chestnut 'Sleeping Gas' saw Julian launch himself into the crowd with a miniature plastic electric guitar. Then, to whoops of joy, he went walkabout, feeling up members of the audience, male and female, before returning to the stage, arms aloft and adoring being adored.

I made as many 'Highlands and Islands' trips as I could over the next few years. The secret was to make sure I went only with journalists I thought of as friends. The journey there alone would have driven me nuts, requiring a lengthy train journey or a couple of flights that ended in a single-engine propeller job like something out of *Only Angels Have Wings*, where you were almost sat in the pilot's lap. One of the best of these excursions involved taking three good friends – music-press vets Max Bell and Gavin Martin, and Pete Clark of the *Standard* – to the Orkneys. The day after we arrived I went with Pete to visit some friends of his who lived in Kirkwall, leaving Max and Gavin in the hotel, where they sat facing a bar stocked with an array of local whiskies. They were on a mission to sample each one shot by shot till they dropped.

They were both a little green around the gills as we journeyed to Hoy on a rust bucket of a ferry the next morning to meet up with Julian. He knew all the ferry times, told us the one to get and assured us he'd meet us on the other side. And he was there, smiling brightly. This was no longer the paranoid Julian hiding behind twitching curtains. After a round of man-hugging we all hiked to the Dwarfie Stane, a hollowed-out rock tomb that was almost an analogy for Julian's plight at Island. Julian wanted some time to himself inside 'to hang', before Gavin squeezed in beside him to conduct the interview. 'I might need a cack so hold your breath,' Julian warned him with an evil grin, while Max and I tried to find our own refuge from the wind and driving rain.

I was making frequent visits to Yatesbury, often accompanying more sceptical companions. 'He's not going to bang on about Mother Earth, stone circles and all that eco-hippy shit is he?' some would ask. 'Don't worry,' I'd be thinking. One of Julian's greatest attributes has always been an ability to turn a potentially dry subject into something highly entertaining. He'd usually drive us around, make a pilgrimage to the man-made Silbury Hill, and then we'd end up at Stones restaurant in Avebury or back at his, where the doubters would soon be all ears, lapping up Julian's every utterance. Anybody I took along, however cynical on the way there, would be buzzing the whole journey back. It's hard to convey just how infectious Julian's conversation is; his enthusiasm is the same whether he's delivering crushing judgements (that the

Apostle Paul was a motherfuckin' lout) or making wild assertions (the seventeen-minute version of 'American Woman' on the Guess Who's *Live at the Paramount* is awe-inspiringly crass). The hardest thing is to keep up with Julian's stream-of-consciousness chatter as his conversation zigzags from environmentalism to pre-Roman history to the occult or Bill Nelson's *Axe Victim*.

Everything is delivered with the same confidence and backed up by mind-boggling sources. He is impossibly well read: his reading list might encompass insurrectionary rock critic Lester Bangs's *Psychotic Reactions and Carburetor Dung*, MC5 manager John Sinclair's *Guitar Army*, philosopher Colin Wilson, archaeologist T. C. Lethbridge, Robert Graves or *The Complete Jung*. So you sit opposite him simply agog as he quotes Vachel Linsday's essay about Chaplin and how Chaplin's films are the portal by which Victorian music hall entered the twentieth century, or reveals how he's filled with what George Gurdjieff called 'Being Duty'. 'It's the artist's job to teach and heal without you feeling you've been taught', was a common theme of his. Only Julian could draw inspiration from T. S. Eliot's essay 'The Metaphysical Poets' to explain why he made *Fried* and *World Shut Your Mouth* in rapid succession, because, to paraphrase Eliot, 'We artists should not sit around on our arses but should bring forth something to educate, to edify and to entertain.' Whether he's summing up Eliot's essay accurately or not, those final three verbs offer the perfect appraisal of Julian's 1990s work ethic.

A few months before heading off to the Scottish isles again in the autumn, Julian delivered his fourth album to Island, *Julian H. Cope*. Island hated it. Julian told the *Highland News* that 'the managing director [Marc Marot] said it was the most sonically unappealing album he'd ever heard.' So he agreed to a record a few more 'listenable' tracks but insisted he would not remix anything, retaining the prevailing abrasive sound and textures. So the eleven-track *Julian H. Cope* became a three-sided, sixteen-track album. The last thing Island had wanted was another sprawling double-vinyl effort, yet irrationally they were now perfectly satisfied with an expanded and no less extreme version which now sported a title that their printers found so blasphemous, they wouldn't touch it. Julian had agreed to change the title to *Jehovahkill* at Island's behest because they thought *Julian H. Cope* was potentially offensive.

Released in October, *Jehovahkill* was another astonishing achievement, and took Julian's esoteric interests even further, musically and lyrically, than *Peggy Suicide*. The album added a healthy dose of metronomic krautrock ('The Subtle Energies Commission', 'Necropolis') but hadn't discarded intense melodic balladry or riffy guitar-driven rock. 'Upwards at 45 Degrees' was a magnificent, slow-building psychedelic rocker about extraterrestrial contact. And he was touring these songs acoustically in the wilds of Scotland just as *Jehovahkill* landed in stores. A week later the story leaked out that Island was about to ditch Julian because 'his critical appeal is on the up but his commercial appeal is dropping'. Just as this was confirmed, a fourth show on the 'HEAD ON' tour was added at London's Town and Country Club – the first three nights had already sold out.

Julian's dismissal from Island caused unprecedented fury in the music press. *Select* published a 'Drude-Aid' form, to be sent to Island MD Marc Marot himself, asking why, instead of Julian, he didn't drop any number of 'lame head' acts like the Christians, the Cranberries, Gavin Friday and even U2? Julian's popularity surged and he became a cause célèbre. Marot rang me and accused me of deliberately conspiring against him, before telling me I was sacked. I told him quite truthfully that I could take no credit for the adverse reaction to Julian being dropped and that I'd figured I was off the payroll since the artist I was looking after had already been dumped.

Fittingly, Julian leered from the front cover of the first *NME* of the new year, under the headline 'Endangered Species', and in the accompanying readers' polls Julian came second in the Best Male Artist category to the immovable Morrissey, and third in *Melody Maker*. He would never be as popular again as he was in the aftermath of *Jehovahkill*. Deal or no deal, his prolific outpourings and recordings were unstoppable. Just before he'd been dropped he'd readied a new instrumental meditation album with Donald Ross Skinner. *Rite* comprised lengthy, mostly instrumental jamming freak-outs ideal for listening to while 'sucking on enormous spliffs'. The album was made available by mail order only via Julian's own set-up, KAK Ltd; it was the first release on his new MaGog label. Far from being a stopgap operation KAK became a financial and creative lifeline for Julian's future musical outbursts and, soon, his literature. *Rite* was followed a few months later by *The Skellington Chronicles*, which combined the original album with a new *Skellington 2*.

The MaGog albums were effectively tiding Julian over. He was in no rush to sign another deal, and with songs simply spilling out of him he was already recording the final part of his visionary 1990s trilogy, before returning to the Highlands and islands again, concluding with a week of dates at the Edinburgh Festival. He told Radio Clyde: 'The new album is based on the "Autogeddon" poem by Heathcote Williams.'

In March 1994 Julian signed to the new Chrysalis-backed Echo label, which opened for business with *Autogeddon* in July. In the US he signed to the hip (formerly Def) American label, which had a strong anti-Establishment image. American's A&R executive Mark Geiger told *Billboard*: 'I don't care what he does or what he makes, we'll put it out.' *Autogeddon*'s most prevalent rants were against the idea of personal motorised transport and its impact on the environment. The irony was not lost when the album's announcement in the press coincided with Julian passing his driving test. 'It's a very weird trip,' he said, now the proud owner of a gas-guzzling Range Rover. The more measured and often semi-acoustic *Autogeddon* met with a more muted response than its predecessors, before being trumped within a month by the first instalment of Julian's autobiography, *Head On*, which brutally and evocatively recounted his story up to the break-up of the Teardrops.

Since completing it in 1989 Julian had been unsure whether to publish it. To the rest of us it was a case of, 'Why on earth not?' He was worried that any publisher would want to remove large chunks of the narrative for being libellous, so Julian's manager Seb Shelton looked into the cost of self-publishing through KAK Ltd. *Head On* was published by MaGog Books in

August 1994, and by its third edition a year later had sold ten thousand copies. Julian asked me if there was anything I thought he couldn't get away with. I advised him to take out the references to Courtney Love; he kept them in, but she is referred to only as 'The Adolescent'.

Head On read like he was talking directly to you, a conversational style that was effusive, razor-sharp and littered with his own linguistic dude-isms. He even showed that hearing about somebody else's drug experiences isn't necessarily boring, as they descended from wide-eyed and innocent craziness at Rockfield in 1979 to the hair-raising adventures of the Teardrops in Australia in 1982. It's a relentlessly funny litany of petty jealousies, clashing egos, bitchiness, betrayal, serious chemical abuse and unhinged debauchery. His eye for character is sharp too, but nobody is described more ruthlessly than Julian himself, often depicted as a self-serving failure.

Echo indulged Julian by releasing the debut album by Queen Elizabeth, an extreme synthesizer duo he formed with his most constant 1990s collaborator Thighpaulsandra. *Queen Elizabeth* comprised two formless thirty-minute experimental pieces that critics and many fans found execrable, but it was never meant for those who wanted Julian to remain the way they preferred to remember him – as he was in the 1980s. Julian was happy to comply with their desires next time, but the twenty-track double album *20 Mothers* still erred towards being cosmically huge and sonically imbalanced. Written to order, 'Try Try Try' was his first hit in five years. A pointy-hatted Julian, dressed in lurid patchwork kecks, appeared on *Top of the Pops* twice, but the album had its darker side, taking swipes at familiar targets. It was almost immediately eclipsed by another book. *Krautrocksampler* indulged Julian's view that krautrock was the most visionary art form of the twentieth century. He made no claims for it to be a definitive reference book, but he struck an enticing balance between fandom and finicky detail, with plenty of context and insight. An intriguing dilemma had arisen: it seemed that Julian's two books were now branding him as someone to be taken more seriously as a writer than a musician.

20 Mothers proved to be his last album for American. The label that said he could do what he liked wasn't happy that he refused to come over and play live or do promo in the US. He had had a vision in 1995 that warned him not to visit California, because if he did, the world would end.

In January 1996 Julian came out in public support of the Newbury bypass protesters. Asked to present *Top of the Pops*, he was the perfect host, but was kitted out in full Newbury eco-warrior battle gear and was brandishing slogans, prompting a record number of complaints to the BBC. It coincided with his third album for Echo, *Interpreter*, a more agreeable mix of Moog pop and bubblegum krautrock this time. The extensive notes offered the usual polemical tirade, wherein the born-again eco-warrior lobbied against greed, cynicism and industrial blight. *Interpreter* is the album that has most undeservedly slipped through the cracks in Julian's canon, and it presented him as a funny, literate, spiritually-conscious maverick. Its two singles both peaked at no. 34; the album made no. 39. They marked his last chart entries to date. Echo were always supportive, and Julian did what was asked of him within the bounds of what he found acceptable, but it was the right time for both parties to move on.

Julian chose not to seek another record deal, and hasn't to this day. He had the KAK/MaGog mail-order infrastructure in place, which he took to the next level in May 1997, when his Head Heritage website was launched with the release of *Rite 2*. Above all, Julian knew he needed to devote the next eighteen months to completing his research and focus-ing on writing *The Modern Antiquarian*. He had a major publishing deal, and when asked he would now say his label was HarperCollins. They had signed Julian through Thorsons, its 'mind, body and spirit' imprint, first created in the late 1920s. Head Heritage took care of everything else. Julian really pioneered and explored the possibilities of an artist-run website, Head Heritage putting the usual lazy, tawdry efforts of his con-temporaries to shame. The amount of original content he provided was astonishing, all written in the same giddy, informative language of his books. Through Head Heritage he was able to enhance the myth of Julian

Cope by taking on a new mantle as the Archdrude of Wessex. He now had an outlet that allowed him to write whatever he wanted and have complete control over his recordings. He was answerable to nobody.

No record company has ever indulged Julian as unreservedly as HarperCollins after he delivered *The Modern Antiquarian* at the beginning of 1998. It was an extraordinary feat, achieved through seven years of tireless, thorough research and field work. During the first half of 1998 Julian would drive up the M4 on a regular basis to discuss the layout and design of the book, armed with ideas even he thought were outrageous. He wanted full colour on every one of its four hundred-plus pages and wondered if somehow those pages could also be laminated, and whether it could be housed in a sturdy slip case. Even in Julian's wildest dreams he reckoned this was asking too much, but instead Thorsons actually upped the ante. We'd meet at their offices in Fulham, and I can't remember Julian ever being so content. *The Modern Antiquarian* was the most ambitious and striking book to hit stores that year, very cool on the outside and divided into seven rainbow colours on the inside, and despite a £30 price tag the first print run sold out before Christmas.

Its publication came just a month short of the twenty-year anniversary of the Teardrop Explodes forming, and almost fifteen since Julian appeared naked beneath a turtle shell on the cover of *Fried*. I finally felt vindicated for all the crap that had been said and written about him. Here was Julian Cope, Renaissance man and scholar. Try dismissing him as an acid-damaged rock nutter now. We managed to get him on the front of the *Sunday Times* magazine, and there he is on the cover dressed like Molly Parkin. He's wearing a three-quarter-length fake fur, with matching animal-print leggings and ankle-high laced DMs, and his hair wrapped in a furry headband. I should have known better. He revelled in being rock's cosmic joker but had, in his own inimitable way, become the most resilient artist and performer of his generation.

There was no way I was going to work with the Mac-less Bunnymen. For years I'd managed to steer my way through the minefield of working simultaneously with the Bunnymen, Julian and Bill Drummond, but this was a straight choice between Mac or the Bunnymen, and I'd already nailed my colours to Mac. Their sole album without Mac, *Reverberation*, was released in November 1990, dominated by a far more psychedelic, guitar-driven sound that accorded with Will's hand on the tiller. I saw them play live once, and it was weird. I couldn't get my head round hearing old Bunnymen songs or even their new ones without Mac singing them. Nor could fans and critics. *Reverberation* was poorly received and widely ignored, but those same fans and critics couldn't accept the idea of Mac without the Bunnymen either.

Mac's second album, *Mysterio*, was a severe reality check. He'd been touring with a band he'd put together called the Prodigal Sons, which included guitarist Mike Mooney, as well as young bass player Edgar Jones, who was simultaneously fronting his own group, the Stairs. They'd been holed up in a residential studio on the outskirts of London for months during 1991, trying too hard to strike a Madchester groove but too out of it to notice it was already passé. I went to the studio a few times and came away in a chemically induced state thinking that what I'd heard was fantastic. In the cold light of day the recordings were too unfocused, and they were largely rejected by WEA. They had high hopes for a cover of 'Lover, Lover, Lover' by Mac's beloved Leonard Cohen, but it barely scratched the Top 50. An accompanying tour was shunned by fans. The London show at the Town and Country was the nadir. It drew less than six hundred people, with the balcony area closed and darkened to avoid embarrassment. Mac had been justly proud of *Candleland*, but his self-esteem hit an all-time low after *Mysterio*.

I saw a lot of Mac during 1991 and 1992, till he was dropped by WEA in 1993. I had a rented flat in Stoke Newington, and he'd stay there sometimes, but he still commanded plush record-company-paid-for hotels, usually in Holland Park, and we spent many a long night innocently getting smashed, the two of us either talking gibberish or pondering our fates. Then, with his career in a slump and no reason for him to leave Liverpool, we lost touch for a couple of years. It wasn't till June 1994 that

I saw a brief news story in *Melody Maker*, asking if anyone had information about missing tapes of recordings made by Ian McCulloch and Johnny Marr. The sting was in the tail, where it was added almost inconsequentially that Mac and Will were writing and rehearsing together again and forming a new group. Both stories came as a surprise to me. The McCulloch/Marr liaison remains a mystery. In January 2012 Marr told *Uncut*: 'The first ten days of us writing together was very creative, and then it lost track in a sort of Mancunian/Scouse haze. It's a long story which ends with the hijacking of the van that the master tapes were in, on its way from my house in Manchester to Ian's place in Liverpool. It's actually a great way for that project to have ended.'

Mac and Will were playing together again, under the name Electrafixion. Through Rob Dickins, the group's sole album, *Burned*, was released in 1995 and featured two songs from the lost Marr tapes. From a distant vantage point it looked to have done OK, and one of the singles extracted from it, 'Sister Pain', went Top 30. I never saw them play live, but on record Electrafixion were louder and noisier than the Bunnymen. Mac and Will appeared to have learnt from the mistake of not touring in the US, where Echo & the Bunnymen's cult status was now growing. They were being talked up by Kurt Cobain and Courtney Love, whose group, Hole, recorded 'Do It Clean'. Other US bands – Flaming Lips and Pavement among them – were covering Bunnymen songs, and by their final US tour in the summer of 1996 Electrafixion were increasingly covering Bunnymen songs as well. The band was the tentative first step towards becoming the Bunnymen again, explained Mac. 'I held out because I needed to know if we could stand each other's company again. I needed Will as a foil but we needed Les 'cause he was the engine.'

They had a new manager in Paul Toogood. Paul had known Pete and had helped to sort out his estate after his death. It was Paul who told me the Bunnymen were getting back together and that they all wanted me to handle the press. I liked him a lot and we became great friends. I hadn't seen Will and Les since Pete's funeral and put off making a decision till I'd heard the album. It was only about 50 per cent as good as the glories of their past work, but even 50 per cent was good enough for me. The clincher was that it wasn't being released by WEA: they had signed to London Records. They recorded their first album in ten years in January 1997, in a small studio called the Dog House, just outside Henley-on-Thames. It took less than a month, with the strings, horn parts and vocal arrangements completed at Abbey Road. 'We owed it to ourselves not to have left it where we did ten years before,' said Mac. 'We proved our point again, and I think that more than anyone else who has got back together, we did it with real dignity.' He told me this in 2001, long before the present culture of bands reforming was commonplace. 'If we could not have come back with a great record, we would never have done it. We weren't just cashing in. We had a Top 10 single – straight in, as big a hit as we'd ever had.'

Before anything was released, however, they wanted to prove themselves onstage. It was another smart move. I never doubted that they would cut it. They made their live return on 14 May at Cream in Liverpool, and three days later played the Mercury Lounge in New York, the start of a month of dates in the US. The live shows were nothing but a complete vindication of the decision to return, and few disagreed with the *NME* review of the Liverpool show. 'It's impossibly good,' wrote James Oldham. 'The first comeback in history not to be dogged by a nauseous sense of distress, the first one to actually sound important.' The real test was always going to be how well the album measured up. Titled *Evergreen*, the first single from it was 'Nothing Lasts Forever'. It was vintage Bunnymen, spine-tingling stuff from the moment Mac sings, 'I want it now,' even if nothing else on the album came quite as close. And that really didn't matter, because the Bunnymen's first new single in ten years crashed into the charts at no. 8 on 28 June. Two weeks later *Evergreen* also reached no. 8.

'The new Bunnymen songs are more personal,' said Mac. 'I'm not singing about anything different to *Ocean Rain* but it's less obtuse. I'm less cryptic these days.' For old fans the directness was important. The Bunnymen had fucked up in 1987, shattering their belief in the group they loved, and nothing any of them had done since had made amends. *Evergreen*'s reflective sense of atonement, with tender pleas such as 'Just a Touch Away' and 'Forgiven', papered over some of its duller moments and, having let themselves down, effectively restored the past. They had been the coolest band of the 1980s, they said and did the coolest things, and of course the cocksure attitude that Mac the Mouth perfected made him a role model for Ian Brown, Shaun Ryder and Liam Gallagher, who sang back-up on 'Nothing Lasts Forever' (he happened to be in the next studio). It bolstered Mac's conviction that the Bunnymen could still be valid and not just seen as a bunch of old tossers making a comeback.

I remember us checking in at the Paramount Hotel in New York, prior to the Mercury Lounge gig, and Primal Scream were checking out. Bobby Gillespie and Mani came straight over to say hello. I knew then that the Bunnymen were cool again. Will, as ever, was more pragmatic: 'It did feel like we meant something again, however much I might have mistrusted what people were saying about how great we were when they'd just ignored us for ten years.' The six months from the point we started doing interviews in May 1997 went like a dream. It was quite clear that, for a while at least, the three of them had rediscovered the ties that bind.

1998 should have seen them go from strength to strength, but the group was effectively derailed when in April they were the unlikely choice of the Football Association to record England's official World Cup song. 'On Top of the World' dated from the Johnny Marr collaborations. Giving in to considerable record-company interference, the eventual release, under the name England United, featured the Spice Girls as guests, with additional vocals by Tommy Scott from Space and Simon Fowler from Ocean Colour Scene. The project had galloped away from Mac's original idea for the song, and the single, released in June 1998, was something of a flop, spending just one week in the Top 10. As a football song it lacked any lyrical hook that could be chanted from the terraces. Its tone was almost downbeat and melancholy. It was perfectly fitting for an England side that performed as badly as the record.

Will and Les had wanted nothing to do with England United, distancing themselves from the whole shabby affair. The damage was done, and Will and Mac were at odds once again when they went back into the studio a few months later. 'I felt like I was having a nervous breakdown,' said Will. 'We had a pretty good year after *Evergreen* but recording with the Spice Girls was just cherry on. The next album . . . my heart's not in it. Nor is my guitar very much. I felt left out.'

'We are our own worst enemies sometimes,' agreed Mac. 'I know he hates that record. I resented Will's lack of involvement and interest, and he felt he was being pushed out, so he resented me.' Les felt they'd gone back to where they were in 1987 and left the band soon after recording commenced. With Will's input negligible, *What Are You Going to Do with Your Life?*, released in April 1999, was to all intents and purposes an Ian McCulloch solo record. He's the only one pictured on both its front and back. It's a compelling album, but it's no longer Echo & the Bunnymen.

I was always much closer to Mac, but there is a line you should never cross in a working relationship that goes beyond being professional. I crossed it a few times and so did Paul Toogood. He did the decent thing and ceased managing the group. It was another sad blow; he had been a major architect of their successful return, but in getting too close to Mac he crucially alienated Will, for whom it became 'unless he goes, I go'. I should have cut and run myself.

On 23 August 1997 a twenty-three-minute 'comeback' performance at the Barbican was announced in *Time Out*. It represented the entire lifespan of Bill Drummond and Jimmy Cauty's latest appellation, 2K, which had been inspired by them attending the Queen Elizabeth Hall performance of Acid Brass. The brainchild of artist Jeremy Deller, it featured the then twice national champion Williams Fairey Brass Band performing eight acid-house anthems, including 'What Time Is Love?'.

The sole 2K performance took place on 17 September, having been postponed for two weeks after the death of Princess Diana. Even the artists formerly known as the KLF could not disrespect the nation's mourning with a project titled 'Fuck the Millennium'. Judiciously edited to '***K the Millennium', it was to be released as a single a month later on Blast First.

From the start people were either disappointed that the so-called comeback lasted only twenty-three minutes or questioned why they were coming back at all. It was an infringement of the 1992 declaration that they had left the music business. Although that had said 'for the foreseeable future', the purists among us considered that by returning at all they were going back on their word. Either way people felt let down. 'That's the whole point', said Bill and Jimmy to anybody who was able to get a comment out of either of them. The impression I got was that they didn't really know why they were staging a comeback, and had they not committed to Blast First and Mute Records they would have scrapped the whole thing.

Both the single and the overly contrived live performance were rare failures. The concept was unusually muddled, one that failed to reignite past successes, despite playing heavily upon them. 2K recycled a number of old ideas, not least another take on 'What Time Is Love?', and they took out full-page K Foundation-style press announcements.

It reminded me of the ill-fated 'Kylie Said to Jason'. Mute Records had that same conviction that '***K the Millennium' was going to be huge just because it was the KLF. I sat in meetings where nobody considered the possibility that the single would not get played on the radio. 'Seriously', I said, 'have you counted how many times they use the word "fuck"?' There were far too many to bleep out. And *Top of the Pops* was never an option. So, far from surfing in on any kind of pre-millennial polemic, '***K the Millennium' was three years adrift of the zeitgeist. Nobody gave a ***K.

Bill brought in Ken Campbell to direct the performance, an extended bells-and-whistles version of '***K the Millennium' onstage. It began with Mark Manning (aka Zodiac Mindwarp) as an axe-wielding 'salvationist' in a vicar's collar and gold lamé suit, and a rendition of the K Foundation anthem 'K Cera Cera'. Two coachloads of placard-carrying

Liverpool dockers had been bussed down to chant, 'Fuck the millennium. We want it now!', a choir of Viking boatmen sang 'For Those in Peril on the Sea' and the Williams Fairey Brass Band pumped out the 'What Time Is Love?' riff. Bill and Jimmy spent the entire performance chasing each other round the stage in motorised wheelchairs. Bill was cradling a white swan in his lap, plucking its feathers. It was one of many mixed messages being sent out. Was it anti-royal, anti the millennium, anti-religion, anti the government and union leaders, or simply anti-everything?

Bill and Jimmy, wearing pyjamas and with their trademark horns strapped to their heads, were made up to look like ninety-year-olds who'd just escaped from a care home. It was a nice touch that presented the antithesis of the usual comeback, whereby artists desperately try to look younger. It may have been a coincidence that Echo & the Bunnymen's comeback was happening just as Bill and Jimmy were struggling to record '***K the Millennium' in June. Bill wrote in his journal that month that 'comebacks were pathetic and sad . . . the desperation of all concerned to exploit whatever they can from the myth while trying to convince themselves – if nobody else – that the band were still relevant'. I couldn't detect any irony in Bill's comments.

He and Jimmy were ill at ease with many aspects of the project that they couldn't control. They were cajoled into doing an interview with *Channel 4 News* before the show, and in character, with the old codgers feigning deafness. They simply said 'Don't know' to all the questions posed by the increasingly frustrated interviewer. Jokes about the show 'getting us out of the house' and its short duration meaning that could get to bed early were too pat. MTV was given the same treatment.

Reviews of the Barbican show were largely negative. The *Guardian*'s comment that it was 'a glorious, jaw-dropping mess' was one of the better appraisals. It had been a jumbled, surprisingly dated affair that failed to make any point whatsoever by trying to cram too much into its twenty-three minutes. For some the brevity was its best attribute.

Later, in the early hours of the morning, Bill and Jimmy scaled the National Theatre building again, this time painting its walls with '1997

What the Fuck Is Going On?' Aside from the ever-faithful *NME* news desk and *Time Out*, I saw nothing about it anywhere else. A spokesman for the National Theatre thought it had been a protest by disgruntled Diana fans.

Twenty years later Jeremy Deller spoke about it (he had by then won the Turner Prize in 2004). 'We always wanted it to be a mess, but it didn't add to the mystique and mythology of the KLF and the K Foundation, which continues to grow,' he said. '2K stands out as the exception. It's more or less forgotten.' By the time of the millennium itself, Bill's explanation in his book *45* declared that the show was a success and that 'the record stiffing at number twenty-eight in the charts was just what the doctor ordered. We had not only blown it, we had destroyed whatever remnants of credibility, bankability and myth we had left.' Jimmy was more circumspect: 'Some things like "Fuck the Millennium" can be absorbed by the better things we've done.'

14 : KNOCKING AT THE DOOR OF THE COSMOS

1990-8

I was always drawn to outsider artists. As a rule they ranked high on adventurousness and originality and were usually accepted or applauded only later. I see Echo & the Bunnymen as outsiders; they certainly were to begin with. Julian Cope, Lawrence, Bill Drummond and Jimmy Cauty, and Jim and William Reid would make most people's team sheets, but pretty much everybody I ever worked with fell into the outsider category. I'd argue that David Gedge does too. The names that follow all unquestionably qualify, and significantly four of them came to me via Paul Smith, who was another outsider. Another crucial characteristic is that everybody here helped changed things by not playing by any rules other than their own. That certainly applied to Sun Ra.

Sun Ra, Central Park, 4 July 1992, sharing a bill with Sonic Youth and magically
making the sun appear on an overcast Independence Day in New York City
(*photo: David Gahr*).

Sun Ra claimed to be an angel from the planet Saturn, and this strange allegation has overshadowed the fact that he's one of the most important figures in jazz. He's had an increasingly potent influence across many other genres since his death in 1993. Perhaps the world is catching up with the man who from the late 1950s usually led a big band, most commonly known as the Arkestra. When you suddenly find yourself working with somebody regarded as one of the greats, you have to pay due respect. Some of Sun Ra's music left me cold; most of what I'd read or heard about him left me awestruck.

So I felt genuinely privileged and not a little apprehensive about meeting Sun Ra in June 1990, when he arrived in London for a handful of shows with a seventeen-piece Arkestra, whose core – tenor saxophonist John Gilmour, altoist Marshall Allen and singer June Tyson – had been with him for almost four decades. Tyson was the latest of these to come under Ra's spell, after he discovered her singing in Harlem in 1968. She was effectively managing the band day to day and looking after Ra during this week in Britain.

Sun Ra was seventy-six then, or thereabouts (in earth years at any rate). He was born in Birmingham, Alabama, in 1914, and given the name Herman Poole Blount. After 1952, having legally changed his name to Le Sony'r Ra, he would focus on a form of Afro-futuristic music and philosophy, his Arkestra wearing brightly coloured Egyptian costumes onstage, while his music would take on an astral dimension.

Sun Ra steered his variously named bands into the space age with blasts of free-jazz energy but encompassing the styles and techniques developed over his years in jazz. It was sometimes pure entertainment, sometimes impressionistic and sometimes dauntingly improvisational. The balance between these facets varied from show to show. The June tour was the first of three visits to the UK in 1990. Paul Smith also brought him over in October to play the Hackney Empire, and in August he played at the Edinburgh Festival. He'd been commissioned to write a piece entitled 'Music for the 21st Century' by the organisers of the Edinburgh International Jazz Festival. He ignored the commission:

"'Music for the 21st Century'," he told one interviewer, with typically sardonic sparkle, 'I wrote that in 1965. I work ahead. I'm writing my 30th Century music now.'

It had been fraught trying to organise eighteen people who collectively had an attitude that ranged from naughty schoolchildren to *que será, será*. Jane Burridge, who ran Blast First in the UK with Paul, was tasked with the initial problem of trying to get details regarding who was actually coming over. That they were allowed into the country at all involved a certain amount of sleight of hand over work permits and some quick thinking when confronted by UK immigration officials on arrival. None of that concerned me. Once she'd figured it out, Jane gave me a list of who was who and what they played.

The Liverpool date came first, on 8 June. We took over an entire rail carriage when the Arkestra travelled there, filling it with the band and crew members, plus Paul and Jane, and a journalist and photographer from the *Wire*; the carry-on luggage and instruments included the five-foot-long drum made from the trunk of a lightning-struck elm tree which, onstage, produced a deep boom like a monstrous clap of thunder. Hanging out with Sunny, as we all came to know him, filled me with apprehension. He was an outlandish musician, showman and remarkable intellect, but a charming, spiritual soul who always had a mischievous twinkle in his eye. 'I'm famous and infamous, cussed and discussed,' he said at one point, and it could have been Tom Waits speaking. Waits may well have learnt a trick or two from the master. Ra's mission was 24/7, almost literally; he was renowned for very rarely sleeping. That alone kept the Arkestra on their toes: he could call a rehearsal at any time of day. Everybody kept their wits about them in his company. As you'd expect from a man who'd travelled the universe, his knowledge was profound and scholarly, in subjects including numerology, theosophy, metaphysics, theology, divinity, history, ethnomusicology and plenty more beyond my ken.

On the train, feeling intimidated, I resorted to a little small talk and asked him about the Disney repertoire he was due to play at Brixton

Academy two days later. The response would have been oddly normal had it not been Sun Ra speaking. 'I saw *Mary Poppins* again,' he said in his soft, calm, southern voice. 'It's fantastic, a masterpiece. They were doing this "Chim Chim Cher-ee" dance and I thought what they were doing was the very soul of England.' If I was meant to laugh, I suppressed it, but I wondered if his whimsy was intentional since he was speaking completely poker-faced to a star-struck Englishman. 'When we play in my home in Philadelphia,' I overheard him tell one interviewer in Liverpool, 'even the spiders come down from the walls to listen. Everything in the universe loves music.' Imagine a playful Jehovah's Witness, if such an oxymoron is indeed imaginable. That was Sun Ra. He'd answer direct questions about music or his background, but if you asked him a question, mostly he'd veer off on a lengthy, twisting train of thought that was hard to follow. One time I overheard him saying that he'd been to Jupiter, even though he knew people might not believe it: 'That's why I'm always singing about Jupiter. I was taken there by a guide, looking down at this little planet.'

Ra was very anti-drugs and maintained strict control over his band members. Those who had been with him for forty years were respectful, but some of the younger ones (the average age of the outfit was around forty) found his regime of 'no drink, no drugs, no loose women' more challenging. There was a certain amount of clandestine smoking and furtive lacing of soft drinks with spirits, and plenty of surreptitious exchanges away from the glare of Sunny and June.

The Liverpool gig at the Bluecoat provoked the wildest and keenest audience response of the three shows. It was an onslaught of massed percussion: the six-strong back row of the band consisted of a double bassist and five percussionists; others in the seventeen-piece outfit also doubled on additional percussion, including another long-timer, James Jackson, on bassoon and the lightning drum. Ra was dressed in rainbow-coloured priest's robes and was sporting a natty red goatee to match his hair. Once you see the Arkestra in their full glory incorporating elements of a space-age soul review, you understand where George Clinton got the idea for his Parliament-Funkadelic thang. At the University of London Union the show closed with a space rap incorporating 'Space Is the Place' and one of the Arkestra's earliest recordings, 'Rocket Number Nine', the band echoing Ra's invocations as they skipped offstage in a conga line, leaving Ra to croon that he dared to knock at the doors of the cosmos. The second London show at the cramped Mean Fiddler in Harlesden was twice as long, the first set fraught with technical problems but with more Disney repertoire – a revamped 'Teddy Bears' Picnic' was hysterical. By the second set a series of wild exultant percussion pieces and some frazzled horn explosions and dissonant brass were finally too much for me. He never did play 'Chim Chim Cher-ee' either.

Paul and I once took Sun Ra shopping on London's Denmark Street. It was near closing and the young shop assistant had no idea who this ageing, flamboyantly dressed shopper outstaying his welcome was. The lad was impatiently drumming his fingers on the counter, so I went to placate him, while Paul watched over Sunny as he hobbled around trying one effects pedal after another. The boss suddenly emerged at the counter, wondering why the shop was still open. I apologised, before asking, 'Don't you know who that is?' I told them. The assistant still looked blank, but the boss's eyes lit up. 'It's like having Hendrix in the shop', I explained to the assistant, his boss nodding in agreement. Paul brought Sunny a 'heavy-metal' guitar pedal. Sunny had no idea it was a modern-day music genre, but he liked the name and went on to explain how the laws of physics were different on his home planet.

They were a magical few days that signalled Paul's revised outlook on the future of Blast First. A few years later he started up a unique multi-media club night called Disobey, which ran for a year during 1994/5. On its opening night on 23 March Disobey played host to the little-known tenor sax extremist Charles Gayle, who judged his shows on the basis of last man standing after his customary upper-register aural assault. In the months that followed Paul organised and programmed a series of disparate events, presenting an unbearable barrage of noise by Caspar Brötzmann, readings by Iain Sinclair and Kathy Acker, Finnish techno duo Pan Sonic and a talk by Cynthia Plaster Caster. The club usually took place in the cramped, box-like upstairs bar at the Garage in Islington. It was the antithesis of an 'arts' venue, where Disobey managed to overcome any elitism and pretentiousness. It was always a good night out.

In 1991 Sun Ra suffered a series of strokes and was admitted to a Philadelphia hospital, where he famously gave his birthplace as Saturn, which was verified by an understanding doctor. After three months of rehabilitation he was back on the road, but thereafter he was confined to a wheelchair, with his left hand impaired. In 1992 I was fortunate to see Sun Ra and his Arkestra one last time, this time supporting Sonic Youth in Central Park on 4 July 1992. The Arkestra line-up had changed little in two years, and I was warmly greeted by members of the band in the artists' enclosure, which didn't go unnoticed by Sonic Youth. It did wonders for my underdeveloped cool quotient. A near monsoon overnight threatened to stop play and it was as overcast as Headingley cricket ground in early summer, but almost as if scripted or ordained, the sun appeared just as Ra and the band took to the stage in red and gold kaftans and turbans. Ra now guided the band from a wheelchair that served well as a throne. The show was heavy on Afro rhythms, with veiled dancers weaving across the stage. When Sonic Youth came on, Thurston, an avid Sun Ra collector, announced: 'I'd like to thank Sun Ra for bringing the sun out, because that doesn't happen all the time.'

Sun Ra died in 1993. The Arkestra continues to this day, but with June Tyson and John Gilmour both long since gone.

Sonic Youth were as fired up and frenzied as I'd ever seen them that afternoon, playing half a dozen songs from the new album, *Dirty*. 'Hey, Park Avenue, wake the fuck up,' hollered Thurston. They did too. Next day some residents on Fifth Avenue filed complaints about the noise. The night before Sonic Youth had warmed up at CBGBs, under the name Drunken Butterfly. I'd last been there to see the Ramones, almost ten years before. It was a relief to see that the place hadn't been given a facelift. It was the same claustrophobic burrow, and Sonic Youth's short, grinding, screeching set ended with the familiar closer 'Expressway to

Yr Skull', whose ten-minute torrent of noise caused an earthquake effect that threatened to bring the roof down.

A week earlier I'd taken Steve Lamacq over to New York for an *NME* cover story on Sonic Youth. We did the interview in the boardroom of the Geffen New York office. 'Look how fat the seats are,' Kim was saying as I took my leave. After the interview we all wandered downtown, and photographer Kevin Cummins unfurled his idea for the cover shot. He'd bought an American flag, which he wanted to use as a prop. They were happy with the irony of posing with it, but he also wanted to set fire to it. None of them were too keen on the idea, but in the end we found a discreet side street, where Thurston followed through with his usual bravado, holding up the burning flag for the shot and then hoofing it.

Sonic Youth had come a long way in the ten years prior to inking a deal with Geffen Records. Being on a major label would have been unthinkable once for Sonic Youth, who had been nurtured in the vibrant US underground scene of the 1980s. It was a scene that had been spearheaded by bands like Black Flag and Minor Threat, through labels like SST and Dischord. Hüsker Dü, Minutemen and Meat Puppets were the break-out bands, but Sonic Youth added another dimension. Just as the SST bands cleared a path for Sonic Youth in the mid-1980s, so Sonic Youth inspired the next generation, most famously Nirvana, but also the Pixies, Mudhoney, Throwing Muses and Pavement, among others. I went over to Dublin in late August 1991, where Nirvana were supporting Sonic Youth at the Top Hat nightclub. Thurston was holding court to a couple of fanzine writers, one of whom asked what his group's goal was. 'To be able to get away with doing anything,' was his throwaway reply. It's a pretty good summation of Sonic Youth's abiding musical and spiritual *raison d'être*. No other group sounded like them; that's why their deal with Geffen was so crucial in setting the tone for the new decade.

Key to them signing to Geffen was not so they were on the same label as Cher and Whitesnake, or that it was a five-album deal for $300,000; it was that they had complete creative control. Not having the latter was a deal-breaker. By signing they established a precedent for other alternative bands. It signified: 'If it's OK for Sonic Youth, then it's OK for us.' Sonic Youth's Geffen debut, *Goo*, was released in July 1990 and reached a respectable no. 32 in the UK and extended their sales base in the US. There was still plenty of trademark clanking guitar instrumentation and nothing that resembled a pop song as anybody else knew it. It was enough for Sonic Youth diehards not to despair and made the point that the group still did things their way.

Nirvana's *Nevermind* was released at the end of their European dates with Sonic Youth. Six months later it had sold three million copies in the US alone. It had been produced by Butch Vig and, in a much-talked-about twist, he produced the next Sonic Youth album, *Dirty*. They usually produced and mixed their records via inter-band democracy, so Vig was the first proper producer they had worked with. Thurston, the man with an answer for everything, was quick to point out that Vig had produced some of the very first hardcore singles in the US, notably underground heroes Killdozer. For Geffen, using Vig was turning the tables. This time it signified: 'If you like Nirvana, then Sonic Youth are OK too.' *Dirty* sounded nothing like Nirvana; it sounded like Sonic Youth but was as close as they were ever going to get in terms of delivering a more palatable sound. *Dirty* went on to become their most commercially successful album. In the UK it reached no. 6 – the highest chart placing they would ever attain – and produced two Top 30 hits in '100%' and 'Sugar Kane'. The only downside was being hailed as 'the godfathers of grunge'.

Sonic Youth had a real and calculated presence in Europe during 1991 and '92, and I spent more time with them then than ever. I always said I found Sonic Youth aloof, but I realise now that I was just as aloof towards them. Thereafter their UK visits were largely promotional stopovers around albums or brief tours. In that situation I was no more than a hired hand. That's the norm. When American bands have a record out or tour, either somebody from the label or an independent PR gets taken on. I had no complaints that I was just the guy who did the job in London; it was a case of 'nice work if you can get it' and well paid, but the visits became fewer and farther apart. In 1993 they played the Phoenix

Festival, and didn't play in the UK again until the spring of 1996, followed by another two-year gap.

Sonic Youth worked with Butch Vig again for 1994's *Experimental Jet Set, Trash and No Star*, which despite a lack of presence still made the Top 10 in the UK charts. They'd held their ground, but it wasn't to last. *Experimental Jet Set* had been recorded and mixed in a month, with two weeks off in the middle, using the same studio where they'd recorded *Sister* in 1987. This wasn't the big sound of *Dirty*. This was Sonic Youth retreating back into a more private shell, where they remained, and sales worldwide had slumped by the time 1995's *Washing Machine* was released. They were no longer the 'godfathers of grunge' and were back where they were far more comfortable: as the figureheads of avant-rock again. My appreciation for their music grew exponentially in the time I worked with them. Some of the albums I love even more today. I often return to *Sister* and *Evol*, and to *Daydream Nation*, *Dirty* and *A Thousand Leaves* in particular, after which we went our separate ways.

A Thousand Leaves was accompanied by another fleeting, week-long UK visit at the end of June 1998. It was the best job I ever did with Sonic Youth, the only time I broadened their press base to national level. Beyond the faithful Sonic Youth were always a hard sell. Their profile had almost exclusively been defined by the music press, so it was a shock when the paper that had always been most supportive decided to turn on them. PRs often talk about being stitched up over a bad review, a feature that never made the cover as promised or sometimes one that never ran. I hadn't really been stitched up in twenty years, not in any way that mattered, but when the *NME* assigned hatchet man Steven Wells to do the next Sonic Youth piece, I smelt a very large rat.

I knew it was a set-up and said as much to the group beforehand. They were avid *NME* readers, so they knew about Swells's reputation, and their arrogance was their undoing because they thought they could handle it. So despite my warning and suggestion we should just say no, the interview went ahead. I sat a few tables away from them in the hotel restaurant where it took place. That was another mistake; it's never good to do interviews over meals because you can ridicule anybody's eating habits. It was raucous and lively, and it sounded as if they gave as good as they got, but of course Swells had the last word, and the ones in print. Anybody is an easy target if you take an underhand, one-sided stance that says everything about them is shit and turn everything they say into something that makes them look stupid or nerdish or egotistical or condescending. This was nothing less than a vitriolic three-page character assassination. Swells branded them as 'elitist and effete tossers', 'NY art wankers' whose music is 'corporate whore shit'. And those were the best bits. Under the headline 'Old and Indie Way', and with a particularly unflattering full-page photo running alongside, the piece read as if the grudge that certain factions within the *NME* had been harbouring for ten years was finally being vented.

I'd barely read it myself before manager John Silva rang me to say, 'You'd better call the group. They are pissed.' I never called them. I was pissed too, with the *NME* and with them. And I was angry with myself for not protesting more that we should have turned down the feature. In 1998 Sonic Youth didn't need the *NME*, and the *NME* didn't need Sonic Youth. Ringing up and saying, 'I told you so', would have given me no satisfaction whatsoever. A week later Keith Cameron, who sat on the other side of the *NME* fence, gave *A Thousand Leaves* 9/10, but it didn't make up for the paper's in-joke at the artists' expense. I'm sure the group are long over it, but it still rankles with me twenty years later.

'So why do you live in Colombia?'

It's the question Andrew Oldham gets asked as often as any other about the Rolling Stones, Marianne Faithfull or Immediate Records. And there's always something in the inquisitor's self-satisfied tone that says, 'I'm sure nobody's asked you this before.'

For over forty years now Andrew has been an expat living in Bogotá. I imagine him living like somebody out of a Graham Greene novel, but before he cleaned up in 1995 he was more like James Woods's ravaged war reporter in *Salvador*. He lives mostly in a flat in the north of Bogotá, with the Andes on one side and a smattering of upmarket restaurants on the other. 'Colombia gave me a life,' he is fond of saying, 'when I didn't have one.'

So why Colombia then? Well, he met and fell for Colombian actress Esther Farfán in 1974, when she was appearing in Willy Russell's *John, Paul, George, Ringo . . . and Bert* at the Saville Theatre. They moved to New York and then to Colombia, and were married on Valentine's Day 1977. Andrew plays with the facts. He's a master of that art. 'There are three sides to every story,' is how his brilliant autobiography *Stoned* opens, 'yours, mine and the truth.' He once said he was first offered cocaine during a meeting with Warner Brothers executives at the Savoy in 1974; another time he said it was only after moving to Bogotá. It set up a great pay-off line: 'I never touched cocaine before I got here. Then I really touched it.' Or another time: 'That wasn't the reason I moved there but given my habits, it certainly kept the price down.'

When I first met Andrew in 1992, he was at the tail end of a twenty-five-year period of being wasted and unemployable. Three years later he managed to get clean, but I'm glad I got to witness both the before and after Andrews. I maintained an ongoing working relationship with him from 1992 onwards, whenever there was a reason for him to bring me on board – including four books – but I first got the call in 1992, through his old partner in crime, Tony Calder. He was coming to London to launch Immediate 3.

The original Immediate label was started up in 1965 by Andrew and Tony; two years later Andrew and the Stones parted company, and in April 1970 Immediate collapsed and was liquidated. Things moved fast in the 1960s. It was impossible for me not to jump at the chance of working with the infamous pair. Tony may always be cast as the second fiddle, but he managed Marianne Faithfull and in the post-Immediate years was instrumental in the phenomenal success of Eddy Grant and Jive Bunny. OK, the less said about the latter, the better.

Andrew and Tony always talked a good talk and fought a good fight, and the two rakish characters did their best to fuck up the music industry, and major record labels in particular, during the four years they ran Immediate. In that time Immediate gave many big acts a leg up: the Small Faces, Chris Farlowe, Fleetwood Mac and the Nice, among others. Jimmy Page was one of Immediate's in-house producers, along with Mick Jagger, Keith Richards, Steve Marriott and Andrew himself, trying to emulate his idols Phil Spector and Brian Wilson. He paid for press ads to declare that the Beach Boys' *Pet Sounds* was up there with Rimsky-Korsakov's *Scheherazade*, telling the world before anybody else that Wilson was a genius.

With its eye-catching graphics and smart slogans Immediate has been an inspirational template for almost every British independent since. Stiff, Factory and Creation all followed suit, but what Immediate had in common with most of the labels it preceded was the capacity to release more that was shit than shined. The second incarnation of Immediate came in 1975, which, said Tony, 'lasted a lunch and a dinner' before a gunpoint altercation in the south of France ended it abruptly. Immediate 3 lasted two years, in name at least, and the old pros still talked a good talk, but nothing was ever released. They were a great team, a kind of bad and badder, with Tony happy to play the not entirely straight man. Andrew came up with a new mission statement for the label. Immediate 3 was 'Happy to be apart from the general malaise,' as opposed to the original label's celebrated axiom, 'Happy to be part of the industry of human happiness.'

So I was pinching myself when Tony and Andrew hired me to look after the relaunch of Immediate after twenty-two years. 'It will', said Calder in one of the initial press releases, 'become the most successful and innovative independent of the 90s. There will be books, TV shows and lots of hits.' None of which happened, although they did record a version of 'Woolly Bully' with the much-hyped latest bad-boy group Fabulous. Andrew had wanted them to record a version 'Get Off of My Cloud', and their single was meant to signal the label's jubilant relaunch. The so-called pop terrorists, fronted by *NME/Face* journalist Simon Spence and photographer Martyn Goodacre, had already been dropped by Pete Waterman's PWL and they quickly ended up in dispute with Immediate. They were managed by journalist James Brown, who claimed that the negotiations collapsed because Andrew was now up against a generation of his own bastard children.

We may have been fortunate to have been spared most of the projects talked up for Immediate 3. These included projected albums by Bill Wyman, Brian Wilson, who was then between deals, and German hard-rock band Backbone Slide, and an anti-smoking compilation of British metal bands in association with the appalling Death cigarettes. Another project was a series of *Music for Dining* albums that would provide background music for dining at home – French, Chinese, Italian and Indian, of course. 'An ideal way to spice up your takeaways,' said the *Daily Mirror*, under the headline 'Top of the Poppadums'. Film and TV ideas included a series about rock managers that went as far as a meeting with Rowan Atkinson's production company, until Andrew passed out in front of them. An animated version of a new all-star recording of the Small Faces' *Ogdens' Nut Gone Flake* and a remake of *Expresso Bongo*, with Al Pacino and Brad Pitt in the roles originally played by Laurence Harvey and Cliff Richard, both fell at the first hurdle.

Hanging out with Andrew was all I could have hoped for. He was wild and unpredictable; his daily routine was fuelled by snorting quality coke from home and munching anti-depressants, washed down by sweetly pungent Italian grappa, the smell of which always announced his arrival long before he came into view. And unless you were on the receiving end, he was deliciously funny. We did tons of press, everything from train-spotting Immediate fanatics who wanted to know if it was Jimmy Page playing guitar on the Masterminds' 'She Belongs to Me' to the inkies and broadsheets who wanted him to retell familiar tales so they could retell them to their readers. We did interviews around lunchtime and going into the afternoon, before Andrew was too out of it, usually in the lounge of the Draycott Hotel in Chelsea. In the afternoon there was always an air of civilised communion. A still youthful-looking Mark Wynter, a 1950s teen idol turned actor who was Andrew's first-ever client, or a jolly Sir Tim Rice might pop round for a chat, but by the evening the ne'er-do-wells, dodgy business types and general hangers-on would start turning up. Fired by grappa and coke, Andrew's short fuse would be burning low and he'd get cranky and less tolerant. I'd usually made my exit before then. I'd decided early on to be straight and professional around Andrew and not get off my face. I wish I'd been around when a journalist challenged him about whether he really dangled transgressors out of windows back in the old days. His answer was to grab the writer and push him perilously close to the edge of a fifth-floor balcony.

Immediate 3 was already a thing of the past by March 1995, when *Abba: The Name of the Game* was published, a biography of the Swedish group that was credited to Andrew Oldham, Tony Calder and Colin Irwin, a long-time journalist for *Melody Maker*. They'd talked Sidgwick & Jackson into publishing it. Andrew found it hard at times to keep a straight face at the idea that Abba were the greatest songwriters of all time. He even had trouble remembering which one was which, but having initially been asked to provide an introduction to the book, Andrew was surprised to find his old partner had credited him as a co-author. It was even Andrew's name that came first below the title. The biter had been well and truly bitten.

After three decades of drug addiction – a regular smorgasbord of prescribed and non-prescribed drugs – Andrew eventually cleaned up in 1995. 'I realised I was being called to the happy hunting ground,' was his colourful description. 'I was just weeks away from checking out for good.' He signed on for a nutritional 'purification' programme in Glens Falls, upstate New York, that saved his life. Two years later, having fixed his body, he embraced the Scientology programme to 'sharpen' his mind. Scientology worked for him and he'd say it 'jump-started' a means of returning to a productive life again after thirty years. L. Ron Hubbard has his own one-liners, one of which is that you need to do something productive in life. That creative need for Andrew was fulfilled this time around by writing, and discovering whether he could write under only the influence of himself.

When we met a year or so later, he was a changed man. He was warm and friendly and polite, whatever the hour and whomever he was talking to. You can't beat even a bad minor-public-school education. It was twelve noon and he was having lunch. His dietary regime and eating timetable were rigid, and accompanying a bloody steak his only drug intake now was a substantial quantity of nutritional pills that he'd pour onto a plate like a mountain of Smarties, slowly munching his way through them one at a time while talking more lucidly but no less tangentially than before. 'You have to be as obsessive about wellness as you are about sickness,' he explained like a true believer, always quick to defend Scientology to sceptics. He never preached. When I had heart trouble in 1998, he rang regularly to see how I was, but he made no attempt to 'fix me' beyond sending me literature that I might find helpful about the dianetic nutritional route he had taken. I didn't understand it at all, and he never pressed the point.

I have Jackie Leven to thank for my working with Bert Jansch. I'd had no contact with him in fifteen years. Doll by Doll had broken up in late 1984, and soon after Jackie was attacked in the street and nearly strangled. He couldn't sing for a year and a half but during the enforced lay-off he cleaned up, dragging himself out of heroin addiction. He was now trying to help others with addiction and mental-health issues through a charity he had co-founded in 1985 called the Core Trust. Core – an acronym for Courage to stop, Order in life, Release from addiction, Entry into new life – used holistic methods like acupuncture and psychotherapy to help addicts. Princess Diana was a patron. It was a much mellower Jackie Leven who began recording again in 1994 after signing to Cooking Vinyl. He suggested that I should handle his press, beginning with two exquisite and emotionally draining albums in rapid succession, *The Argyll Cycle* and *The Mystery of Love Is Greater Than the Mystery of Death*. Jackie's forte was an ability to switch effortlessly from solitary melancholia to uplifting choruses. He drew on the blues and his Scottish roots to create his own twisted folk sound, but a torrent of releases diminished the potential level of interest in the media. He never made that one defining album but never delivered any duds either.

Jackie was a lovable rogue, gregarious and charming, and a teller of tall tales onstage and off. Some of them were even true. Did he go to school with Gordon Brown in Kirkcaldy? Was his own brand of Leven's Lament whisky nothing but rebottled Bell's? Did he meet Bob Dylan in a Berlin hotel bar sometime in October 1988? He claims to have travelled with him by train from Berlin to St Petersburg in Russia. During the journey he showed Bob some song lyrics he had written, and Bob suggested he set them to the melody of 'One Too Many Mornings', crediting the song – 'As We Sailed into Skibbereen', from *The Argyll Cycle* – to Leven and Dylan. Some spoilsport Dylan nerd eventually pointed out that Dylan was known to have been somewhere else when the alleged trip happened.

We stopped working together at the end of the decade. He found love and moved to a remote part of Hampshire, living opposite the local pub. Jackie stayed with Cooking Vinyl and released a staggering twenty-six albums by the time of his death in 2011.

That was my introduction to Cooking Vinyl, an undeservedly unfashionable label that was founded in 1986, but which outlived almost all of its contemporaries. Its boss Martin Goldschmidt kept the label afloat through the hard times that followed the collapse of Rough Trade distribution in the late 1980s by concentrating on low-cost contemporary folk music. To absolutely no fanfare whatsoever, Martin signed Bert Jansch in 1995 and released *When the Circus Comes to Town*. I'd hero-worshipped Bert for almost thirty years. Martin was renowned for penny-pinching, but little did he know that I would have taken Bert on for nothing. *When the Circus Comes to Town* was Bert's first album in almost five years and his first collection of original material in ten, during which time all of his solo albums had been recorded for tiny UK or European independent labels and been overlooked. By comparison, Cooking Vinyl was an established label, and even pushed the boat out a little on production. The recordings were wonderfully reminiscent of his finest work of the 1960s, and it was Bert's best by far since 1973's *L.A. Turnaround*.

The time was right too. The expanded music press benefited Bert, because the likes of *Q*, *Mojo* and *Vox* hadn't existed to write about him

271

before. The broadsheets were willingly sniffing around, and a four-month residency at the compact 12 Bar Club in Denmark Street presented a week-by-week opportunity for people to see him. Then fifty-one, Bert hadn't changed beyond filling out around the girth. He was the same tousled-haired, casually dressed figure I'd first seen play in 1968 as a member of Pentangle. He still had that too-cool factor. To see him on top of his game in such an intimate club recaptured the spirit of Soho in the 1960s. It was the perfect script. The 12 Bar was within walking distance of the great folk-music haunts of the past, like Les Cousins, on Greek Street, and Bunjies, just off Charing Cross Road.

Once word spread Britpop's finest began asking to be put on the guest list, including members of Blur, Suede and Pulp. They all watched in awe and wondered why he was playing in a hundred-capacity venue. I don't feel able to comment on his guitar playing, but I took William Reid along. Bert sat, as usual, hunched over the guitar, wrapped up in his own timeless music. William had positioned himself in the front row, spellbound, and offered the perfect technical appraisal: 'How does he play like that? He must have a fucking invisible third arm.'

I was shy and star-struck around Bert, but all through the summer I'd take people upstairs after the show to meet him in what passed for a dressing room or else we'd sit on the stairs. He hadn't a clue who I was, nor the people I introduced him to. I was a stalker on a mission. I'd mumble incomprehensibly, and he'd answer back in an equally soft, apprehensive manner. I couldn't tell Bert he was a hero; it would have embarrassed him more than it would me. Nor could I hold up a batch of impressive write-ups. Bert was never comfortable with the adulation of others. He'd shrug it off. He just did what he did, which was exactly what he'd been doing all his life.

Bert's second Cooking Vinyl album was too long coming. *Toy Balloon* didn't appear till March 1998. Although there were plenty of contemporary artists who would happily have collaborated, Martin kept holding out for Jimmy Page. That was never going to happen, however much Page openly admired Bert. I suggested Bert could work with Sonic

Youth. Lee and Thurston were up for the idea, if Bert would come over to New York, but Martin didn't want to put his hand in his pocket. Bert had never heard of Sonic Youth. I reminded him that in 1973 he made *L.A. Turnaround* with Mike Nesmith, and he'd not heard of the Monkees either. The idea of Bert playing with Lee and Thurston was such a missed opportunity. It would have been a great story. We'd done the career re-appraisal and played the 'rediscovered 1960s legend' card, so there was nowhere to go with *Toy Balloon*. I didn't work with him again till his final album, *The Black Swan*, in 2006. I also played an incidental part in helping reunite Bert with John Renbourn and, in turn, getting Pentangle back together. When they played the Royal Festival Hall in June 2008, I took great delight in the fact that, like them, I had also been there forty years earlier to the day.

In 1998 Paul Smith brought both New York punk duo Suicide and author and Merry Prankster Ken Kesey over to the UK. Kesey and his amiable psychedelic sidekick Ken Babbs toured here during August, including two nights at the Barbican, plus talks in Dublin and at the Edinburgh Festival. The dates heralded the launch of a spoken-word label called King Mob. Seven years in the planning, King Mob's manifesto was: 'Music begone! All music is dead, reduced to nothing more than competing background noise. Only the human voice can save you.' It was a far cry from Martin Jarvis reading the classics.

King Mob's aim was to release cult fiction read by its authors, which took a leaf out of the Beatles book. Apple Records had brought Kesey to London in 1969 to oversee a project involving authors reading their own work on a series of albums that Paul McCartney christened *Paperback Writings*. Unlike Apple, King Mob did actually release a batch of titles, which comprised Kesey and Babbs's notorious Acid Test recordings; urban portraits by Charles Bukowski, recorded in 1968; cult writer Stewart Home's *Pure Mania*; Iain Sinclair's London riverside fable *Downriver*; Ken Campbell's *Wol Wantok*, a crazy, instantly learnable new language; and a proto-rap oration by the Black Panthers' Bobby Seale.

Kesey's visit overshadowed rather than heralded the launch of King Mob. The advance press was mountainous, although I didn't enjoy ferrying Kesey round to do interviews. In between them he was grumpy and unappreciative. He was a hard man to warm to, but he knew how to turn on the charm when the tapes were rolling.

He turned it on for the shows too. Clad in a Stars and Stripes waistcoat, and underneath a Stetson, Kesey was a compelling, mesmerising performer. He told entertaining and touching stories about meeting the Beatles, delivered an elegy for John Lennon and gave a lengthy account of three teenage dropouts who made a pilgrimage to his Oregon farm (where the Pranksters' original magic bus was rusting away) during the week of Lennon's death. He even carried off a twenty-minute hipster children's tale about Tricker the squirrel, who gets one over on an angry bear called Big Double. 'Are you still tripping?' asked somebody in the audience. 'Are you kidding?' came the reply, amid a torrent of laughter. One reviewer likened Kesey's guru-like command of the crowd to Graham Chapman's character in *Life of Brian*. Kesey wasn't the Messiah, but nothing he spouted was going to shake the loyalty of those who flocked to see him.

The following year Kesey returned, this time travelling round in a new version of the Magic Bus, with a motley crew of hippies of all ages occupying its seats. They went 'In Search of Merlin', performing at Cornwall's open-air Minack Theatre on a drizzly 11 August to coincide with the solar eclipse. The bus then chugged its way to Brixton Academy. The 'Where's Merlin?' pageant was the supposed highlight of a show that had sold less than a hundred and fifty advance tickets out of a four thousand capacity. The biggest cheer from an eventual five hundred onlookers came when the curtain opened to reveal the bus. Not *the* bus, of course, but a bus. For a while they were happy to suspend disbelief, but it was amateur hour, culminating in the laughable Arthurian pageant itself. It resembled a school Nativity play, but was nowhere near as professionally staged. Kesey, in a top hat, presided, but the charming man who had been so enthralling at the Barbican had become more Captain Mainwaring than Captain Trips.

Kesey was a tired-looking and often forlorn shadow of the man I'd met a year before, and once again the press build-up had been hefty. I was glad there were so few reports. I was convinced the reviews were spiked out of respect for his countercultural glory days. The tour had been overly ambitious, seriously flawed and anarchic for all the wrong reasons, but nobody wanted to dent Ken Kesey's mythical status. It proved to be his final trip. Kesey died of liver disease two years later, in November 2001.

By comparison, Suicide was painless. On 9 March 1998 Blast First re-released the duo's classic 1977 debut album, *Suicide*. In the run-up to its release they played the Garage in Islington over four nights. The odd couple, Alan Vega and Martin Rev, were warmly welcomed back, the celebrity rock turnout confirming the extent of their influence. Jarvis Cocker, Andy Weatherall, Barry Adamson, Depeche Mode's Martin Gore and Soft Cell's Dave Ball all spun discs, as did Tim Gane of Stereolab, who with Bobby Gillespie, Jim Reid and Jason Pierce (from 'Breathalysed', as Vega kept calling them) formed an unofficial past and present Brassneck reunion. Julian Cope and Will Sergeant must have been there in spirit. Tim Gane nailed why Suicide were so significant: 'Their debut album is probably the greatest "rock" record not to use a guitar.'

I bought the Suicide album in 1977, on the Red Star label run by former New York Dolls manager Marty Thau. I could now add them to my collection of classic Bowery groups I'd worked with. *Suicide* was the flipside to the Ramones' debut album, a simplistic pop formula of a very different kind featuring Rev on vocals and Vega on 'instrument'. Rev's heavily echoed vocals, peppered with grunts, screams, sobs and whimpers, are delivered over Vega's droning two-note keyboard and ominous, pulsating drum machine, and the album still sounds fresh and exciting and scary.

They did a lot of interviews while they were over and were surprised that they kept on coming. 'This is more than we've done since the album was released,' said Rev. They liked to remind everybody that they'd never split up, although most of their recordings over the past twenty years had been apart from one another. The two men were opposites and looked as much like cartoon figures as the Ramones. Both wore enormous dark shades, but Vega was smaller and stockier, never without his beret, and a little grouchier. He drank, smoked, ate meat and loved cats. Rev was square-faced, with a mane of hair, and was a teetotal, non-smoking vegetarian with an allergy to fur. I found this out when we did a photo session in my office space in Old Street, where our three cats caused him to come out in blotches.

They had a lot to live up to at the Garage. The anticipation was intense, as they played to an audience that was too pleased to be there to be disappointed by a forty-five-minute art-punk cabaret set that honoured their debut album with a crackling 'Rocket USA', a truncated 'Frankie Teardrop' and a bristling 'Ghost Rider'. Best of all was a song called 'Juke Box Babe' (from Vega's 1990 album *Alan Vega*), where he borrowed from '96 Tears', 'I Wanna Be Your Dog' and 'Sister Ray'. Despite their outsider status, they were disarmingly modest and ambivalent about the reverence they'd been afforded by two generations of musicians. In that, they had much in common with Bert Jansch.

15 : MY PATIO'S ON FIRE

1995-9

I left Metropolitan Wharf in 1995 and moved to a newly converted warehouse space on Old Street, opposite St Luke's church, then an empty shell with no roof. *Dazed and Confused* magazine was based on the ground floor, with a rather less trendy Turkish takeaway next door. Sara Lawrence began working with me immediately after I moved in. I'd known her for five years. She'd been a freelancer for *Melody Maker* and on the staff at *No. 1* magazine, before becoming an independent PR herself for several years. She was my first assistant to have any prior PR experience and was amazed that I seemed to do so little. I wasn't haranguing journalists all day or sending mass mail-outs, and I was still in the dark ages. I worked

Gorky's Zygotic Mynci: Euros Childs, John Lawrence, Megan Childs and Richard James, just before recording *Bwyd Time*. One of my greatest disappointments was that Gorky's didn't become bigger than Genesis (*photo: Martin Goodacre*).

on an old golf-ball typewriter that was at least electric, but Sara dragged me into the computer age. Before long I even had a mobile phone and an email address.

Although only two floors below me, *Dazed and Confused* never wrote about any of my groups, until we took on Elastica and they did a cover-story fashion piece about guitarist Donna Matthews. Elastica were one of the leading lights of Britpop and, for me, by far the coolest and best group in the pack. I couldn't have cared less about them recycling the Stranglers and Wire, their self-titled debut album was thrilling, angular, guitar-driven new-wave pop. And live they galvanised such energy that it was irrelevant that the line-up was three-quarters female and had most male writers salivating. They would have been a great group in any era. So when Elastica came my way in spring 1996, my first thought was, 'Why?'

Their press had been handled by John Best since their first single in late 1993, and he can't be faulted. It would have been impossible to contain the acres of coverage that self-generated over the next two years. John was part of a select circle of publicists who had divided up the spoils of Britpop, most of whom I hardly knew at all. Elastica came to me because I wasn't in that clique. I was undeniably older and allegedly wiser. I was respected, supposedly a safe pair of hands. I'm always reminded of a line in *Chinatown*, delivered with such iciness by John Huston as the odious Noah Cross: "Course I'm respectable. I'm old. Politicians, ugly buildings and whores all get respectable if they last long enough.' Elastica wanted somebody to get them off the media treadmill, and it was easier for me, being outside the melee of Britpop. I'd never met the group. I was bliss-fully ignorant and did my best to remain so. It's much simpler to deny what you don't know about.

Elastica had spent much of 1995 focusing on cracking the US, their relentless twelve months on the road winding up with them playing at Australia's Big Day Out the following February. They'd hardly been home or released anything new in over a year, but press interest remained heightened because of Justine Frischmann's relationship with Blur's Damon Albarn. It placed her centre stage in the Britpop circus. She

278

was one half of its royal couple – or 'Blur indoors', as one tabloid wag described her.

My immediate impression was that Elastica were burnt out by the rigours of touring and the pressures of sudden stardom, and 1996 was a quieter, transitional year with no undue pressure. They played their first UK shows in over a year headlining the second stage of the first V Festival in Chelmsford and Warrington on 17/18 August. Original bassist Annie Holland had walked out in the US and had been replaced by circus-family girl Sheila Chipperfield, and ex-Fall keyboard man Dave Bush had also been brought in. He was no stranger to volatile behaviour, having been sacked by Mark E. Smith after five years. The new line-up went down a storm. A rumoured new single remained only a rumour, but in all confidence we announced that Elastica were now recording their second album, for release in spring 1997.

A sultry-looking Justine appeared on the cover of the first *NME* of the new year. The day of the interview a gossipy piece appeared in the glossy magazine *Elle*, where the writer – a friend of Justine's – wrote about 'Britpop's favourite lovebirds' following a dinner engagement with them that Justine thought was a friendly get-together. Justine was livid about her privacy being violated, and while the *NME* piece was positive, it was a little innocuous. I didn't want to fall into the trap of pandering to unnecessary requests. Six months earlier Elastica had been on the cover of *The Face*. Justine, Donna, drummer Justin Welch, me and writer Chris Heath had a great four-day jolly in New York. We'd flown there purely to do the photos, which made little sense, but I wasn't complaining. *The Face* cover had appeared in a vacuum in the summer, and after the *NME* cover I knew we shouldn't do anything else till the album was finished.

It turned out to be a long two-and-a-half-year wait before anything new was released at all. In between the rumour mill had been churning away over serious drug problems and a group in turmoil: Justine and Donna weren't talking, recordings had ground to a halt and Justine and Damon's relationship was on the rocks, with Justine cast as either a priv-ileged rich girl or some kind of femme fatale. We'd get calls most weeks.

We were once asked if we could confirm that Donna had died of a heroin overdose, but usually it was people asking whether Justine and Damon had split up or had Elastica disbanded. We just kept a lid on it. A spokesperson denied everything and said nothing. The spokesman hadn't a clue. In August 1998 Donna did leave the group and Justine and Damon finally broke up. We still had nothing to add, except to say the group were carrying on and still recording. Nobody was too interested in that.

It wasn't until May 1999 that another new line-up was announced (ex-Linoleum guitarist Paul Jones replaced Donna and Annie Holland returned), as well as an interim 6 Track EP to coincide with a bunch of dates, culminating this time in the August Bank Holiday Leeds and Reading Festivals. Having played no shows in two years they proved once again they could still cut it live. The EP was downplayed and wasn't chart-eligible so as to ease the burden of expectation. The ploy didn't work. If these were 'works in progress', including a live track, a droning instrumental and one of Donna's home demos, then they didn't bode well for the second album, which was currently being mixed. *The Menace* finally appeared in March 2000, five years after Elastica's debut. It was dissed in the *NME*, where it was rated 6/10, with a bitchy parting shot: 'See you. Wouldn't want to be you.' It didn't set the tone, though. Most of the reviews were more constructive. *The Menace* was an intermittent triumph that encompassed the chaotic eighteen months before Donna left and a frantic six weeks during which the present line-up picked up the pieces. The group were always going to be on a hiding to nothing. The album was almost incidental to the media. It simply presented them with the opportunity to rake up the stories about drug abuse, band inertia and friction, and to drag up the disintegration of Justine and Damon's relationship, which Damon had put under the microscope on Blur's album *13*.

Justine once said I'd done a great job by keeping them out of the papers for so long, but in the run-up to *The Menace* we blitzed the press. Not just the expected music titles; Justine was all over the broadsheets and glossies, but everything that was written was about the baggage of the three 'Ds' – Donna, Damon and drugs. The press onslaught warranted an entry in the *Guardian*'s 'Hard to Avoid' section. 'This week: Justine Frischmann is promoting Elastica's new album just about everywhere.' It made little difference. The album charted at no. 24 but dropped outside the Top 75 a week later. They were relieved the album was finally out there and soon behind them. They toured the UK and Europe, playing most of the major festivals, then went to Japan and the US over the next six months. As ever they went down a storm, but in October 2001 they officially announced they'd split.

If any two groups fought against the tide of Britpop, it was Gorky's Zygotic Mynci and Stereolab. My introduction to Gorky's Zygotic Mynci was their third album, *Bywd Time*, in June 1995, when I eagerly took them on. I drew a rather perverse connection between *Bwyd Time* and the Grateful Dead's fragmented third album *Aoxamoxoa*, with its eerie mix of folk forms and experimentalism, which included sucking nitrous oxide for maximum vocal weirdness. *Bwyd Time* was a no less perplexing mix of pastoral folk and indulgent experimentation, with added British prog and psychedelia, but like the Dead they did some serious larking about and added silly Pythonesque voices. *Bwyd Time* begins with a tinny piss-take disco track, after which they break into the sublimely moving 'Miss Trudy', about a music teacher who has a moment of madness and throws violins across the room. I was well and truly sucker punched.

I was convinced Gorky's would be huge and the only comparable group was Genesis, whose naive acoustic whimsy and dark humour initially stood them apart from the prevailing blues rock. Like Genesis, Gorky's came together as school friends, though nothing as grand as Charterhouse – in their case it was Ysgol Bro Myrddin school in Carmarthen. In chief writer and singer Euros Childs they had as reluctant a star as Peter Gabriel had once been, blessed with a voice as gorgeous as any I'd heard. Success wasn't to be, and by 2001 they'd beaten That Petrol Emotion's record, becoming the only group with eight UK Top 75 singles without ever making the Top 40. The charts never mattered to them, nor sales, so they never considered they had failed or were underachieving. They were a classic Brassneck group. Gorky's adhered to their own rule-book. Rule one is the same for all bands: the music comes first, and you fight to do everything your way. In that, Gorky's were sticklers.

Euros, the son of two teachers, and John Lawrence, the son of a town planner, formed the band in 1990 with classmate Richard James, the son of a police chief inspector. The official and simplest explanation of the group's name was that 'Gork was school slang for dim-wit, zygotic, we hijacked from GCSE biology classes, and mynci is just a misspelling of monkey.' The most familiar line-up was completed by Euros's elder sister Megan, who played violin, and drummer Euros Rowlands, who was the son of Dafydd Rowlands, a renowned poet who held the office of Arch-Druid. For those still seeking evidence that Gorky's were a batty bunch, then Euros 2's Druid dad was the final proof. The sub-Tolkien cover of *Bywd Time*, which saw them donning wizards' costumes and wearing bishops' mitres on the inner photo, was further confirmation. These misconceptions never left them, branding them variously as eccentric, quaint and quirky, while their music suggested baffling 1960s hippy influences like Kevin Ayers, the Bonzo Dog Doo-Dah Band and the Incredible String Band.

'The *NME* was always obsessed with the idea that we took mushrooms and psychedelic drugs,' moaned Euros, 'purely because of the type of music we played and because we didn't write conventional rock 'n' roll lyrics. We didn't need drugs to come up with what we did. We enjoyed messing about; we joked somewhere that we lived in a caravan and the *Bwyd Time* sleeve was a wind-up. Things like that stuck but if anyone says don't do it, then you do it. *Bywd Time* has that attitude running through it.' It was the group's breakthrough album, and they toured beyond the Welsh borders and began to get prominent reviews and features in the *Sunday Times*, the *Independent* and the *Guardian*, among others. The crazy Welsh school kids could no longer be ignored and they were responsible for putting Welsh-language pop on the map, ahead of the likes of Super Furry Animals and Catatonia, who would become far more commercially successful. 'The idea of a Welsh scene was purely a geographic convenience in the music press,' said Euros, 'and they wrote about Welsh pop as if it had never existed before. Why shouldn't we sing in our own language? It was insulting and fitted an English stereotype that Wales was some sort of backwater.'

I was forty-five when I started working with Gorky's. They were half my age but looked younger. Gorky's were shy, nervous, friendly, but with a disconcerting habit of breaking into their native tongue and laughing out loud in unison. I often felt like a teacher trying to quell a noisy classroom. When I mentioned that I'd seen Captain Beefheart, Tim Buckley supporting the Incredible String Band and had interviewed Gene Clark, they were agog – probably amazed that I was still alive. It was my standby way of winning groups round. It was only ever the music that mattered, and the promotional chores that came with it were a necessary evil. Gorky's mixed playfulness and cussedness in equal measures in the face of continuing, often insulting and patronising questions. They were a nightmare to interview, and even harder to photograph.

Gorky's signed to Mercury and released the first of many near-hits, the dreamy but disarming 'Patio Song'. It preceded the breathtaking *Barafundle* in April 1997, yet another mind-bendingly subtle shift of musical direction. It was a warped acoustic folk album but with the harmonies and musical irreverence of *Friends*-era Beach Boys. The album even had a medieval feel to it. Euros and Megan's dad played in an early-music band, so they borrowed a crumhorn, a shawm and a hurdy-gurdy. The record was magical and dazzlingly ambitious, but its sales weren't enough for Mercury. When their next album, *Gorky 5*, sold even less, they were hastily dropped at the end of 1998.

They went to Beggars' affiliate label Mantra, and only a year later *Spanish Dance Troup* was their best shot yet, a gentler statement, with some of their more contrary stylistic quirks less exposed, but once again it failed to nudge them up a notch. John left the group in 1999, and some of the craziness left with him. They gradually adopted a more bucolic, alt-folk sound that was several years ahead of its time. Gorky's weren't cut out for the kind of success they were capable of achieving or the bruising experience of a music industry that was infuriated by their stub-bornness, particularly a refusal to release multiple-format singles with additional tracks because they thought this was exploiting fans. Their tarnished innocence prevailed, along with a boundary-less quality that never found a wider audience. I stuck with them, and they stuck with me till the last of their nine albums, *Sleep/Holiday* in 2003. They broke up that year and finally told the rest of the world three years later.

On the face of it, Gorky's and Stereolab were totally different groups, with backgrounds and ideologies that were miles apart, but scratch beneath the surface and they had far more in common than separated them. Both groups vigorously demanded and maintained complete control over their music and neither viewed the notion of courting the press as anything but extraneous. As for cultivating an image, that was equally unimportant. Gorky's were awkward, but Stereolab baffled journalists. They provoked the notion that you can't take the laboratory out of Stereolab, and journal-ists were wary of their intellect. They were pop boffins but, scariest of all, the core duo of East End-born Tim Gane and Parisian Laetitia Sadier also happened to be Marxists – 'running dogs of bourgeois revisionism', said one writer. I began working with them at the beginning of 1997, ahead of their ninth album, *Dots and Loops*, in September.

From the outset Stereolab were an independent group – though signed to Elektra in the US – and after 1993 everything in the UK was released by their self-financed Duophonic Ultra High Frequency Discs. They were an incredibly prolific band and as vinyl junkies created an eminently collectible catalogue: every album had a limited-edition vinyl release, plus mail-order-only seven-, ten-inch and tour singles, which built up a committed fan base. They were a self-reliant unit, which from my point of view meant that I never got to know them as well as I'd have liked. They may have taken their music seriously, but they were good to hang out with on the too rare occasions I did.

Stereolab's music was fluid and musically flirtatious. Some would say too much so. It shifted across krautrock, 1960s Brazilian psychedelia and old Moog synthesizer albums, seductive French pop, Latino jazz, muzak, disco pop, post-rock and, latterly, techno grooves to create a futuristic world drawn from the past. It was a neat trick, but for all their experimental traits their truest musical instincts were pop. They floated above scenes and fads, but by default the brief trend for easy listening and space-age pop in the mid-1990s helped gain Stereolab some recognition, and in 1994 singles such as 'French Disko' and 'Ping Pong' picked up radio play. 'Ping Pong' could well have made the Top 40 but for their independent distribution. It would have been something if it had. Its sunshiney Free Design-style vocals disguised a lyric that was a critique of capitalist economics. Stereolab were invited to tour with Pulp in 1995 but couldn't resist winding up Pulp fans puzzled by their combination of motorik drone and mood muzik. Laetitia would announce, 'This is our last song,' to ironic cheers, before adding, 'but it's very long.'

Dots and Loops raised their profile at the right time, just as the stranglehold of Britpop was loosening. The album was produced by John McEntire of Tortoise and Andi Toma and Jan St Werner from Mouse on Mars, who, like Stereolab, were part of a *simpatico* set that also included the High Llamas, Nurse with Wound, Labradford and Broadcast. They presented a united front of intelligent, thoughtful, more left-field musical aspiration. Most of the groups I looked after around this time had a certain commonality. Gorky's toured with Stereolab, who did a major US tour with Sonic Youth. Sonic Youth played dates with Spiritualized, and in the past they'd supported the Jesus and Mary Chain. Jason Pierce was a great fan of Gorky's, who had opened for Spiritualized at their first major show after the release of *Ladies and Gentlemen* in June 1997, and Megan played violin with them. Jason likened Gorky's to *Smile*-era Beach Boys, when Brian Wilson's crafted sounds were matched by Van Dyke Parks's oblique lyrics. Kate Radley's stepfather once said that Jason spent an entire summer afternoon lying in the garden listening on a loop to that song about 'the patio catching fire'.

When Spiritualized shared a bill with Sonic Youth at John Peel's Meltdown festival on 1 July 1998, it was the last time I saw the line-up that, in the main, had been touring since the release of *Ladies and Gentlemen*. Kate Radley had left around the Royal Albert Hall show in October 1997, and Julian Cope collaborator Thighpaulsandra had been brought in. They added sax player Ray Dickaty, but the core group comprised Sean Cook on bass (he joined in 1993 and played on their 1995 album *Pure Phase*), guitarist Mike Mooney and drummer Damon Reece, both of whom joined soon after. Previously, Damon had had the unenviable job of replacing Pete de Freitas in the Mac-less Echo & the Bunnymen line-up. I'd known Mike since the Bunnymen's 'ley lines' tour in 1983 and we hung out after the World Trade Center show, where it soon came out that he, Sean and Damon were unhappy about their low wages and session fees. All three left the band at the end of 1998, by which time they had ceased touring, and they were officially sacked the following April. It was an acrimonious end to a line-up that had always transcended the limitations of a six-piece group in realising Jason's trance rock and narcotic visions.

It was the only sour note in what had been a particularly smooth, enjoyable and close working relationship with Jason. In the months leading up to the release of *Ladies and Gentlemen* we settled into a routine, whereby interviews usually took place at a Hoxton bar/restaurant called the Electric Light Station, near Shoreditch church. Jason was fashionably lean and always fashionably late by anything up to an hour. Once he arrived he'd sit chain-smoking Marlboros while nursing bottled beers. He had a cool, deadpan approach to answering questions, all handled in a quiet, considered manner. Incessant smoking and the lighting of cigarettes provided a natural pause, not to think of an answer, but for effect.

As the circle of journalists widened to people new to Spiritualized, they'd be surprised on meeting Jason to find that he was healthy-looking, well turned out and shattered the preconceptions he toyed with in lyrics that explicitly referenced his taking heroin. I never once saw him stoned; he balanced intoxication with being in control. Jason was certainly no wasted junkie and occasionally adopted Hunter S. Thompson's line that 'If I'd really done everything people say I've done, then I'd be dead.'

Groups change labels, change line-ups, change managers and they change PRs. I'm not equating what I do to the work of a producer or musician, but getting the right PR at the right moment is significant, and for the few years we worked together between 1997 and 2003 Jason and I had a natural understanding. Once or twice in interviews he was asked why the press reaction was greater this time around, and he would nod in my direction. Jason finds it hard to acknowledge success as anything other than something abstract and refuses to accept that *Ladies and Gentlemen* is Spiritualized's greatest album. 'What's happened is that the public are more informed about us – thanks to our publicist. We're taken more seriously.' I always appreciated the acknowledgement, even if I was being damned by faint praise.

In 2001 Spiritualized returned with *Let It Come Down*, an even more capacious musical work. Three years in the making, it featured a hundred-piece orchestra, a gospel choir and a new hand-picked group. This time Jason scored and orchestrated everything himself from scratch. It was a painstaking process, singing all the parts into a Dictaphone, then carefully transferring them to piano, on which Jason had only rudimentary skills. He wanted to dispense with effects and studio techniques and create the sounds purely as played by each individual musician – 'in the room', as he would say. *Let It Come Down* was magnificently orchestrated and the songs were no less personal, but it failed to connect in the same way as its predecessor. I find it impossible to say what was missing, although for me of course *Ladies and Gentlemen* had been a one-off experience. There was something so unique about it. The specific circumstances in which it was created and the manner in which it was executed to perfection in every detail meant that it couldn't be replicated.

Two years later the stripped-down *Amazing Grace*, recorded in under a month this time, saw Spiritualized move from Dedicated and BMG to the independent Sanctuary group, where its release felt like a comedown. It was regarded with less importance, certainly in the press. It was a cathartic album for Jason, a necessary primal rush of garage rock after the more suffocating *Let It Come Down*. 'She Kissed Me (It Felt Like a Hit)' was full of blazing fury, but the album's highlights were once again the strung-out ballads. I knew it would be the last time I worked with Jason.

Throughout June 1998 I'd begun to experience a shortness of breath that gradually got worse. If I walked any distance, it felt as if my chest was about to explode. Pretty soon I couldn't even make it to the corner shop to buy cigarettes without stopping for a breather, and I gave in to Sara's insistence that I see a doctor. By then we were in a relationship. I went for a health check on 14 July and was referred to a heart specialist, who told me I had congenital coronary heart disease and that I'd need a bypass operation. Much as I wanted to, I could not put it off. For the time being I could at least function more easily with the aid of GTN spray, but hanging over me was the knowledge that on 2 September I was booked in for triple heart bypass surgery. I asked Sara to tell people I was away. Ten days later I was home again, and soon after could at least give the impression over the phone that I was back working after a bit of a break.

It all happened so quickly that I had already decided to take on Mercury Rev, and it was a done deal before I found out about the bypass surgery. It had been a ridiculous year, and we were still busy. In June we'd had Sonic Youth in town, Spiritualized were winding down and the England United single was released as the World Cup got under way. Then Kesey and Babbs arrived in August, *Gorky 5* and David Gedge's more lavish, post-Wedding Present duo Cinerama's *Va Va Voom* were released, and *The Modern Antiquarian* was just months away from publication. Mercifully, Elastica's album was delayed. I also had to move from Old Street to nearby Clerkenwell in August, and the timing of the upheaval wasn't great. No wonder I was in a frazzle when Mercury Rev's *Deserter's Songs* came along.

I didn't know much about the group, but they had a reputation for drug addictions, onstage fighting and major line-up changes, with only Jonathan Donahue and Sean 'Grasshopper' Mackowiak remaining from the group that first came together in Buffalo, New York, in 1989. Three years after the last album, *See You on the Other Side*, which had pointed towards a more accessible direction, the pair had moved to the Catskills, in upstate New York. The Band's Levon Helm and Garth Hudson were neighbours in nearby Woodstock, and their fleeting presence on *Deserter's Songs* was enough to give the album a reference point. It was a door into Mercury Rev's new brand of dream-like Americana, casting off any reminders of their previous wayward, indulgent recordings and chaotic live shows. Outside of a dedicated few music journalists, most people were coming fresh to Mercury Rev and everybody embraced *Deserter's Songs* with almost messianic zeal. It was instantly appealing: a broad palette of pastoral beauty, gentle psychedelia, backwoods country, wobbly noises and even a hint of Broadway ('Endlessly' sounds almost like Gershwin). 'Delta Sun Bottleneck Stomp' meshed jug-band hoedowns and house beats; it was remixed for a single by the Chemical Brothers, who immediately declared *Deserter's Songs* to be the best album of the year. Mercury Rev's box of tricks was so strange that, as one reviewer observed, it featured sounds probably last heard on a Perry Como Christmas album back in the 1950s.

We sent out promos in early August, and by the time it was released two months later it was already being hailed as the undisputed album of the year. In twenty years I'd known nothing like it. Right across the board it received the most astounding reviews. It bettered *Ladies and Gentlemen* and Mercury Rev began to be viewed by many as a more peaceful, nocturnal counterpoint to Spiritualized. I genuinely believe that our involvement as PRs helped effect that transition and its acceptance.

Jonathan and Grasshopper came in for a week of promo at the end of August. Sara did all the legwork, while I sat around freaked out with dread. The day after they left I went under the surgeon's knife. I only met them a couple of times, but it was the same old story with me and visiting American musicians. I found them, and Jonathan in particular, too self-important to like too much. When the follow-up album *All Is Dream* was released in August 2001, we did an even better job. In terms of its mood and courageous sweeping musical ambition it was the better album, and the acclaim it received replicated the unprecedented praise that *Deserter's Songs* had been given. Next album they went in-house for their PR. It felt like a kick in the teeth, but Jack Lemmon's calming voice echoed in my head once again.

In the months that followed my operation I thought long and hard about my life and the job I'd been doing for the last twenty years. The level at which we were operating and the success we'd had for a pro-longed two-year period were quite phenomenal and had somehow crept up on us. Brassneck PR was still on a roll as we crossed into 1999. It was hard to let go or heed the advice to take it easy, and when I was given the opportunity to work with XTC, I jumped at it. The first of two albums, *Apple Venus Volume 1*, was released in February 1999. Its companion piece, *Wasp Star*, followed a year later, both through Cooking Vinyl.

These were the first new recordings by XTC in seven years, as they had famously refused to record for Virgin Records again. Now down to the last two founding members, Andy Partridge and Colin Moulding, after guitarist Dave Gregory had been booted out during recording for being a negative presence, both albums were compositional triumphs of orches-tral pop, typically infectious, intricate and off-kilter, and with shades of Vaughan Williams. XTC were one of the few groups whom, back in the 1980s, I'd have killed to work with. Their punchy, Talking Heads-influenced debut *White Music* had been released in 1978, just as I was starting life as a PR. They were *Top of the Pops* regulars between 1979 and 1982, when I'd be there with the Undertones and the Teardrops. The hits dried up for XTC too, but albums such as *English Settlement*, *Skylarking* and *Oranges & Lemons* were fabulous, and Andy Partridge, perceived as another of the great, troubled 1980s eccentrics, was clearly one of pop's finest auteurs. They were my kind of group. I never dreamt I'd get to work with them, and when I did I never expected it to be anything but short-lived. XTC haven't recorded anything since *Wasp Star*, although I carried on working with Andy for another ten years after he set up his own label, Ape Records.

The work certainly hadn't eased up in 1999: aside from XTC, Mercury Rev had a momentum that carried them through till the end of sum-mer, while the second album by the re-formed Bunnymen, the return of

Elastica, Kesey's disastrous magic-bus tour and albums by Stereolab and Gorky's made for a full-on year. During the summer I was asked to work with Death in Vegas, whose label Concrete was bankrolled by BMG. *The Contino Sessions*, released in September, was another hypnotic, dark, zoned-out album that placed high in the critics' polls and was our third consecutive *NME* Album of the Year. I was a little dismissive; it was déjà vu all over again. Death in Vegas was the brainchild of graphic designer and club DJ Richard Fearless, recently joined by producer/engineer Tim Holmes. *The Contino Sessions* was shoegazing for the club culture. It managed to pack a strong emotional punch, which belied its creation in their small cluttered basement studio, the Contino Rooms, situated off the Gray's Inn Road. They brought in a series of guest vocalists: Iggy Pop, Bobby Gillespie, Jim Reid and One Dove's Dot Allison, who weaved an atmospheric, gothic web on the album's best-known song, 'Dirge'. You've almost certainly heard it without necessarily knowing who it's by.

Death in Vegas were nominated for a Mercury Prize in 2000 and invited me to the do. They were party animals. They demolished all the booze on the table in rapid time and were regularly disappearing furtively to the toilets. I declined both the legal and illicit stimulants with surprising ease, thinking how glad I was that this was no longer me. They partied on elsewhere, leaving their heavy-duty bronze Mercury nominee's award on the table. I lugged it home, where it now props up a bunch of books in the back bedroom.

My heart op had given me the perfect way of resisting the sort of social pressure that went with the job. I could more easily make my excuses and leave. I'd bought a flat in Islington in 1999 and now worked from home rather than living in an office space. The difference was palpable. I was approaching fifty and it was a relief to finally feel able to start acting my age. I didn't slow down, but quite naturally almost everything I'd been involved with since the mid-1990s would run its course within a few years.

My long association with Echo & the Bunnymen came to an abrupt end. In 2001 the group – now just Mac and Will – were signed to Cooking

Vinyl, which had become something of a post-punk care home for acts whose major-label days were behind them. Their new album, *Flowers*, was their first since the acrimonious *What Are You Going to Do With Your Life?* It wasn't great; Will and Mac tried too hard to appease one another, and the results were lacklustre. That same year I wrote notes for a four-disc Rhino Records retrospective called *Crystal Days*. Mac took exception to some of what I'd written for the accompanying booklet, specifically about his drug-taking exploits. It was mostly through veiled references and in-jokes such as 'Echo & the Buglemen' and 'no snow, no show', and was by no means a betrayal since Mac had talked openly about it in so many interviews, but he rang me from the US and called me a traitor. I was really angry after he hung up. I knew I hadn't divulged any trade secrets, but I couldn't understand why he'd not read the notes in advance. Although that was the label's responsibility, I was left thinking I should have ensured rather than assumed that everything had been checked beforehand. So I quit. I'd been in two minds about carrying on in 1999, when I thought that Echo & the Bunnymen wouldn't last out the year. How wrong could I have been? Twenty years since Les left, Mac and Will are still keeping the group alive. They've learnt to tolerate one another's differences, largely because they don't hang out together and don't see each other except when it's called for.

I don't regret much, but I wish I'd patched things up with Mac. Echo & the Bunnymen are the group I'm still most associated with. They were part of my world for over twenty years, as a group and as individuals. I had a strong link to Liverpool too, and I worked with a number of other artists from the city whom I've not touched on here. To this day I meet people who are surprised I don't have a Liverpool accent. Echo & the Bunnymen had a huge impact on my personal and professional life, which would have been very different had Seymour Stein not seen something in a group with a daft name and a good-looking singer who reminded him of Del Shannon.

My working relationships with both Bill Drummond and Julian Cope were always far more complex. With Bill I called a halt in 2005; with

Julian it petered out a few years later. I'd reached a point where I felt that neither of them required or benefited from anything I could do any more. Bill and Julian have much in common creatively. Both are work-aholics and were juggling so many projects from 1999 onwards that it was hard to keep up. They were too prolific, and I was becoming increasingly frustrated. Bill was starting too many projects that he didn't see through; Julian was releasing too many albums.

Both were writing voluminously. In 1999 Thorsons published the second part of Julian's autobiography, *Repossessed*, and in 2004 they published *The Megalithic European*. His follow-up to *The Modern Antiquarian* was no less a feat of extensive on-site research, requiring extensive travelling throughout Europe, but in between he found time to undertake lecture tours, including two at the British Museum, and to curate events at the South Bank and at Hammersmith's Lyric Theatre. On top of that, between leaving the Echo label in 1997 and the end of 2005 he released at least ten albums, including side projects such as Queen Elizabeth's *Queen Elizabeth 2: Elizabeth Vagina* and glam power trio Brain Donor, neither of which I cared for. But in that time he recorded what I saw as three 'proper' song-based albums: *Rome Wasn't Burned in a Day*, *Citizen Cain'd* and *Dark Orgasm*, all of which were played down. It was maddening. Despite characteristic self-indulgence, deliberately jarring production levels and unsettling instrumentation, they represent some of his best work and plenty of grossly overlooked songs. Julian was happy to let people discover these albums themselves. For the publicist in me, it was galling to be so hog-tied.

It was a similar situation with Bill's output. His autobiographical collection *45*, which was published in 2000 by Little, Brown, and his self-published *How to Be an Artist* two years later were the most rewarding and involving for me. Bill wasn't making albums any more but instead was racking up a series of activities, as he'd call them, that came under the collective umbrella of the Penkiln Burn. These included the production of a pack of cards titled *Silent Protest* and the foundation of the Intercontinental Twinning Association, the Soup Line and

No Music Day. What I found exasperating was that I knew that if Bill was going into somebody's kitchen to make soup, all I had to do was ring up the *Guardian* and they'd jump at the opportunity of sending a journalist along. But as far as I could see none of it was going anywhere, till in 1994 Bill set in motion his idea for the conceptual choir The17. It didn't evolve fully for a couple of years, by which time it had become his primary focus, at the expense of the other activities. The17 was a wonderfully abstract idea, but by then I'd moved on. In 2008 Penkiln Burn published *17*; it will change the way you think about and listen to music. Many of Bill's other abandoned 'activities' have since become facets of his extraordinary 'The 25 Paintings World Tour', which launched in 2014 and continues until 2025. I should have had greater faith.

I didn't work with Jimmy Cauty at all after 2K. He was more comfortable working as an outsider artist and for a long time now has worked closely with the Clerkenwell-based L-13 Light Industrial Workshop. He came to greater attention after his run-in with the Royal Mail over his Stamps of Mass Destruction, and more recently his 'ADP Riot' tour, a short film with Debbie Harry that premiered at Tate Modern, and his creation of the 'model village' for Banksy's anti-art theme park Dismaland have brought him further recognition that he's neither sought nor is too bothered about.

Jimmy's consciously lower profile made it easier for him to avoid what was always the most tiresome aspect of my working with Bill and Julian: too many writers and editors couldn't get past their reputations as tricksters and weirdos. I could do nothing to change that and it wore me down. Julian has always purposefully challenged the notion of the serious artist, but it nagged away at Bill. Bill is always harder on himself than on anybody else; he doesn't respond to praise and I'm not sure he's ever completely satisfied with anything he's done. I can certainly relate to that. He and Julian both deserved better from the media and from me.

There's a strong spiritual bond between Will, Mac, Bill and Julian, no matter whether any of them are speaking to each other or whether they've spoken to one another in decades. I was one of very few common links between them all, but I was always very conscious that I hadn't been in Liverpool in 1977. There is something deep inside them that binds them by an invisible thread, a consequence of the circumstances that aligned in Liverpool to bring them together. It was an incredible moment in time that can't be explained, and certainly not by the fiction of ley lines running underneath Mathew Street.

I carried on as a PR and shifted into catalogue work, handling remastered and repackaged reissues of what was essentially my seventies record collection. I even found myself working with many of my teenage folk heroes – Bert Jansch, Richard Thompson, John Renbourn, Pentangle, Shirley Collins, John Martyn and Michael Chapman among them. That was a new and different kind of buzz; I was content to be grazing in the long grass with musicians older than me for once. I'd finally accepted my lot as a 'respected' or 'veteran' PR, and I can now blissfully identify with the ageing lawmen cast adrift in a modern world and confounded by new technology in Sam Peckinpah's beautifully autumnal *Ride the High Country*. When Randolph Scott's Gil Westrum tries to lead Joel McCrea's Steve Judd astray to steal a gold shipment, Judd is having none of it. 'All I want,' he says to his old friend, 'is to enter my house justified.'

SOURCES

INTRODUCTION
2 'It's all about looking', Max Bell, *Evening Standard*, 26 June 1998

CHAPTER 1
13 'With a lot of these new wave people', *Sounds*, 1 January 1977
14 'materialistic and decadent superstars', Mick Farren, *NME*, 19 June 1976

CHAPTER 3
50 'Room after room reveals', Max Bell, *NME*, 28 July 1979
59 'a chilling, harsh environment', Nick Kent, *NME*, 24 February 1979
61 'We're very much into musicals', *Sounds*, 19 April 1980
63 'He was everything the rest of the Bunnymen', Bill Drummond, *Mojo*, 14 April 2014
64 'our egos aren't big enough' Paul Morley, *NME*, 28 June 1980
65 'Form your own opinions', Deanne Pearson, *The Face*, August 1980

CHAPTER 4
74 'I knew it wouldn't be long', *The Face*, August 1981
74 'I didn't want everything to sound the same', Tom Cox, *Guardian*, 15 October 1999
75 'I was really forged in Liverpool', ibid.

CHAPTER 5
86 'Brian wanted to say', Paul Rambali, *NME*, 8 November 1980

218 'Teenage fans screamed in horror', *Daily Star*, 13 February 1992

218 'We looked into our souls', Danny Kelly, *NME*, 29 February 1992

CHAPTER 13

237 'There's nothing worse', Bob Stanley, *Melody Maker*, 24 February 1990

237 'You don't have to put out', ibid.

238 'So he and I would manifest', Mark Beaumont, *NME*, 26 August 1995

242 'the managing director said', *Highland News Group*, 11 July 1992

244 'I don't care what he does', *Billboard*, 2 July 1994

249 'The first ten days of us writing', *Uncut*, January 2012

250 'It's impossibly good', James Oldham, *NME*, 24 May 1997

255 'We always wanted it to be a mess', Ian Harrison transcript, Liverpool, 25 August 2017

255 'the record stiffing', Bill Drummond, *45*, Little, Brown, 2000

CHAPTER 14

258 '"Music for the 21st Century"', *The List*, 17–23 August 1990

265 'elitist and effete tossers', Steven Wells, *NME*, 2 May 1988

266 'There are three sides to every story', *Stoned*, Secker and Warburg, 2000

269 'I realised I was being called', ibid.

CHAPTER 15

287 'What's happened is that', Max Bell, *Evening Standard*, 26 June 1998